Accountable Advertising

Accountable Advertising

A Handbook for Managers and Analysts

SIMON BROADBENT

**Admap Publications
in association with
Incorporated Society of British Advertisers
Institute of Practitioners in Advertising**

First published 1997

Admap Publications
Farm Road
Henley-on-Thames
Oxfordshire RG9 1EJ
United Kingdom
Telephone: +44 (0) 1491 411000
Facsimile: +44 (0) 1491 571188
E-mail: 100144.3077@compuserve.com

A CIP catalogue record for this book is available
from the British Library

ISBN 1 899314 61 X

Typeset in 11/12.5pt Times by Admap
Printed and bound in Great Britain by
Biddles Ltd, Guildford and King's Lynn

Contents

Part 1

Part 2

Part 3

8 Modelling   149

Appendix

List of Figures

For my son Tim

To listen well is a second inheritance.

– Publilius Syrus, 1st century BC

Acknowledgements

Many advertisers I have worked with, both in the UK and in the US, have shared with me their data, their hopes and their fears. These include: Cadbury, Heinz, IBM, Kellogg's, Kraft Jacobs Suchard, Mars, Mercedes, Mitsubishi, Müller Dairy Products, Nestlé, Perrier, Procter and Gamble, Prudential Corporation, Rowntree, Royal Mail, Tropicana, United Biscuits, United Distillers and Visa International.

I have enjoyed working with my colleagues in The Brand Consultancy, Helena Rubinstein and Oliver Bolitho. All the techniques described have been developed with the resources of Leo Burnett and The Brand Consultancy.

I am grateful to Nick Phillips, Director General of the Institute of Practitioners in Advertising, who gave permission for the use of Advertising Effectiveness Awards material, and has sponsored this book. John Hooper, Director General of The Incorporated Society of British Advertisers, is the joint sponsor. Nick Bertolotti, of Arthur Andersen, helped develop the Continuous Budgeting model.

All errors are mine, but I have been very greatly helped by comments made by Tim Ambler, Patrick Barwise, Steve Gatfield and Stephen King.

We see nothing until we truly understand it

— John Constable

You see, but you do not observe

— Sherlock Holmes

The virtues of a superior general are to estimate the enemy situation and to calculate distances and the degree of difficulty of the terrain so as to control victory. He who fights with full knowledge of these factors is certain to win; he who does not will surely be defeated.

— Sun Tzu, c 500 BC

How to Use This Book

Introduction

It is no longer enough for the marketing director to determine how much it is right to spend on advertising. That was the assumption behind *The Advertising Budget*, which I wrote nearly ten years ago. He (or she – I ask the reader to make this change throughout) still has to make this decision, but must now do more – justify it. In today's business climate, top management and finance take too keen an interest in this budget to leave it to marketing alone.

Marketing management should work with an analyst in order to present the budget successfully. This is the person responsible for looking at historic marketplace data, deciding whether previous advertising met its management objectives, and advising what to do next.

The manager's recommendation is made to people who understand accountability though they are not advertising specialists. The object of this book is to bring the firm's communication decisions up to the accountability level of other investments.

This is a handbook. It does not pretend to review the literature. It is a manual based on day-to-day experience. It will have two sorts of reader. First, all those concerned directly with the budget decision: chief executive officer or managing director, corporate strategist, finance director and budget controller, brand owner, marketing management, advertising agency account manager and planner. Second, the analyst who does most of the work described here.

The managers start with strategy and teamwork, and end with decisions. The analyst is more like a detective or scientist, whose aims are understanding and measurement. The analyst begins with the brand and the marketplace, takes a point of view, rooted in the data, about the forces which shape behaviour, evaluates the levers and suggests which to pull.

The book therefore spans a wide range. Many people are involved, so many that their skills and interests differ dramatically. After reading a draft, Stephen King commented that many managers 'don't try to make advertising accountable at all – because it's never occurred to them, or because they don't think it can be done, or because they're too busy getting on with it to have time for such intellectual stuff, or because they're frightened to know the truth'. Others 'want simple rules of thumb, not realising or wanting to realise the complexity of the issues or the dodginess of the data'. I hope that somewhere in their organisations there is an analyst who will persuade these managers to make a serious attempt. There are 'those who do want accountable advertising, but normally rely on judgment and interpretation because they are worried about the obscurity of the maths and fear being blinded by science'. I believe these managers will see that a hard look at the numbers does not preclude judgment, and that often it is not as hard to do as they imagined.

Part 1

This first part of the book sets the scene; it describes management and marketplace, money and communications. For analysts, it is an introduction to a complex world which they would be tempted otherwise to oversimplify. They need to understand where the brand's objectives and budget come from, the realities of the marketplace and of advertising.

The material is handled by managers every day, but the perspective described here will help them. They are under heavy pressure – in the time available and on the financial results they have to deliver. What sounds simple and obvious when read calmly and as a general statement, especially in Chapters 2, 3 and 4, may get squeezed out when the heat is on and compromises are being made. That is why the arguments put forward here are such a necessary foundation for the rest of the book, making accountability a natural consequence.

Chapter 1 is a general introduction to the work ahead. It defines 'accountability' and 'advertising'. It describes the battlefield; it discusses what is important to managers and how they should work with analysts. It issues the challenge: most advertising can be made accountable.

Chapter 2 is about brands from the company's point of view: advertising helps to make them valuable. It is about the company's objectives and how to ensure that the brands serve the company's purposes.

Chapter 3 sets brands in the marketplace, and in the consumer's mind, against a competitive environment. These places are very different from the boardroom.

Chapter 4 builds profit from the marketplace results and the financial data. The budget for the brand is set out in the way used in the rest of the book.

Chapter 5 is about our mental model of advertising's effects. In what ways do they further your company's objectives? Exactly how do communications work for you? There is a wide variety of possible views here, but the team must agree on their expectations in their own case.

Part 2

Now the two partners, manager and analyst, meet and work together. In case history fashion, they solve the problem of making their communications spend accountable. Both sides will learn from this story how it can be done.

Chapter 6 turns the general description of Part 1 into a realistic situation. It shows how the techniques I recommend produce conclusions which can be applied in practice. It does not describe the methods in detail while it tells the story, but it refers forward to Part 3 where they are explained.

This example is a combination of several projects I have worked on. Everything described has actually happened. Details have been changed to protect the innocent. The numbers have been adjusted, to prevent identification and to make the conclusions more apparent, but are based on real data.

Part 3

This part shows how the analyst does the job. It is also an explanation of the analyst's craft for the manager. It shows the power and the limitations of the methods; hence the manager will understand what is going on and he can ask the right questions about his own case. In many companies, the manager does this work himself.

The purpose is to detail the methods which the analyst uses to make the situation clear, to quantify effects, to add financial evaluation and so to recommend decisions. There is a sensible, methodical and tested way of approaching and organising the data, and of drawing conclusions. In the Tables section, there are numbers on which the reader may try out some of the techniques.

The tasks suggested in this part are more than worthwhile – they are the only way we will ever get close to the truth. I have not oversimplified. The challenge is for those who do want to know, who find generalities unsatisfying, and who are ready to work. I do not want to give 'woolly answers to vaguely expressed questions that appeal to the undiscriminating because they are absorbed without effort.'

Long before we get into what many think of as 'analysis' there is work to be done collecting and presenting the relevant data. Nothing more complex than an average and a plot may be involved, and these may be very revealing. If you cannot 'see' the answers in properly re-worked data there is a good chance they are not there.

Chapter 7 tells how the first job of the analyst, after assimilating the business situation, is to inspect historical data, to decide with the manager which are the most meaningful items and how these should be interpreted. If you are evaluating a campaign, you re-visit its objectives and compare the findings with how they were expected to look. You discuss the results with people working at the coal face because there are always factors not revealed in the basic data. You get them ready to show the manager.

This chapter is about description only. Never rush into more complex techniques without these preliminary steps. The answers often emerge more easily than you expected, or you will at least get strong indications of what to look for later. By immersing yourself in the subject you will build up in your mind ideas about how the category works and what affects the brand.

A man was building a cabin and taking longer about it than his neighbours. He had been supplied with screws to join the planks to the framework. He had been expecting to use nails, and was trying, with little success, to hammer in the screws. The analyst must not dash in with his hammer. 'Have technique, will travel' should not be his motto. Look, listen, learn first.

Some projects will stop at this stage. But part of the situation may be too complex for you to detect directly what is happening: you then have to use a more powerful approach to disentangle the effects of a number of factors. When modelling is used, the purpose is to estimate numbers to describe the effects you believe took place.

Chapter 8 covers modelling. This is a search for a better understanding of the forces which push our brand's sales up or down. We do not expect to model in every case. This chapter is mainly for the analyst, but it also shows the manager how to keep an eye on what goes on in the back room.

Chapter 9 makes the link between the last two chapters and the accountant's cost data. The ideal system allows us to ask what-if questions, and to come up with financial answers. As well as looking back you have to take part in the plan for the future.

Chapter 10 turns the process into checklist form. This takes the manager and analyst step by step through the work to be done. Too often parts are left out, especially the early ones. These omissions make the later work harder to complete and may be fatal.

By going through these steps, you should make your advertising accountable.

Part 1

1 Introduction

This chapter defines 'accountability' and 'advertising'. It explains why it is increasingly necessary to justify the advertising budget. Behavioural and business criteria are more convincing than the traditional communications measures.

Some marketing managers prefer to work intuitively. They become uneasy when a numerical analyst is brought into decisions which also involve creative work. They can in fact learn to work with analysts, and greatly to their advantage. No claim is made that their subject has been turned into a science, only that some techniques help their decisions and ease their meetings with general management and finance.

1.1 The Subject

In this book's title, the unexpected word is 'accountable'. The word is less used in the marketing department than by general and financial management. The purpose of this book is to make its use in marketing more common.

What does 'being accountable' mean? This is explained more fully in the next section, but briefly it means agreeing in advance the *business* objectives for a project, and its *cost*. Then, after the event, it means evaluating the effects, so deciding whether or not the objectives were met, and improving future decisions. This process is still rare for advertising campaigns.

'Advertising' in the title also needs explanation. It is always worth putting in the word 'advertisement' instead, and seeing how the sense changes. 'Advertisement evaluation' is clear enough. It means checking whether the copy you are running is as good as it could be. Most of the work in advertising is about individual executions, is internal to the advertiser and advertising agency, and does not address the questions: Should we be doing this at all? How much of it should we be doing? These decisions have already been made; the purpose is to carry out the job efficiently.

Evaluation of individual executions is not the subject of this book. The methods most used for that purpose are qualitative, or from survey research about noting, recall, awareness and changes in brand image. These tools play a part in campaign evaluation, but as diagnostics about how the advertisements perform, rather than as substitutes for behaviour or as ends in themselves.

'Campaign evaluation', close to the subject of this book, is different. Yes, it may address the effect of individual executions, but it is also about how the brand is doing in the marketplace and about what else affects its sales. It is a harder task; there are many other factors affecting your sales, and in comparison with all their effects, what advertising does is minor (usually, and when only the short term is considered). You are looking for ripples in comparison with waves.

Accountability is an even bigger task: you look beyond the marketing department; you include justification of the budget. In the course of doing this you need to address several technical questions, which the book also covers.

'Advertising' needs explanation in another sense. Other sorts of communication can be made accountable in exactly the same way, by the same methods. This is discussed in Section 1.3.

1.2 What is 'Accountability'?

Accountability drives many management decisions which were previously made less formally. It requires that the activity which is studied must produce results which are more or less predictable; the costs to achieve these results are agreed, as are the benefits which will flow from them. These effects must be reported on after the event and they should be compared with benchmarks. You judge the effects against your business and management objectives, both in the marketplace and on your budget. The findings are used to plan future steps in what is a cyclical and learning process.

Advertising has too rarely been accountable in this sense, and so it is usually poorly managed. This statement may outrage some campaign owners who claim their advertising 'works'. They mean they have detected, even measured, advertising *results* – comments in focus groups of consumers, awareness and recognition of the advertisements, changes in brand image. From such effects, which are genuine and valuable, they claim their campaigns are 'effective': this can be a weasel word, sliding easily into 'worth it'.

But such measures are not set as business objectives, and working with such surrogates sits uncomfortably with other managers in the firm, especially with accountants. 'Keeping the books' is now a minor part of the work which accountants do. Their major jobs are to organise the setting of financial targets and to monitor financial progress. The effect they have had is to create a view of the firm as primarily – even exclusively – a money-making machine for its shareholders and managers. The annual or quarterly bottom line has often become an obligatory objective, rather than one of several targets. In response, other departments have cut costs and made themselves accountable. Incidentally, few query whether this short-term pursuit actually makes the firm more profitable in the long term.

Advertising is still run differently. It is hardly understood by many who pay for it; its objectives are set in communication terms; its budget is subject to whims; no one is too sure about the real returns – and so advertising budget recommendations are not much trusted. You can see this in the switch to other marketing methods, which do produce countable results. In the battle over the total budget for the brand, no advertising appropriation is now unchallenged – and as often as not it is raided in times of need.

The purpose of this book is to raise advertising decisions to the same level as other investments, as soundly argued and trusted as much. It should not be permitted as an indulgent exception in the boardroom. The book provides ways to analyse history, in order to evaluate the contribution already made. Once a track record has been established, and the team has a better understanding of what advertising has done for the brand, then forecasts about the worth of investment in it will be more relied on. The accountability gap between marketing and other activities will be smaller.

Advertising managers *want* this to happen. They would like to have the accountants as partners, not judges. That is what this book is for.

This does not mean that the standards applied to advertising should be any *tougher* than for other choices. Risk cannot be removed from any business decision. The comments above apply to some extent to other activities which are less tangible than manufacturing – and in this decade we have seen more and more of this country's turnover in intangibles. Promotions, loyalty schemes and the sales force are all examples of investments for which the real return is hard to evaluate. In fact, communications should be no harder to make accountable than they are. The firm is also making concrete choices – raising capital, hiring staff, building factories and offices, and buying products from outside suppliers. All of these decisions were once based on forecasts. Interest rates change, the new director may not deliver, building costs overrun, production speeds or delivery dates were optimistic. But in all these cases, targets were set and estimates of best and worst cases were provided. No one could be sure whether the decisions would pay off and no one expected total accuracy. Judgment was inevitable, and it was trusted because explanations were provided for the numbers.

In a 1995 survey, half the finance directors interviewed, and over a third of the marketing directors, agreed that the advertising business had not been properly accountable in the past decade. Less than a tenth were completely satisfied with the effectiveness of their marketing activities. Many commented that it was difficult to decide on the criteria; more that none of the techniques intended to do so was totally accurate. Hence, the majority agreed that their systems do not give the information needed to manage marketing effectively. A 1996 survey found that finance directors wanted to measure the effectiveness of the marketing budget more than any other. They also showed less enthusiasm for spending on marketing than on budgets supporting training, information technology, or research and development.

It follows from the needs to match results against business objectives, and to satisfy top management and accountants, that accountability must be about behavioural effects. The advertising trade will continue to be in trouble if it takes the advice (given in 1996) of a management consultant that 'advertising objectives can rarely be set in terms of sales results', and continues to work, as the recommendation continues, only with awareness, brand images, stated purchase intentions, and so on.

Advertising management should aim to be data-based whenever possible, and explicit about assessing risks and balancing probabilities. Certainty is not promised, but the reduction of uncertainty is very likely to be achieved. The criterion is not that your model of the marketplace will be exactly right – that is not expected – but that decisions are improved and justified.

In the boardroom, the defender of the advertising budget is most helped by evidence that advertising contributed to the sales of the company's own brands. Testimonials from other companies, case histories about other products, generalisations about the proportions of campaigns that work or pay off – these have their own value. But a single analysis which concluded that last year's spend paid off is worth all nine volumes of *Advertising Works*, the collection of successful stories about other people.

That is why this is a practical handbook.

1.3 Only Advertising?

Advertising is taken here as the most common method of paid-for communication. It means using the traditional media, especially the television screen and all it carries – from terrestrial to satellite channels, time-shift and commercial videos. It includes newspapers and magazines. There are other well-known media – outdoor, from posters to taxi-sides and signs at outdoor events, radio and cinema. Many other ways of communicating exist – the product itself and the pack, point-of-sale material, direct mail, database marketing, price cuts, promotions which are more than just price cuts, loyalty schemes, other store activity, staff on counters and forecourts, telephone sales clerks and those who deal with your invoice queries and complaints, door-to-door, sample drops, sponsorships, licensing, the computer screen, brochures, exhibitions, trade shows, and so on. The list of peripheral media is very long. Each medium presents its own opportunities and they will not be addressed in detail. I do not claim that they all work like TV or print, only that the principles of accountability can be applied to them too. Their effects can be evaluated using methods parallel to those described here. In some cases, the evaluation is easier – interactive, direct response and database marketing are examples – and a growing proportion of all advertisers now use such channels precisely because they are more easily accountable.

'Advertising' is to be understood very generally, and other communication techniques are also referred to.

There is one major exception to this wide definition. This is not a book about developing new campaigns. It is about evaluating campaigns already in the field – the only secure way. They may of course be on air for the first time. Creating advertising, whether for an existing or a new product, is a special skill. Predicting its success is unusually difficult: the hothouse where creative development takes place is very different from the world of realistic ad exposure and of brand competition which you face in due course.

1.4 For What Sort of Business?

The firm selling packaged and advertised goods through supermarkets is in fact an exceptional advertiser. Far more companies which advertise are selling services, or make technical and financial products, or are recruiting staff. I cannot say 'products or services' every time, just as 'any other form of communication' would be a clumsy addition, but the reader is asked to bear these qualifications in mind.

Most has been written about, and most of the research has been done on, consumer products sold through middlemen of some kind (supermarkets, corner stores, independent financial advisers, pharmacists, car dealers, or counter staff), and supported by advertising. Groceries advertising is accountability's core problem area, of which the other cases are variants, some easier to evaluate, some as hard. The principles in other cases are identical and the translation from the language used here should be straightforward.

There is one way in which every business is the same, and which is at the heart of this book: it competes. If you do not have a direct competitor today, you will tomorrow. To do battle, you have to differentiate yourself – you have to brand. Communications are a powerful tool in this war.

The book stresses competition in another way. What your competitors do may affect your sales, often as much as your own activities. A large part of analysis is about understanding this – and also using their case histories to help you see how the category works. Competitors are both enemies and instructors.

Everyone communicating with a mass market, in whatever way, should learn from this book.

1.5 Science or Craft?

Only a small proportion of advertisers look methodically at even the most obvious behavioural data with the intention of disentangling advertising from other effects. It is like the Dark Ages when measurement was unknown, inspection of nature was heretical, and instruction was by rote. For many marketers, Galileo and Newton might never have been born. They think the scientific method is something which applies to other activities – not to marketing. Learning is what they buy when they recruit people, not what they acquire about their own brand.

Making advertising accountable is an easier task than they think, but it does imply the first difficult step: the will to know. It is certainly not a job separate from normal management. It uses traditional management skills. The conclusions are not reached solely by judgment: you need data, a few analytical tools, and the time to use them. I ask no more expertise than many researchers, analysts and advertising agency planners already have. These skills need to be applied by you *now*, to *this* brand and *this* campaign, not at some other time and by someone else.

It is only in marketplace data that the clinching results can be found. Both words matter here: 'marketplace'– not laboratory, theatre test, focus group or interview; and 'data' – so that the findings are numerical. Here we hit another apparent difficulty. Some statistical skills are needed. These are not excessive: arithmetic and plotting describes the bulk of the work and there is little here that should put off the average brand manager.

Chapter 8 does introduce some formulae and uses regressions. For those who find these difficult at first, explanations are given and everything is also covered in textbooks and in computer package manuals. The two cultures – statistics and marketing – have to stay married but are uneasy together. The work is sometimes necessary – not always, as the answer often emerges long before you embark on the harder parts. But if the answers are not obvious, trying to make advertising accountable without any number work is like reading a book in the dark – it is simply a contradiction. On the other hand, an analyst who uses techniques to take a brand apart, and then cannot put it together again, will not understand the consumer, who thinks holistically. Judgment which makes use of statistical output, rather than swallowing it whole, is the answer.

A manager who claims it is too hard is opting out of responsibility. Often the practical solution is to form a partnership between an analyst, who is by training not scared of the work, and a manager, who knows enough to ask the right questions.

It is not claimed that marketing has become a science, or that we can predict exactly the outcome of an advertising campaign, or calculate the return from it to the nearest pound. These are impossible dreams in our craft. But it is claimed that some of the *methods* used in science (measurement, statistics, even equations) give us insight and improve judgment. Just because the same methods are used in the laboratory does not mean that we are pretending to *be* in a laboratory. The man in the white coat gets clearer benefits than we do – but what we get is a whole lot better than if we did *not* use the methods. Our aim is to estimate with more precision, but still to estimate; to convince, not to prove.

There are extreme views about analysis in the advertising business. Many people believe that the real problems are qualitative – they will get nowhere by studying tables of data; conclusions from numbers are likely to be unimaginative. Experience and common sense – these are their real touchstones. Such beliefs are not all wrong. If a conclusion from analysis does contradict common sense, it is probably false. But, whether an advertising budget should be half a million more or less; how much of a sales rise was due to the promotion – questions like this cannot be answered by experience alone: a hard look at the facts does help. I do mean a *hard* look: a naïve glance can mislead.

The contrary extreme is to think that if you give an analyst a jawbone, he can unfalteringly reconstruct the whole skeleton. No such claim is made here. We may learn more; we cannot know it all.

For the analyst, the problems which the book tackles have numerical elements *and* a qualitative overlay. Numbers on their own very rarely solve a marketing problem, but numbers-based judgment is the ideal aimed at. The good analyst uses as much experience and judgment as any manager, but builds on a bedrock of fact.

For the manager, these two aspects may be in the other order. His problems are mainly qualitative with some numbers attached. In the grand scheme of things a manager in charge of communications is right to put feelings first, since this is how consumers decide. A difficulty is, does the consumer have different feelings? The only way to understand the consumer properly is to start with behaviour and then interpret it. The argument again begins with numbers. Do not argue about the priority: obviously we need both.

It is this dilemma which gives the book its character. Managers do not know enough about analysis; they are only occasional users. The book is designed to help them. Analysts rarely see the bigger picture which the manager has to interpret; they too seldom contribute in a way the manager understands and trusts. The book should help them too.

The question, 'How do I make my advertising accountable?' is also unusual in that it needs people with different skills, and who normally have different priorities, to sit down together. They have to learn a common language and agree a common agenda to reach a shared decision. The chief executive, the entrepreneur, the accountant, often do not have the patience, the time or the expertise. The analyst or researcher often does not have marketing experience. This book is an attempt to bring them together. The work of the analyst takes up more of the space because it has been least understood and practised, and so needs most explanation.

A good manager, while reserving the right to make decisions, should rely on the analyst for independent and informed advice. The worst can happen when a manager reacts badly to disagreeable advice, which may challenge received opinion or threaten comfortable positions. Unfortunately, it may also be unwelcome because it is hard to understand. These are often the reasons why research budgets are such a small fraction of advertising budgets: why spend £100,000 to improve the worth of £10 million on advertising if the answers will not be appreciated? The manager–analyst relationship should be such that the analyst's opinions are always clear to the manager. But what the manager wants to hear should not determine what the analyst says, and what is said should not cause a rift.

1.6 The Challenge

I have written this book because most advertising *can be made accountable*.

Can, because the company has to decide whether to take this trouble. The reason for the traditional belief that we cannot know whether spending on advertising was worthwhile, is that few people have invested in the analysis required to measure the effects of campaigns in the marketplace.

Made, because work is needed. If the firm feels it is not worth it – that the data cost too much, that the analyst cannot be afforded, that there is no time – well and good. But managers about to offer these excuses should first weigh the value of decisions involving many thousands or millions of pounds. If they choose not to pay for illumination they should not complain that they are in the dark. Yet that is the position of too many advertisers.

They could fairly say, 'I have decided not to try,' but they must not say, 'It cannot be done.'

While wondering whether to make its advertising accountable, management faces a problem which mixes strategic thinking and common sense, understanding human nature, statistics and finance. Unless all of these skills are employed, the solution is unlikely to be found. With all five, and if there is a solution, it will usually be found.

Business and financial criteria are central in this book. Advertising is not different from other tasks like manufacture and sourcing, logistics and personnel. It has a business justification or it has none.

The objective of this book is to find this justification: to help people who need to defend their advertising budget.

No one can guarantee that a specific campaign *is* paying back until they have done the necessary work – and found a positive result. The answer will not always be favourable. It is possible that the analysis produces results – but they tell you that the campaign is not sufficiently effective and so new copy is necessary, or the money is better spent elsewhere. These are hard conclusions to accept, and the possibility that this is so can be one of the reasons accountability is not sought.

It is also possible that analysis will fail to deliver, since there are a few circumstances in which it is actually true that no reliable measure of effect can be made.

The position of this book is certainly not that *all* advertising *is* economic – in fact some definitely is not. Nor is the book claiming that a clear-cut answer can *always* be found to the question, 'Is my advertising a sound investment?'

The truth is not as extreme. It is that the relatively small cost of analysis, using data which are available to most advertisers, is worth spending because it answers one critical question: '*Can* I find out whether my advertising pays off?' Analysis has a good chance of answering other questions which every advertiser worries over: 'Should I spend more, or less?', 'Should I spend on something else?', 'How am I doing compared with my competitors?' It will illuminate other marketing decisions at the same time, particularly, 'Have I got the price right?'

More optimistic and determined advertisers who have used the methods now available have a competitive advantage. They spend more heavily behind advertising which pays back, they change ineffective campaigns more quickly, and they withdraw from uneconomic situations.

Making communications accountable is not only looking backwards and deciding whether or not decisions were correct. The ideas in this book are used to forecast, to evaluate future scenarios, to draw up better plans and so to improve business decisions. These applications will be demonstrated, as well as the analysis of history.

To repeat the main point: if you follow the process recommended, you are likely to get a reasonable estimate of whether your advertising investment is worthwhile.

Notice again the reservations:

- You have to *follow the process*, you have to take the trouble to collect the data and other information required, and you have to study it. The work may not be easy or come cheaply. You may not have, and cannot get, the appropriate numbers about sales and about your category – in which case you cannot begin. In most cases I have come across, the data existed but had not been collected in one place, it had not been studied properly and the necessary analysis had not been done.
- You are *likely* to get a result, but there are exceptional circumstances when it is not possible – success cannot be guaranteed. The proportion of cases where the job can be done is certainly far higher than is usually assumed. 'Success' means here that the evaluation is made and you know whether or not management objectives were met, at the expected cost. Once more, it does *not* mean that advertising is necessarily worthwhile.
- You will get a *reasonable estimate*, not certainty. The level of success, and of rigour in the arguments, will be at least as high as for many other commercial decisions.
- No one knows in general how much advertising pays off. Too few know, in their own cases, whether their business objectives were met. My own guess for the proportion of campaigns meeting that criterion is under 5%. Probably half of all campaigns have some measured result, in the sense defined in Section 1.2, which is not the criterion aimed at in this book. If you do not know 'which half is wasted', it is time you found out. Only a minority make this attempt, though the majority could succeed. Of those who do try, there are very few who fail for technical reasons, and not many who fail because they do not have, or cannot afford, the data and expertise. The majority have the data but do not make the attempt, or make it inefficiently. This book is to encourage them to try, and to raise the efficiency of the process.

2   Management Objectives

The analyst has to understand the company's view of their brands. Account-ability is based on business objectives, and this chapter describes these being set. The starting point is where the brand is now and where the company wants it to be. Examples of objectives are to increase or defend sales volumes, to defend brand price while not losing volume, to support share prices, to improve short-term profit, to demonstrate cost-cutting, to create famous brands and admired advertising, and to keep a cash cow alive – as well as personal goals. The chapter prepares the analyst for objectives which may not be expected; the manager is reminded always to keep the bigger picture in mind.

From the management's overall objectives, the marketing and communi-cation objectives are decided. The communication task is not an end in itself: it has a higher purpose.

2.1 Motives

One purpose of this chapter is to explain that 'accountability' is not a simple and unvarying concept. It depends on objectives which are specific to the situation, and perhaps temporary. Objectives need to be agreed by manage-ment and shared with the team before the analyst can check whether communications serve the company and the brand well.

The analyst is often surprised by the complexity and fallibility of the real world. The personalities and the hidden agendas are part of the situation. Managers are people. They do not set the brand's objectives in stone, nor always in a dispassionate, logical way.

As well as business objectives they have personal goals: a bonus, or a promotion to the next job. Prestige and power go with big budgets: there is an incentive to spend. They also go with profit: there is an incentive to cut costs. A famous advertising campaign confers fame on its patrons: there is an incentive to be part of the team which makes the well-known ads for ...
A few advertisers genuinely see themselves as patronising an art form, Benetton being the most conspicuous example. So the objectives which managers set are not always impartial, and may even be bad for the firm. An unnecessary change in copy when a new manager arrives, spending cuts at the end of the year just to make company profits look good – these are not done for the sake of the brand.

Business objectives for a brand are never as simple as 'It should make a profit', though this is often said. Perhaps so, but over what period? Can you really afford to invest now for a return next year? The answer management gives to this question is one of the most revealing insights into the company.

Is the priority to servicing borrowed capital – and how patient is the lender? Or is it to shareholders – in dividends, in the share price? How is 'shareholder value' measured? By return on capital employed? By operating profit compared with the cost of capital in the category (some industries are seen by the City as more risky than others)? Or by some other accountancy criterion?

The company is more important than the brand. The brand may be milked, it may be sold. Not everyone in the firm, including the analyst, is privy to such priorities.

In addition, not all brands are there for self-sufficient reasons. Some brands are spoilers – there to block competitors as part of a larger strategy. Others are cash cows, or kept alive to justify a tradition.

The vision of the firm, if it has one beyond making money, is an important element of brand strategy. Is there a mission on product quality? On being the category leader in innovation? In volume? In value for money? Is it part of the objectives to fill production capacity? To protect the workforce?

Who sets and embodies the long-term future of the product, who is responsible for the well-being of the brand, or its service to the firm's greater needs? This is the brand owner: the person who can balance the firm's goals and the decisions for the brand. It is important that the manager, to whom the analyst reports, either is, or has the confidence of, the brand owner. Another person to be identified (possibly the same), makes the final financial decisions.

2.2 The Brand – to the Manager

The brand owner is like a farmer and the brand is his field. He may sell it, he may mortgage it in order to buy another, he may create a dust bowl with poor feeding and overcropping, or he may support his family and pass the field on, enriched, to the next generation.

All of these are legitimate business objectives and the choice is made at a level usually above the brand manager's and certainly above the analyst's. In this book, I discuss very briefly: valuing the brand when it is sold; the possibility of milking it; the difference between short and long-term profits; and I describe in depth the nourishment and sustaining of the brand through communications. It is this last which is the normal assumption, but be prepared for alternatives.

First, I have to define what the brand is, in order to explain how objectives should be set. Note that there has been a school of thought which held that 'branding' was something bolted on as an afterthought to a (separate) product. This is not so: a brand is holistic in the consumer's eyes and it includes – in fact may be predomoinantly determined by – aspects of the product. Some well-known and recommended definitions follow, and in Section 3.1 I give one for the analyst.

A brand is a combination of
– a name, and/or other symbols,
– and its mental associations among customers and others which enhances the
  value of the product or service.

This definition is by Patrick Barwise. An equally valid one is by his colleague at the London Business School, Tim Ambler:

A brand is the promise of a bundle of attributes that someone buys and provides satisfaction. The attributes may be tangible or invisible, rational or emotional.

Both are made more dynamic by Stephen King's comments:

The difference between products and brands is fundamental.
A product is something made, in a factory; a brand is something bought, by a customer.
A product can be copied by a competitor; a brand is unique.
A product can be quickly outdated; a successful brand is timeless.

These three quotations give us the essentials to look for when you come to your own brand and management's objectives for it.

I examine in this book the 'enhanced value' which a branded product possesses. Remember that I write throughout this book 'product', but of course services are included. What is the evidence that this value has been created? Where did it come from? What is it worth?

You must look for this value among 'customers', for it matters that someone 'buys' and that they get 'satisfaction'. It is in their minds that the value resides, but it has to be shown in their behaviour. Of course the product itself has value, and you should know about that; it is usually much the largest element in the consumer's satisfaction. But it is not only the 'tangible' or 'what you can kick', in the accountant's phrase for physical assets, which accounts for brand choice. In many categories, products can be, and are, quickly imitated. In blind tests there is little to choose between them. What makes the brand chosen, some of the time, by some people, in preference to competitors, is also 'emotional' and potentially 'timeless', though it will need refreshment.

One definition reminds us that the brand consists partly of a name and/or symbol, so part of our search must be about memories and recognition of these. And it resides in the 'mental associations' and 'attributes' called up by the name, symbol and product; so these are also to be investigated.

A great brand is 'unique' in some way. There must be differences, real or imagined, between the brand and competitors. You must look for these differences and decide whether they are strong enough to produce the required added value.

2.3 Brand Essence

Brand Essence is defined by Helena Rubinstein as the enduring, competitive position of the brand expressed in a unique way. It is a set of words used by professionals working on the brand. It is also the idea which the words describe. It is therefore *not* only the 'image' of the brand, from the point of view of buyers and users, though this plays a part. It is certainly not just an advertising slogan, but is the considered view of management. It sums up their property, which has to be communicated internally to suppliers and to distribution channels, as well as to consumers.

It is a reduction or summary of four different aspects, and expresses whichever of these (or some combination), is the most descriptive of how the team see their brand. The four are:

(a) *Functions*: What is it? What is it for? What does it do?
(b) *Differences from competitors*: How is it different? How is it better?
(c) *Image*: How do people feel about it?
(d) *Source of authority*: What does the company (making it) stand for?

For the team to reach agreement on these elements and on their summary they study what is known about the brand and its competitors. The essence is usually defined as where things are now, and then again as where the team want to be. Thus both business and communication objectives are defined.

2.4 Commissioning a Brand Audit

A brand audit is a review of the brand's present position. The first step in setting a goal is to agree where you are now.

There is often confusion about what a brand audit is *for*, as well as how it is done. Two steps are recommended. First, review the purposes given in Section 3.2, where carrying out the audit is also described. Second, list the headings for all the information you have about the brand and its competitors, including data which might be bought or collected. Possibilities are covered in Chapters 3 and 7.

2.5 Setting Objectives

Determining business objectives starts by understanding your brand and its current situation. Assume these are known and that a brand audit has already been carried out. When you know where you are, and when you appreciate the larger business objectives of the firm, then the business goals for brand management can be set. These should be *both* for the long term, or strategic, or visionary, *and* for the short term, or tactical. They must be about the financial goals as well as about marketplace strategy and tactics. The effect on the brand budget of reaching these objectives should be set out. It is preferable – but a counsel of perfection – that all of these should be known before the team agrees marketing objectives and lays down criteria for communications.

There are three steps to take next. The first is about essence, or at least about part of it, brand positioning. What is the brand to stand for? The second is about the part communications are to play in this, or the objectives for communications. Third, what the ads should say or communicate.

There is a semantic slip here it is easy to make. 'Objectives for communications', or what communications should achieve, is at a higher level than 'communications objectives', or what they should communicate. The last step is a decision about the creative brief, with which this book is not concerned.

In my experience, marketing objectives are combinations of targets under no more than five headings, and often two or three. These are the major dimensions of most objectives:

- Product
- Costs
- Volume
- Price
- Distribution.

Product usually means for these purposes product quality, both real and perceived. Steady product improvement, and bursts of innovation, are the normal task of both production and marketing (new products are also important, and launches are a special situation). All marketing is easier with a superior product, and this is our goal. 'Superior' may be defined by any benefit which consumers see as there, and these are not all material. To get *perception* of added value is often a major communications objective.

Cost reduction is another normal job, and marketing has a part to play by keeping internal costs to a minimum and raising the efficiency of processes and of products bought in (creative work, media scheduling and buying).

Volume (or category share) and *price* are two essential dimensions in marketing plans. Together they define *revenue*, another criterion. With cost data and the rest of the brand budget, they define *profit*, often the ultimate criterion.

In many categories, the product variations within a brand (pack sizes, vehicle models, tickets for the front or back of the aircraft), have very different profitabilities. The trial size, the entry point model, economy class – these are not where the bottom line benefits most. Lifetime value is another aspect of profitability to be remembered. Management must be careful not to define 'volume' too loosely in these cases. Remember the law of unintended consequences, which says here, that once a goal is defined, operational managers will interpret it in the easiest way for them.

With the sales department, getting high and good quality *distribution* is a constant objective. This never comes easily and may have to be paid for. It includes activities which draw attention to the brand at the point of sale, position in a display and in the store (including shelf space or facings), plus various aids to getting attention or a message across.

In other words, some of 'distribution' is communicating something about the brand, and conversely communications can, via the sales force, help get distribution.

The priority given to the different dimensions varies enormously from case to case. It is traditional, though it should be questioned, that financial and short-term criteria come first. The quarterly revenues and the profit stream may be the inviolable goal to which all else is sacrificed. Shareholder value gets priority. It is taken for granted that shareholders can, and do, unconcernedly switch investments continually to the current, short-term highest performer. This also encourages dispositions and acquisitions or other financial engineering. In other words, saying profit is 'ultimate' means it is the supreme criterion to which everything else gives way. It is the end in itself.

The paragraph above is a typical US and UK view. In contrast, some Far Eastern operations put marketplace criteria first, meaning continual improvement of product quality, and the growth – or defence – of market share. The long-term objective is to ensure survival of the firm. Every week's sales figures are still closely studied, but concentrating more on how the brand is doing versus competition than directly on financial performance. Profit is still ultimate, but now that means it is at the end of a successful process.

This is not an abstract discussion. On the contrary, it is practical and central to the definition of accountability. If this year's profit were truly the only criterion most businesses would stop advertising. In practice, the first point of view can lead to cuts in research and development, raw material quality, and sometimes in communications. These are where easy savings can apparently be made; the results do not show for a little while. Cuts are next made in price to retain volume. On the other hand, the virtuous circle can lead to gains in both price and sales volume; hence revenue and ultimately profit – but how hard this is to follow in the typical Western environment.

Objectives should be prioritised: often a minimum must be met for criterion A, then B must be maximised. It makes all the difference in the world to be told, 'profits must be at least …, after this, get good sales volume', rather than, 'maximise profit'. Or, 'improve product quality to get a score of …, so get a distribution gain of…,' rather than, 'improve quality and distribution'.

Note that criteria are often contradictory, indeed the tension created is sometimes deliberate. You can get the required profits, perhaps, by raising price, but at a cost in volume. Or, you can get the volume and perceived gain in product quality by advertising, but at a cost in immediate profit. Ideally, you need some kind of model to guide you in keeping the right balance, but most people do not have one and they rely on instinct.

The objectives may not even be feasible. It is only when the plan to meet them is being drawn up that this becomes apparent. The process can be circular: the team returns to top management if necessary to suggest alternatives and to get guidance on priorities. Section 9.10.4 gives an example.

For similar reasons, the plan may be revised during its implementation as new circumstances emerge and threaten our success. It is a mistake not to have a clear plan; it is also a mistake to stick rigidly to a plan which is not working out. Sometimes the corrections cannot be merely cosmetic: it becomes clear that the objectives themselves should be changed. It is normal that the planning process is circular and iterative.

Remember also the company objectives. Sometimes a brand stands virtually alone with only a financial link with the company. More often, the brand benefits the firm in ways wider than its balance sheet. But it can also happen that the provenance of the products is more important than the products themselves. The seller wants the buyer to return – for after-sales service, for upgrades, for other products. The values created by the brand and its communications must attach themselves firmly to the supplier. When this is the case, the brand's objectives should include providing these benefits to the firm. The 'guardian' of the parent company must be satisfied as well as the brand owner.

Finally, note that *all* marketing activities should be set against the same, agreed objectives. Store promotions are an example. You may write: 'Design a promotion to defend sales by appealing to loyal buyers,' or, 'to increase penetration by appealing to occasional buyers'. Alternatively, your purpose may be to block competition from display, or, by selling two-for-one, to take some sales from competition. It may be simply to accede to retailers' demands in order to avoid confrontation. Increased profit need not be part of these objectives: money is being paid out for strategic reasons.

2.6 Communication Objectives

After the firm has set business objectives and the team has agreed the marketing plan, it is time for the manager to set communication objectives. Often they flow simply. If a volume decline is to be stopped (the business objective), and a loyalty scheme is designed to do this (the marketing plan), you might write: 'Communicate the new loyalty scheme to current buyers so that you do not lose penetration.' Or, if a product improvement is planned to attract a new target group and improve volume, then: 'Communicate the product improvement to this group so that volume is increased to so-and-so.'

In other cases, you need a more extensive view of what communications can achieve. This enlarges the objectives which are possible, and means that you may agree on more than one. Chapter 5 suggest this wider view.

When recording the objectives and the brief, it is strongly recommended that, as in the examples earlier, *the business and marketing reasons are always given* for the communication objective: achieve A *so that* B follows.

The reason for this advice becomes clear when you evaluate your achievement. If all that was required was a communication result, then a survey before and after the campaign would be an adequate check. But that is not the *real* purpose: '... so that you are able to maintain your price premium without losing volume' means that you will measure price and volume too.

It is also recommended that when you state the objective you also say *in what way the result is to be judged*. This forces you to be explicit; it becomes an important part of campaign briefing, which is the ideal time to start planning evaluation.

The *time by which the result is expected* should also be stated. You will find that the debate between the short and long term is often critical. This applies both to the times when data collection stops, so determining how long is available for consumers to be influenced, and when the evaluation is to be reported.

If a volume increase is called for, the *source of business* should be specified. It is recommended that a specific *number* is given: '... so that you get a share increase of two category percentage points' – and then the main source of business – 'from younger buyers of Brand X'. This is again to ensure management has thought through what it is calling for.

These recommendations are so important they should be made rules in your company. They are now repeated:

- Agree a *communications objective* and give the *business and marketing justification*; there may be more than one objective.
- State the *way* in which the achievement of the objective(s) is to be judged.
- State the *times* by which the result is to be achieved and the evaluation completed.
- If volume increase is expected, state the *source of business*.

2.7 Examples of Objectives

The recommended collection of case histories about the effects of communications is the series *Advertising Works,* which prints the best papers submitted for the effectiveness awards competition run by the Institute of Practitioners in Advertising. This scheme requires evidence of marketplace effectiveness by the toughest criterion – at the bottom line. Further, the papers are written for an audience which is potentially hostile: 'I think factors other than advertising are the real reason for the situation you see.' The fact that the media used are mainly traditional advertising, and not necessarily from a wider field, is less important than the lessons to be learned. These translate to other communications too.

In volumes 6 to 8 of *Advertising Works* there are 61 case histories which show what objectives were set for business, marketing and communications. We also learn – in these cases – that they were economically met. From these I have drawn up the following suggestions for the most frequent objectives, which come under the following headings:

- Increased volume or share
- Volume and quality of response
- Adding value, to make other activities work harder
- Morale and performance of our own staff
- Relations with channels of distribution

– Launching a new product (trial).

Increased volume or share is the most frequently set business goal. In a category with stable sales volume it is logical that a larger share is unachievable for about half the competing firms, however effective their marketing – my gain is your loss. *Maintenance of volume or share* can be hard work and is often more realistic.

Rather than by conquest, volume growth may come from increasing frequency of use, or loyalty to your brand. Suggesting cereals as a snack rather than a breakfast dish is one example. Offers on pack which mean repeated buying to get proof of purchase is another.

A further technique is to encourage growth of a sector, rather than of brand share. This is reasonable for a brand with a large share, or when the potential for the sector increase is a softer target than switching from a competitor, as with credit cards.

Maintenance may be replaced by minimum loss. It can be a sensible company strategy to block a competitor's planned entry into a category, or keep him to low volume, by launching a brand into the same sector. This brand is not necessarily there for growth or profit reasons. Similarly you may pre-empt a positioning, or category motivator claim, by using it ourselves.

Volume or *share* may be set directly as advertising objectives. In this case a different and important addition is required. 'By' is the converse of '*so that* ...'. For example, 'We require a share increase of two category percentage points *by* adding to the perceived value of the brand and *from* younger buyers of Brand X.'

Note that some research measures used may not cover all the sales actually stimulated by the communication. The take-home buyer may not be the main user. Two share points for an alcoholic drink in groceries may or may not correspond to similar increases among specialist off-licences or in on-licences. Communications may do more for one type of customer than another: which sort are you measuring? More on whether the measures are representative appears in Section 7.2.

For direct communications, volume (enquiries, coupons returned, phone calls made) should be qualified by some measure of 'quality'. This may be a description of the responder (high net worth, owner of a motor bike, lifetime value, etc), or of the response (ultimately converts or makes a purchase). It is likely to be the job of communications to create or trigger demand, and among the right sort of people, but actual sales may depend too much on the product to be a fair criterion. Financial and durable products provide examples. The behaviour required may be to call a broker or visit a dealer rather than to buy a policy or a car.

Adding value is a very frequent communications task. Again it needs amplification. What exactly are the dimensions by which the 'value' is to be enhanced? An example: 'Add to perceived value by communicating the resale value of the car.' In addition, and as usual, the way the effect is to be measured must be stated – by behaviour in the marketplace? By survey? Note that *how* you cash in the value depends on other activities. You may hold price and take it in volume. It may be more profitable to raise price, hold volume and raise revenue this way (without increasing costs due to added product sold). Your promotions may work better – indeed the irony has been noted in cases of communications making promotions appear more effective than before, with the result that communications money is cut.

An acceptable *price* may be set on its own as a goal. This looks like a very practical way of stating 'value', but it is not recommended. It suffers from the complication that, as stated above, volume is related to it. Usually you will sell a certain volume at one price; less at a higher price. What is an 'acceptable' price can be tested only by the volume sold. So volume turns out to be the criterion again, and price is really a statement of the difficulty or otherwise of meeting it – and of the way in which the desired profit will be made.

Similarly, reaction to price changes may be stated as a goal: a low price elasticity when our relative price rises, for example. Insensitivity to distribution loss is another measure of this type. Again this is a desirable outcome, a sign of a strong brand, a measure of 'value'. It is argued later that objectives in the price–volume–distribution dimensions are all different ways of calling for high Consumer Brand Equity (*see Section 8.7*).

Many other benefits claimed after the event can rarely be set as objectives initially: for example, getting overseas distribution; investment or sponsorship negotiations being improved; or the ability of a bank to enter a new sector of business. There is more on these 'indirect' results in Chapter 5.

Other apparently indirect effects may however be part of a deliberate plan. A building society may, for example, want to be seen in the financial sector as large and successful – perhaps to help in the outcome of a merger. A pension firm may want intermediaries, such as independent advisers, to think of it as suitable to suggest, because the purchasers of the pension will find their recommendation acceptable. Thus the immediate objective is acceptability or saleability rather than specific sales; the part to be played by communications has been spelled out correctly. These are again examples of setting the perceived quality of the product as the communications objective.

The *morale and performance of your own staff* may sensibly be a goal which is spelled out, rather than an incidental by-product. Many people have too few direct contacts with the company they work for. You do not have to be a salesman out on the road to feel isolated. Others need retraining in the way to deal with the public. Bank and fast-food restaurant advertising may be setting an example to counter staff. *Recruitment* of staff may also be helped by a campaign.

Our *relations with channels of distribution* are another field where objectives may be set. Sometimes this means simply advertising in the relevant trade journals. But it also means that consumer communications can help our salesmen in negotiations with the trade. This is partly because retailer buyers – like managers – see advertising at home. More important, it is part of the push–pull process. This means 'pulling' the brand out at one end of the pipeline of distribution by creating consumer demand, and also 'pushing' it in by various inducements to the trade. Of these, the most sensible is a believable claim that the brand will walk off the shelf due to the said consumer demand, and the least sensible (though common), is a trade price reduction. Getting new outlets requires a similar argument.

Launching a new product clearly has a trade dimension in which a similar case is made. Communications has special work to do in creating and positioning the brand, explaining its properties, and getting trial. A distribution target will be set and so will a trial and repeat purchase rate. It is particularly clear on these occasions how difficult it is to attribute success or failure to communications or to the product. *Trial* in a launch is the equivalent of 'sales' for a going product and is the sensible objective to set.

There are detailed examples of objectives and effects in Section 7.8.3, which are all successes from *Advertising Works*. In contrast, three cases are summarised here which show how the process can produce unexpected results.

Examples of objective setting
- A marketing director's bonus was determined by the level of brand name re-call. This was reflected in the advertising brief. Communicating benefits was not an objective and was not achieved – sales fell. But recall rose and so did the bonus.
- The objective was to arrest the decline of a food staple. A long-term pro-gramme was planned to achieve this. The industry committee which faced this problem, and had the plan drawn up, never took action because decisions were blocked by a major producer who said, 'I won't myself see any return from this, since I'm retiring soon.'
- The brand was a cash cow, supporting development elsewhere. Its share was in slow decline, while being supported by a mix of theme advertising and pro-motions. The purpose of advertising was to sustain loyalty by reminding users of the benefits of the product. While the objective was to raise money at a cer-tain rate, the programme worked well. When money was needed at a faster rate, management decided to sell the brand. Had advertising failed?

2.8 The Benefits

There is a last step, already mentioned, before advertising is briefed out. It is essential to accountability, but it is too seldom taken. Its omission is the reason why so many marketers meet only the wrong side of their financial colleagues.

The step is to argue *how much it is worth* to meet the objectives. This brings the accountants in at the right time: the beginning of the plan.

It ensures that the budget is not, 'same as last year plus media inflation,' or, 'so much per case'. Instead, it is agreed how much should be invested so that the objectives should be met.

Later, the question is, 'Will the plan meet the objectives?' Now, it is, 'With these benefits, how much better off will we be?'

To answer the last question, details of the brand budget are needed. If it is benefit in the current year which is needed, then Chapter 4 gives all that is required. At the end of that chapter, an example is given. If it is benefit in a forecast year, then Section 9.10 lists what is necessary.

You cannot be too careful or too explicit in setting objectives. As you saw in Section 1.2, accountability consists in meeting these objectives at an agreed cost. It is no good raising new criteria after the event, or saying first, 'more sales', and later, 'I meant more than that.'

3   The Brand and the Marketplace

The concept of the brand and the purpose of a brand audit are described. The material needed for the rest of the book is introduced by a data review. The most important numbers are volume sales, price, distribution, some survey data about brand qualities and media exposure. The brand can be seen properly only in the context of its competitors, so data about them are needed as well.

The brand has to satisfy both its final consumers and the channels through which it passes to them. Information is needed about our own staff and about retailers or other middlemen.

3.1 The Brand – to the Analyst

Some definitions of the 'brand' were given in Chapter 2. The discussion was from a business point of view. The question then was, how does management view its property, in order to define its objectives?

Now I take the analyst's view, and give a definition which introduces the work in the rest of this book.

This definition starts with the fact that you are to sell a product or service. Before it is there to sell, it has to exist, which means designing and making it at some cost, or buying it in, perhaps with assembly costs; or the people to provide the service have to be hired, trained, housed or transported. The point is that there has to be something physical – even if only a brochure or computer program – and there has to be a budget to underpin it. It is this budget which is the arena for the accountability debate.

The second element was noted in all the previous definitions – that the brand cannot exist in the view of management alone. A brand has to live in the mind of the customer – the purchaser, the consumer, and/or the user.

Finally, the customer always considers alternatives. If there is really no competition, there is no need for branding. The purpose of branding is to persuade the customer to choose yours, rather than another brand. This is not explicitly noted in Chapter 2, and in some firms is not prominent enough in management's minds. There is a tendency to exaggerate the loyalty of 'our' customers, and to ignore or to block out the frightening reality of the marketplace.

Branding exists because the marketplace is ruthless, because the customer is led, completely and properly, by self-interest. All definitions of marketing acknowledge this, but practice sometimes falls short. This is not an intellectual game. No one owes you a living; failure is always at your shoulder. The analyst must never forget competitors. The most fruitful analyses are not those that relate what you do to what you get. They relate what you and competitors offer, and how the customer chooses between alternatives.

To sum all this up in a sentence:

A brand is a product or service, seen through the eyes of the consumer, and the reason why your product is chosen, not a competitor's.

I start with the thing itself, to remind us that it has to be produced and paid for. It is only through the customer that a meaningful definition can be given. The important action is the customer's choice. Branding is there solely to affect that choice. The brand has to be preferred to competitors – for whatever reason.

In order to establish the brand in the consumer's mind, there has to be a name or symbol. Others in the chain between the manufacturer and the consumer value you only because of your worth to the consumer. The consumer chooses you expecting satisfaction. The reason for choice defines why this brand is different from that – a brand is holistic, but can be unpacked, more or less realistically, into a 'bundle of attributes', 'tangible or invisible, rational or emotional'.

Elements in the other definitions fit into this one, but this emphasises the choice, the ever-present threat that the vote will go the other way, the most democratic of all processes – shopping. Shopping is not just buying – someone can do that for you. It is viewing and considering alternatives.

This section is headed 'to the analyst', rather than 'to the manager', as in Chapter 2. Of course the manager shares the views described above. But the manager has to consider other aspects of the brand: the process of getting it made and onto the shelf, and the battle to get the attention and support of top management in competition with other company brands. The analyst can be more single-minded. The preoccupation of the analyst is the essence of marketing: seeing whether the product is preferred by some customers, and why.

3.2 Brand Audit

To make the definition of the brand more precise in your particular case, management may commission a 'brand audit' and the analyst may carry this out. There can be other reasons for a brand audit, and these are now described. Much of the detail is in Sections 7.3 and 7.4, where the analyst's work in describing the brand and the category are covered. On the way, we meet for the first time another piece of jargon: 'Brand Equity'.

There are four major reasons for carrying out a brand audit.

(a) An internal review of the brand's strengths and weaknesses, for general guidance, and to assist management in every area – financial, production, distribution, etc as well as in marketing

By definition, all kinds of data will be used and there will be no attempt to summarise the findings in one number. There will be different results for different parts of the operation. Often the review is part of a comparison of different brands within the company, even across different categories.

(b) An internal evaluation of the marketing function, with a specific objective – to assess the return made on investment

In contrast with the first purpose of a brand audit, you have the task of summarising the value of the brand to the company in a single figure. For the purpose of this book, you need a number to compare with the investment made in order to be accountable.

In an ideal world, you would be able to create a number which is often called Brand Equity. You would measure what this equity is, whether it is going up or down, and how far marketing activities affect this change. If communications add value, you should know how much they have improved equity. You thus monitor and control the marketing function.

Various suggestions have been made about how to do this. A process is put forward in Section 8.7 to define one specific measure, called Consumer Brand Equity, but you should be warned that there is no agreed definition for the frequently used phrase 'Brand Equity', still less a common way of measuring it. Often, it means no more than a collection of the ways in which the brand differs from a commodity. This description is met by the review (a) above. It is then much the same as the result of the brand audit now under discussion. It can be a synonym for brand value or worth, for the price difference above own label, for brand valuation, even for brand essence – concepts which are better kept separate. It may be defined entirely by the opinions of consumers collected in a survey, or entirely by behavioural measures, or by a mixture of the two. Thus it may include the perceptions of the purchaser – the aspects of the brand which he balances against the price – and/or the probability that he actually buys at such-and-such a price.

What nearly everyone does to make communications accountable is to estimate specifically their effect, usually on volume, and not to look at a definition of Brand Equity. You do not then claim to know the value of the brand before and after this addition, only the size of what has been added. This is because of the difficulties in item (d) below.

(c) Part of a category review, using generally-available data, to assess a brand's position in the category

This differs from (a) and (b) in that you have to assess competitors too, and can therefore use only data which you also have about them. The purpose is general, as with the first objective. No summary figure is required as the separate items could lead to different actions. You are describing, not summarising.

(d) A tool to improve defence and acquisition strategies, by putting a financial value on the brand

This is called brand valuation. It envisages the brand as up for sale, or at least bid for. Conversely, management may want to acquire someone else's brand and needs to know what it is worth – or at least how to justify the price asked. I am talking about a different marketplace here from the rest of the book: one in which the right to market brands is bought and sold. A brief comment is made here about brand valuation, but it is not mentioned again.

Even if the brand is not for sale, in a few companies its valuation is calculated, and may be shown in the accounts. To do so is not too hard if the brand has just been bought, but this is a rare event. Valuation is a difficult job if no bid has been made. For valuing the brands of another company the data used have to be available (or estimated).

This is not like the housing market, where enough properties are bought to make valuation possible from the prices of similar houses. Here, the price worth paying depends on who the purchaser is. It is well-known to be greater in practice than the physical assets. If there are synergies between the brand and the purchasing company then the brand is worth more when sold than before. For example, an existing sales force or manager with sourcing skills may be able to take on the extra work more cheaply than in the selling company.

The price depends also on whether there are competing purchasers, which brings egos and reputations into play. Rules for accounting practice are also involved and vary by country and from time to time. Hence a general acquisition value (without a specific selling situation) can be only a very rough guide.

The most reliable method – and this is not saying much, as once it is described its weaknesses are apparent – starts with a forecast of profits. These are multiplied by a capitalisation factor, which takes into account the risks in the situation. Both parts of this expression are poorly determined. Both profit forecasting and risk assessment are inexact.

You have to be careful in this area that you are genuinely describing the brand, and not the company. For example, if the company sells to another company overseas a licence to manufacture and to retail the brand, this certainly makes the brand more profitable to the company. Similarly, by clever financial management profitability may be increased. But these improvements are not to be credited entirely to the marketing management at home. Similar difficulties arise when share price is used, even in the rare cases when it can be related to an individual brand, and this is not a recommended measure.

I have now outlined the four reasons for a brand audit. Their main differences are whether:

- internal and confidential company data are used (a and b),
- or only generally-available data (c and d);
- the different characteristics are left separate (a and c),
- or they are combined into a single figure (b and d).

Carrying out a brand audit is the first step towards setting objectives. Before you decide where to go, you have to know where you start from.

3.3 Marketplace

3.3.1 Marketplace: Trade or Consumer?

There are two sorts of buyer for most brands. The first signs the cheques which the firm depends on for its livelihood. Most often this is a middle-man, a distributor, a retailer, a dealer – 'the trade' as it is often called. But in another sense the firm sells to the final purchaser and user: the housewife buying for her family; the driver looking for a car. There are two market-places you must consider.

In other cases, such as mail-order or business-to-business, there is only one sort of customer with whom you deal direct.

The retailer can be taken as the typical middleman. Some manufacturers would like to return to the old days of retail price maintenance, when they decided what price the consumer should be charged, and the retailer was literally a channel for distribution. This is history in most categories. The retailer is better thought of like any other customer, with the priority on self-interest – and often short term at that.

The retailer thinks mainly about his own competition, in the High Street or shopping centre. Manufacturers are just that – they make products and supply the retailer, themselves in competition with other manufacturers. Some of these supply products to which the retailer adds his own label;

some are labelled by manufacturers. Manufacturers are at liberty to advertise their products to the final consumer; if they do so they are spending their own money, not always wisely in the retailer's view.

Quality and price are the two watchwords, or their combination, value. 'Made by perfectionists. Priced by realists' – how many varieties are there of this slogan? The price charged to the consumer is entirely at the discretion of the retailer. He looks over his shoulder at the prices of other retailers, and his strategy is often to offer enough products at competitive prices to be able to claim he sells bargains to the consumer.

He does not have to have low prices throughout his store, only enough to give the impression that he offers value. Of course, if the shopper hunts for them, this claim is entirely true. Many shoppers do follow this strategy, and buy mainly the brands on promotion. Others pay more: those who are more loyal to a brand – either a manufacturer or the store's own label.

If a manufacturer's brand, or the whole category, becomes ammunition in a price battle, there is little he can do about it. He may see his brand sold below the price of manufacture, he may see his cherished image of quality and 'worth the price' ripped to pieces as consumers are trained to look only for bargains. This is the doom scenario which manufacturers dread, though it can do wonders in the short term for volume. The retailers may seem to him to have gone mad and to be throwing money away. This is not so. Retailers are using one of their principal weapons – price – in their own war, that is, with other retailers. The cost is paid by their income from other categories, for the moment not in a price battle.

Most retailers need to keep some manufacturers' labels on their shelves for several reasons. First, they are a standard in price comparisons between stores: 'They have Heinz Baked Beans at X pence – we have them at Y.' Second, they offer a comparison with own label: 'This the famous Cola at X pence – but ours is at Y.' Third, they do have their own consumers: branding does work, some people come in and buy them.

Other reasons have become less compelling. It used to be that manufacturers set the standards in quality, but often the retailer's brand is at least as good. It used to be that manufacturers created categories: they innovated and retailers copied, but some category developments are now due solely to retailers – branded sandwiches for example. It used to be that retailer brands depended on manufacturers' advertising to train new consumers into what the category is about, by advertising, and of these three, this is the argument which is most likely to hold.

It can be seen that the sales department, selling to retailers, does not have an easy job. It is easier to think short term, to prefer price deals to advertising, to rely on the power they have as the ones bringing back the retailers' cheques, than it is to worry about the brand's long-term future. The marketing department, for whom the analyst works, takes part in debates inside the firm which impinge on the advertising decisions in a way which the analyst has to learn to appreciate. The trade environment is not the main concern of this book, but it can never be overlooked.

3.3.2 Marketplace: The Brand in its Category

Returning to the consumer's view, the supermarket or its equivalent (the forecourt, travel agent, building society, trade magazine), is a confusing place. Prices are continually changing; promotions and coupons and other special offers are always around. Against this background, some reassuring certainties persist: brand names. Most consumers cannot evaluate quality; certainly not for all the brands on offer. Most shoppers are prepared to balance what they have to pay against the reassurance of the familiar.

The choice is being made every day – is this brand worth paying more for? Not only that, but among the brands on offer, why this one? Again, you must never think of your brand on its own, though this is a fault of many who approach the communications task. Hone the survival skills needed in this cut-throat environment.

You have to think of a category, made up of you and your closest competitors, within which you have a share of sales (to the final consumer). It is usually better to explain separately what happens to the category (for example, because of seasonal changes in demand, or because of a trend in total sales), and after that to think about your share.

In this marketplace your communications are only one of many factors which explain *why* you see the movements you do. The job for the analyst is to understand and to reduce to manageable proportions this 'why'. Then, to estimate the numbers involved so that marketplace numbers can be combined with financial numbers.

The main other factors have already been mentioned: price and product quality. Price should always be thought of comparatively – how does yours compare with the rest of the shelf? Price has two aspects which must always be distinguished: first, its average level; second, the temporary variations round this average, because of the price promotions, the special offers, the banded packs, the extra volume and all the devices of markets through the ages. Price points also matter; critical values are determined largely by the first digit. Going up from 37 pence a pot to 40 pence can affect sales seriously; when the competition falls from 33 pence to 29 pence you see a clear result.

The manager must be just as tough on the evaluation of pricing, promotions, trade relations, product development and the rest, as on communications. The question management is really interested in is about *marketing* accountability. There are two reasons why the analyst has to evaluate all the other factors. First, the answers are vital; second, you will never understand advertising effects unless you are able to allow for the others. So this book is as much concerned with price effects (the main determinant of profit), as it is with advertising effects.

You should be as interested in competitors almost as much as in your own brand. Again, you will not understand your brand unless you see it as it really is – fighting for survival against pitiless competitors. What do the data sources tell you about them? How are they distributed compared with your brand? How do consumers react both to them and to you? You are never alone with a brand.

4   The Brand Budget

The financial details about the brand are defined in simple terms. This is so that the manager sees the key facts about the brand, and so that the analyst can extract the few numbers needed later to help decide whether the advertising investment has paid off.

4.1 Definitions

The finance function in the firm determines the language and sets the rules for discussion about the brand's profitability. Conventions differ slightly; in your own case the words and definitions used may not be the same as those you find here, but this should present few problems.

The financial model for the brand is basically simple though its implications can be intricate and details may be up for discussion. In the description which follows these sensitive points are emphasised. The language of packaged goods and traditional media is used – but this is only because you have to have some particular application in mind – and the earlier point must be remembered, that other products, services and media use similar but not identical concepts.

It costs money to make or to buy in and then to distribute the various products. These costs are allocated to the different brands in the company. The money each brand earns is credited to it. Thus for each brand there is expenditure and revenue; the difference is its profit (or loss).

Different pack sizes, variants, and so on complicate the picture, but are ignored here. From one year to the next all the figures change, so forecasts across years result in further calculation. This is not dealt with in this chapter, but in Chapter 9.

The summary for a brand for a single year was, initially and several years in advance, a rough outline. It becomes a forecast; then an agreed budget. During the year it is part actual and part a plan for the remainder of the year. Two or three months after year end it is history.

The timings of the items in the accounting summary can cause confusion. The accounts may show costs and revenue by when cheques are written and payments are received. These are not always the same as the dates in the marketplace year: you may run a television campaign in December but pay for it in January; you may deliver cases and receive payment from a retailer in November and December but the housewife takes a pack from the shelf in February and it is this which shows in the retail audit.

The summary starts with the *quantity* sold; a standard unit is used (kilograms, litres, standard cases).

The *revenue* depends on the way you invoice the retailer. There is a list price, there are various allowances which may be deducted, and incentives given by the manufacturer or demanded by the retailer. These may depend on the volume of the order or delivery method, for example, or be negotiated as a one-off.

These allowances may be deducted from the list price and the revenue calculated from the result. Alternatively, the list price may be used to calculate revenue, so the allowances are treated as a cost (which may be fixed for a period or vary with the volume sold). The difference may look like a quibble, but is important when you come to calculate marginal revenue, and for other reasons. For example, if you treat the list price as fixed (even though you know you are going to discount from it), and count all the differences from it as a cost, then 'retailer promotion' may look very high. It can be a larger figure than advertising and other communications. The City may be told that 'marketing expenditure' is being increased, when actually revenue is being reduced – and the retailer may or may not choose to pass on the price changes. Cutting advertising while increasing discounts (ie cutting prices to the retailer), may look like a simple transfer of marketing funds. The effects may be neither simple nor healthy; at worst, you accelerate decline in perceived brand value.

However it is done, you can arrive at a selling price per unit, plus perhaps a fixed sum, so that total revenue equals this fixed amount plus the quantity sold times this price.

The price paid by the final purchaser is set by the retailer. Broadly, it reflects the list price set by the manufacturer. Changes in prices to the consumer from one season to the next are roughly in line with the manufacturer's list-price change. The relationship is not always straightforward. Retailers usually aim at a profit percentage added to the list price (or bought-in price) across all their brands, but they exceptionally sell a few as loss-leaders below the cost to themselves. They may take allowances on other brands but not pass them on to the consumer. Various forms of price promotion further complicate the picture. Although the association is not exact, I assume here that a percentage rise in your effective price to retailers provokes the same proportional increase to the final purchaser.

Manufacturers' costs associated with each brand are divided into those which are fixed for the year and those which vary with the quantity sold. The distinction is important.

General overheads are usually allocated to each brand as a fixed amount at the beginning of the year. For example, head office, part of the factory and finance costs may be a general overhead. Whether sales go up or down, these are fixed costs in the brand budget. The allocation often depends on a sales forecast – the higher the forecast the more the brand pays.

Other costs – raw material being the best example – clearly vary with the amount you sell (and make – it is presumed here that warehoused stocks are low or constant). Packaging and cartons, warehousing, transport – all these have a known price, and the amount paid usually depends on the quantity made and distributed.

Time spent by the sales force (selling to retailers), other parts of the factory and its staff – these are examples of items which may follow either of the two systems.

Does it pay us to sell one more case, if this sale depends on an investment in communications? This is a key part of the accountability question. It clearly turns on the cost of making and delivering one more case. I noted above that some items may or may not contribute to the costs of the extra case.

The variable costs used later really *should* be variable within your time horizon. That is, a firm should cover its overheads on the initial forecasts, and calculate a cost per case which is genuinely the added cost of making and delivering just one more. Only in this way is the bottom line really maximised by decisions about variable investment.

If you add some of the disputed costs to the sale of the extra case, you may find it appears not worthwhile to do so. This can lead to lost opportunities and reduced profit. You wrongly forgo what could be extra profit because the decision not to invest has been incorrectly made. Try to operate at the genuine margin, when evaluating additional spend, as closely as possible.

Some people object to this on the grounds that not all sales can be treated this way – which is true. They also say that all sales must make a contribution to overheads. Argue these points with accountants who look for 'full overhead recovery' on sales added after the base plan has been agreed. Their argument is misconceived. If you did change overhead recovery across the whole of the brand, including any added sales, over-contribution on the original sales would have to be credited to the communications, otherwise you would over-recover (not that accountants object to this – it is the marketer who should be worried). The result would be the same, but after added complications.

Once this decision has been made, you extend all the *units* sold, or quantity, by your *price or revenue rate*, which gives *revenue*.

You also extend units by the *variable cost per unit*; the result is *variable cost*.

The *difference between revenue rate and variable cost per unit* is called here the *gross margin rate*. Units times the *difference between revenue rate and variable cost per unit* is called here the *gross margin*.

You have now started to write the brand's budget in the form:

revenue – variable cost = gross margin

From the gross margin you have to subtract fixed cost and other costs in order to arrive at profit.

What 'other costs' are these? For present purposes you are to consider communication costs, but it is often the case that promotions and price cuts are considered as alternative activities to communications, so these may also fall in this part of your budget. The rest of the costs are here included as fixed (for example, new product development work, package design and many other items which are key to some people but not the subject of this book).

Even within communications, you must distinguish those costs which are fixed over the year. For example, you have decided to make a film for television but not how much airtime to buy – the production costs are fixed, the airtime is variable adspend. Your concern is now with the parts of the communications budget which have still to be determined and accounted for. 'Fixed' costs here include those you are not going to alter as media spend changes. In another context, production costs for advertising may be variable; here they are fixed.

When you subtract fixed costs and the other costs above from gross margin, the remainder is available for communications and profit, since the budget may be written:

gross margin = revenue – variable cost

gross margin = fixed cost + communications + profit

In this form communications looks like another cost. The more you spend on it, the lower the profit. This view too often prevails. The drive for accountability fuels the desire to lower communications and other marketing spend in order to raise profit.

There is another way to look at the figures.

The costs of making the product and selling it to the retailer are all building the brand and making it available. Without the communications investment, price might not be justified, volume might not be delivered. Then fixed costs could not be paid nor the profit achieved. Marketing activities, including communications, are adding value to the product already in the warehouse; they are pulling it through the delivery pipe; they are responsible for extra profit.

The relevant short-term, marginal parts of the brand's budget are now:

profit from higher price of the brand + profit from additional sales − cost of communications = profit from communications

Note that this understates the return from communications since it relies on only two of its potential benefits (*see Chapter 5*).

4.2 Headings in the Budget and Example

In a more conventional format, I have now laid out the brand's budget in this way:

units sold x price	= revenue
units sold x variable cost rate	= variable cost
units sold x (price − variable cost rate)	= gross margin
gross margin − fixed cost − communications cost	= profit

The example which follows starts the case history which forms a thread through the rest of the book. It appears again in Chapter 6, and is used in many of the later examples.

Example: Your brand's budget
Towards the end of 1995, it was clear that you would see 24,167 tonnes delivered to your customers and that you would receive (from retailers and other middlemen) £94,976k after various discounts and other negotiated arrangements.

It is known that your retail-level research data will report that you sold 19,333 tonnes and that purchasers paid £104,106k. There are two factors at work. The first is the cover of the research source, here 19,333 / 24,167 or 80% of actual sales volume. The second is the cash retained by retailers. If they took £104,106 / 0.8 or £130,132k, then they kept £130,132k − £94,976k or £35,156k; in other words, their margin was 27%. These differences from reported data and your actual budget have to be kept in mind when evaluating the research results − but you have to use such external data because this is how you set yourselves against competition.

The variable costs of production (mainly raw material, packaging, labour, and delivery) are £2,140 per tonne, so the total variable cost is £51,717k. This leaves the gross margin of £43,280k, which is £94,976k − £51,717k.

The first call on this is fixed costs (financial costs, office staff including marketing and their overheads, parent company costs, and so on) which is £25,500k. To this you add the fixed cost of production for advertising or £525k. The amount spent on media for advertising is £3,930k, of which £3,700k is for television time and £230k for magazines, trade press and miscellaneous. Promotions, which are run twice a year, cost including production and in total £1,575k.

You most easily see what is left as profit or contribution by setting out this table:

	£000
Revenue from 24,167 tonnes at £3,930 per tonne	94,976
Variable cost at £2,140 per tonne	− 51,717
Gross margin at £1,790 per tonne	43,259
Fixed cost, including advertising production	26,025
Adspend, or media costs of advertising	3,930
Promotions, including production	1,575
Profit or contribution	11,729
	43,259

There are certain ratios of interest in such a budget when brands in a portfolio are being compared: profit to turnover, advertising to sales (A/S), media spend to media plus promotion, and so on.

Example: Useful ratios
In the example above, profit as a proportion of turnover is 12%.

The advertising to sales ratio, when advertising production is included and revenue is net (the sum cannot be done this way for competitors) is 100 x (3,930 + 525) / 94,976 or 4.7%. An outsider might look at the ratecard value of the time and space you bought – say £4,466k if your discounts were 12%. He compares this with the reported turnover at retail level: £130,132k. Then the A/S ratio looks like 3.4%. The former is the way to compare your own brands with each other, the latter is the only way to compare brands from different manufacturers.

The proportion spent on media advertising including production, of the total of advertising plus promotions, is 100 x 3,930 / (3,930 + 525) = 74%. This looks an unusually high figure, but note that discounts to the trade were deducted before revenue was calculated, and were not counted as trade promotions. If they had been so counted, the ratio would have been well below one half, as is normal. The difference can be critical.

4.3 Breakeven Elasticities

From the budget you can calculate two further ratios of great importance in this book: the breakeven elasticities of price and of advertising. The first means that if you increased price by one per cent, and if sales volume decreased as a result by this (negative) percentage, then you would make the same profit as before. The second means that if you spent one per cent more on advertising, and if sales volume increased as a result by this percentage (a short-term effect is implied, often but not always), then you would make the same profit as before.

For the price elasticity, there are two equivalent simple formulae:

breakeven price elasticity = –price per unit / variable cost per unit,

or   breakeven price elasticity = –revenue / gross margin.

For the advertising elasticity, the formula is just as easy:

breakeven advertising elasticity = adspend / gross margin.

These are proved in Section 9.9.1 and the implications are discussed.

Example of price and advertising elasticity calculations
For price, the breakeven elasticity for the example above is –3,930 / 1,790, or –94,976 / 43,259, both of which are –2.20.

The conclusion is that if you dropped price from £3,930 per tonne to £3,891 (one per cent) and sales increased by 24,167 x 2.20 / 100 = 531 tonnes then profit is unchanged. If you sell more than 531 additional tonnes then you have increased both volume and profit.

The breakeven elasticity for advertising is 3,930 / 43,259 which is 0.091.

The conclusion is that if you spend a further £39.3k on advertising (one per cent) and the short-term volume increase is 24,167 x 0.091 / 100 = 22 tonnes then profit is unchanged. If you sell more than 22 additional tonnes you have increased profit.

Care must be used with such conclusions. The effects of advertising are usually more than short term: competitors may react to price cuts; profit is not the only criterion. But as summaries of the brand budget, and as benchmarks to compare with measured elasticities in the field, the information is helpful.

It is well worth calculating the two breakeven elasticities as soon as you know the brand's budget. These indicate how easy, or how difficult, it is going to be to justify an advertising or a price increase. This is because typical values for the marketplace price elasticity are around –2, and for advertising elasticity, 0.1 (these are indicated by current data and some collections noted in the Appendix).

So if you were to see a budget or breakeven price elasticity of, say, –1, you know immediately that this is probably a smaller number than the marketplace elasticity. But if you saw a budget or breakeven price elasticity of –3, you know this is likely to be a larger number than the marketplace elasticity. The implications of one figure being above or below the other are spelled out in Section 9.9.1. These are concerned with the movements of volume and of profit when you raise or lower price – or your advertising budget.

A rather similar sum is done to answer questions like, 'If we increase volume by 2%, what is the additional gross margin?' The purpose is to compare the additional cash in hand, after meeting variable costs, with what might be paid to get it. Again, be cautious with the answer, since only one of the possible benefits is being evaluated. It may not be only the cash which matters; the status of higher share and the effects of growth on morale can be important and worth paying for.

The sum is straightforward: the additional revenue is the added units sold times price; the additional variable cost is the added units times variable cost per unit. The added cash is the difference. More usual is to multiply the added units by the gross margin rate.

Example: Gross margin as the benefit
If we increase volume by 2% we sell 483 more tonnes. The sum is:

$$483 \times (£3,930 - £2,140) = £865k$$

A cautious management might build in a safety margin and say, 'You may have £600k to spend if you will return 2% more units sold.' A management which believes there are other benefits might say 'You have another £1 million to spend.'

5 How Advertising is Expected to Work

You need to be very clear exactly what your campaign is intended to do. Contrary to the belief of some people, this is no simple matter. Unless both manager and analyst understand and agree on what it is reasonable to expect for their campaign, its evaluation will be imperfect.

There are many ways advertising can affect behaviour, and usually more than one for a single campaign. The main ways include: influencing the consumer's view of brand values and price; pulling the brand up to the advertising's own level of likeability; just being there; stimulating trial; prompting the use of promotions; other immediate calls for action; confirming that a purchase already made was the right choice; and making the trade more helpful.

5.1 No One Way

Decision-makers simplify their ideas about advertising in order to manage it. That is understandable. But to over-simplify beyond a certain point, and especially when you are measuring effects in the marketplace, can be fatal.

The ways different people on the team standardise and reduce their views may not be the same, which can lead to incompatibility. On the one hand, there are usually those who believe advertising is for communication, 'how it works' is about creating brand images in consumers' heads. On the other hand, some managers would be amazed to see a whole chapter on this subject. To judge by the way they evaluate an advertising campaign or a weight test it seems that they believe advertising is simply a tap you can turn on or off with immediate effects; these are on volume sales alone.

Advertising can actually do a great many different things. The range of situations in which it may be used is very wide, and for each situation there is a variety of different strategies and different media. There is *no one way* communications work: you have to define exactly what you expect, in your situation. This chapter might have been called, 'How *these advertisements* could work in *your* situation and against *your* objectives.' The final result is to influence behaviour, but it is worthwhile investigating the mechanism by which this is done.

Nor is there only one result from a particular campaign. Hence, there is no such thing as *the* effect. Nor is there necessarily any effect at all – some campaigns are simply ineffective. They do not reach the right people often enough, they are not motivating, or they are not 'branded', that is, nothing from them is recalled by the prompts at the time of a purchase decision. As an example of having more than one effect, a burst of advertising may produce extra, immediate sales *and also* help justify your price for some time to come by reinforcing belief in a benefit among future buyers. If the immediate sales are economic, bringing in a profit greater than the cost, you may legitimately discount the second advantage as 'additionally, there are long-term benefits'. But if the burst is uneconomic short term, you need to consider the second advantage with care.

Here is a checklist, in a very simple form, of the main ways advertising often has effects:

- It influences the *consumer's view of brand values*, though not as much as does product experience. The result is that the consumer feels the brand is 'for me'.
- It is seen and considered by the *trade*, thus influencing distribution. This makes the brand more available.
- When the consumer comes to consider the *price* for the brand, this is seen as acceptable.
- If there are *promotions* for various brands in the category, it prompts the consumer to use ours and ignore competitors.
- Finally, advertising is a direct *call to action*.

Hence, the consumer is aware of a product to suit her needs, it is available and at an acceptable price, your promotions make it more attractive, and she has recently been reminded to buy it.

'Selling is easy...' I was once told by a marketing director I worked for, 'you just have to think about the sale from the point of view of the consumer, and make your brand the natural choice.'

Advertising most often makes your brand 'the natural choice' in the *first* way above, by adding value and making the brand 'for me'. This can be a slow process and the results can last a long time. A dilemma you meet when you come to measure effects is that this, the most important effect of most advertising, is also the hardest to demonstrate. As already pointed out, product experience (except when competitors are very similar, as for example with petrol), counts for more. The immediate 'call to action' can be less economic, but easier to see.

5.2 The Definition of Effect

The situation now considered is that you have carried out some communications plan. After it has been executed, you observe some situation in the marketplace: so many cases sold at such a price, for example. This observation must be compared with *what would have happened if you had not carried out your plan*. The difference is the effect of the communications.

It is not hard to see a practical difficulty – the hypothetical state '*if you had not carried out your plan*' has not been observed. This is not the laboratory, where you can repeat experiments and compare the result of a treatment with no treatment or with another treatment. Only in direct mail, other database techniques and specially designed experiments is this possible. In most situations in marketing you get only one shot. You either run your campaign or you do not. If you do not, you will never know its effect. If you do, you have destroyed the conditions to compare the results with. In Chapter 8 I discuss various technical ways round this.

Another difficulty is that when you move on from analysis of the past to making decisions about the future, you have to predict effects in an unknown environment. However, here you are in the same situation as in every business decision.

Finally, for analysis to affect decisions it must tell the manager about behaviour: essentially, so many units sold at such a price. But much of the research about advertising is qualitative: what people say goes on in their heads.

It is not only because accountants need numbers about volume sales and prices that you must be wary of softer measures. When they are used diagnostically to help creative development, they are often the best information you can get. When you use these as surrogates for sales measures, you cannot be certain that their face validity (about what they appear to measure), actually corresponds to reality. This is usually because you have yourself made unwarranted assumptions – 'if they say it is creamier, that must mean they will buy more of it'; 'if my lager's scores have not improved that must mean no one is ordering more'; 'if my advertising awareness is up/down, that must mean sales are up/down'. There are real examples of all these assumptions being wrong. The reason for such discrepancies is that advertising's relevance (to real motivations), and persuasiveness (causing behaviour change), can be different from recall, noticeability, image scores, and so on.

5.3 People Use Advertisements

People are bombarded by hundreds of commercial messages every day. Most of them are ignored – or, more accurately, filtered out without conscious attention. Much of the processing of advertising is not conscious. The same is true for much decision-making in a grocery store. The headline 'Want cheaper car insurance?' does not much interest people without cars – or even the car owner who is months away from making this decision.

This example reminds us that it is the reactions of the *target* which interest us. The reactions of people you do not want to influence have little relevance as long as you are not building up antipathy. To the marketer, people are not all equal: some are irrelevant; some are open to persuasion; and others bond with competitors. There may be an average reaction, but it is made up of a very wide range, from apathy to picking up a telephone and dialling your direct response number, or taking some equally positive action.

The example also reminds us that people *use* or process messages: the results are not always what the advertiser wants, but are decided by the recipient. At this stage the consumer, not the advertiser, is in charge. What people take *out* of a communication may not be the same as what you put *in*. And they will normally take out more than one message. Those who pay attention will absorb some fact, such as that flights are now cheaper, or this car costs £11,000. And they will have an impression both of the product – 'oh, they're local flights in the UK,' or, 'it's a family saloon' – *and* of the brand owner, users of the brand and so on – 'they're helping me with this information,' or, 'I don't want to be like the people in the picture.'

Advertisers who rely mainly on direct response sometimes ignore the second sort of response. They complacently argue that cost per conversion makes them accountable already. They seem unaware that the primary measure – response – is not all that is going on: they disregard the values being added to the brand, which may pay off later in all sorts of ways (more attention to later ads, more forgiving attitudes to the product). This is particularly true for the first entrants into direct response for a new category, such as insurance or banking. The first direct advertiser picks up all those ready to take up such an offer. When several firms advertise this way, choice is likely to be more influenced by brand values, so they had better be there.

It is not an obvious waste of money to communicate with an advertisement containing information already 'known'. The recipient may take out something which is not just factual information such as: 'They are still there, talking to me. I'm glad they are taking the trouble'; or, 'I had forgotten how good that looks.'

There are many ways you can segment the target. The reason is that even if two people are 'in the market', and have the same exposure to advertising, they can have very different responses. This is because the strategy they adopt to the brand decision can be so different. For groceries, for example, some housewives have decided to buy the cheapest brand on offer in the category. Others buy whatever brand is on offer, among a group they regard as acceptable. Others rotate purchases among such a group. Some buy only one brand nearly all the time. You can see that advertising can have very different sorts of effect on these different groups. It may be ignored, it may be used as a source of information about deals, it may confirm a habit, it may move a name to the top of the repertoire, it may occasionally encourage trial and help make a convert. Within these reactions, heavy viewers may behave differently from light viewers. And heavy buyers in the category are of greater interest to us than light buyers.

The real world is amazingly complicated when you look at it in detail. It can be segmented in so many different ways, and the different groupings you have to create to make it manageable are not independent. Your target may watch more or less television than average. Your price promotions appeal more to some buyers than others. They may or may not be timed together with your advertising. Sometimes such factors are critical to the analysis; they are meat and drink to advertising planners.

More often, the analyst is concerned with overall effects on sales volume. Others legitimately worry about what goes on in the hearts and minds of the target, and the most relevant ways to segment them; the analyst is initially more concerned with the total of all the shopping baskets or cheques. You know what behaviour you want to affect, and the question here is the relation between the advertising schedule and overall decisions to buy, or not to buy, your brand. Later, and occasionally, the complexities may re-enter.

In addition to the direct effect on the purchaser, you are interested in indirect effects: Does advertising affect the distribution and display of the brand? Does it alter the enthusiasm of those who make and sell it? Does it help to get the financial backing from management for the whole process?

5.4 Not Just Advertising

It is hard to be realistic about what communications do when you consider only the communication and the recipient. Communications do not work on their own.

In a successful firm many different operations are done well: the product is superior; the price is seen as very affordable given the perceived quality; the trade treat it with respect; the source of the product adds lustre, and so on. Communications speed up the effects of these good things. An 'affordable' price may have become so because of values added by advertising: it may be affordable now but it did not become so by itself. The synergy of all these processes makes it hard to disentangle the effect of any one of them and, in particular, the help which advertising has given.

To repeat in different words the point at the end of Section 5.1, advertising simply makes it easier to do business. You see its results indirectly in the popularity of the brand, the success of the promotion, the presence in store.

Note also that an advertisement which prompts a sale may be followed by a favourable product experience; so a further reaction can be, 'That was good, just like they said it would be, I'll get some more.' One of the functions of advertising is to point out exactly what it is in the usage experience that is satisfying. 'The taste *was* tangy', 'the newspaper *was* a good read', or, 'the people I met on holiday *were* friendly'. The advertising, plus the experience, can lead to a repeat purchase. This is called 'framing'. The advertisement directs you to a particular aspect of the product, like a frame holds your eye on a picture. The person subject to this influence is often unconscious of it. The perceived quality is part of the product and the advertisement may then be forgotten. Nevertheless, the advertising is partly responsible for the next purchase.

What has just been discussed is this sequence: advertisement – purchase – experience causing recall of a copy point. Another sequence is purchase – closer study of a later advertisement. For example, the recent car buyer tends to look for confirmation that the right choice has been made, and that the emotional or rational appeal which sold the car is actually backed up. It should go without saying that, with good media buying, those who see the advertising tend also to be buyers anyway, and that a link between ad exposure and purchase may not be causal in the way normally expected.

The perception of quality in a product or service has many sources, not all laboratory-proven or circumstantial. Consumers' feelings of satisfaction and of loyalty are as important to the manufacturer as is purchase itself. Activities which reinforce or improve these feelings are likely to be long-term benefits.

5.5 Head or Heart?

Few buying decisions are made in a totally rational, explicitly argued way. This may sometimes happen, but it is by no means the only or most likely process.

There is an analogy which explains a great deal of what people do take out of an advertisement. Do not think of a communication as if it were like a new line of data in a table – to be coldly assessed, tested for novelty or consistency or whatever. Rather, think of it like a brief meeting with an acquaintance. You may or may not learn something new – most likely not. But you refresh your opinion about her, you renew your friendship, you are pleased to have had a smile from her and to feel accepted and approved of.

Brands are very like other people in this way. It is not only that it is quite easy to answer the question, 'If X were a person, what would she be like?' The point is that you have *relationships* with them. If you are not a homemaker, you may at first think this exaggerated when applied to laundry detergents or margarine. You will probably accept it about products you yourself have chosen: your car, your watch, your PC, your holiday, or your newspaper. It is so with *any* product which people buy, all the way down to business-to-business selling for photocopiers or chemicals. The heart may not always take priority over the head, but as in other aspects of life, it certainly makes itself felt.

When a brand communicates with you, it is reinforcing almost-human links. The unconscious reaction is that the relationship is refreshed. Without advertising (and of course without use and sight of the brand), you would lose touch. The communication is making it easier for you to keep a warm feeling about the brand – and about the brand owner.

The emotional channels tapped in this way may be of many different kinds, just as your friends and acquaintances have many different qualities. Advertising may call on 'category motivators' and fundamental human needs. The first means those attributes prominent in the whole category: nourishment for foods, safety for cars, and so on. The second includes belonging to a group, being respected and other psychological drivers.

5.6 Other Ways

There are no lack of other theories about the ways particular campaigns work – and no reason to doubt that each of them is genuine in its own situation. Usually more than one way operates at once. You do not have to pick from the list in this book, though I cover the most frequent types. Think through what *your* brand's business and marketing objectives are; hence, what *your* advertising is meant to do, and above all *how* it will accomplish it. If you are at the beginning of your planning cycle when you do this, make sure that agreement on the point is recorded in the agency briefing. A useful exercise is to study what your competitors have decided should be the reaction to their advertisements which you should be able to deduce from their copy. Not only what claim or motivation they use, but what reactions they expect. Avoid confusion: do not employ a claim already appropriated, or you may do more good to a competitor than to yourself.

For *launches*, the priority must be to communicate what the new brand is, what it does, why it is different, and to stimulate trial. When products are no longer new, there are still innovations of various kinds, improvements, different flavours and so on to announce. For these the task is much the same, so communication and immediate response are again the mechanisms. Even when there is no real novelty, it is common to emphasise some lesser-known aspect of the product, or to create news in some way.

Persuasion may also be the job for advertising, even without new arguments. Here is one of the classic roles: by comparison with other brands, by demonstration, by testimonial – the advertisement argues, more or less logically, more or less emotionally, that your brand is better, and should at least be given a try.

Occasionally you will see, in the sales plot over time, a 'step' up in the general level when you advertised and it does not fall back. The job done was not just reminder; it was that coveted event – conversion. This is most likely if you have something new to say, and have said it relevantly, and above all persuasively.

Already mentioned are the adding of emotional values and personality; 'framing', or presenting and emphasising benefits which are then attached to the product; reminder or nudging to the top of the repertoire so that a blip in sales is created, but a fall back follows.

This list is far from complete, and two other methods must be included. The first is being famous. This offers the advertisement itself as the benefit. No longer is the main point to argue for the product. The copy is so striking, memorable, amusing, in tune with the concerns of the target audience, gives them such pleasure in itself, that it enters the language. You must not underestimate the advertising-literacy of today's consumer. A soft drink, a coffee, a beer, a snack – all of these may acquire involvement and status purely as a result of their communications, more than because the communications carried some message about the brand's own qualities. A brewer once said that Guinness had three products: draught, canned and advertising.

This route is not often described in textbooks or in technical papers, but is very evident in the trade press. Indeed one of its major channels is the 'trade'. It is work which professionals admire, which wins creative awards, which is 'artistic', emotional, streetwise, knowing. The analyst, who tends to concentrate on communications about brand values, at first finds these characteristics get in the way, the campaigns are too self-indulgent, too clearly for self-advancement, to take seriously. Such aims are not often spelled out in creative briefs, though codewords like 'breakthrough' are used. Leo Burnett's advice, 'We want them to say it's a hell of a product, not a hell of an ad' is not so relevant – here we want them to say both.

Rather than supporting the brand from below, by stressing product values, such advertising pulls the brand up to its own level of likeability and fame. It had better be pulling up your brand and not the brand leader or the category, for the weakness with such work may be its inability to brand, that is, link with you and you only.

The final method is just being there. 'Ninety per cent of life is turning up,' has been attributed to Woody Allen. For much advertising, this is undoubtedly true. Even the shoppers who cannot replay a single copy point often know the brand has advertised; they should, they feel, know something about it even if they cannot recall exactly what. 'If they advertise, they must be all right/reliable/big.' The trade can feel this too.

5.7 Trade

Apart from you and the final purchaser and user, others are involved in the flow from raw material to the buying decision.

Most clearly, the other time a grocery product is bought is when the retail chain pays the manufacturer for it. Retail buyers are human too; they see your consumer advertising and you should make sure they know about it. Advertising helps explain the category and so sell the store's own label, establishes the brand and the manufacturer as serious contenders, and will help the sale off the shelf. So it also helps get the brand onto the shelf, and in general is an assistant to the manufacturer's sales team.

Your own staff also see the advertising. Not only your representative on the road, but your counter and telephone staff (who may get lessons in how to behave), and others not so directly in touch with consumers.

In these and similar ways advertising may have indirect effects which you should understand.

5.8 The Importance of Time

Time is a serious dimension for the analyst. It is not only that most of the data you deal with arrives at regular intervals; it is because effects take place after the actual exposure of the advertisement. But how long after?

To some advertising an almost immediate response is expected. Car drivers stop at the garage for the deal they have just heard about on the radio: 'ring this number', 'fill in this coupon', 'open on Sunday', 'special offer this week'.

'Recency' is a sensible concept. The commercial I saw on Thursday, or the poster half an hour ago is more likely to influence me on a shopping trip on Friday or Saturday than an advertisement I saw last Sunday.

This raises the question of forgetting. As new impressions reach the brain, they elbow out previous memories. It is not that these disappear – it is thought that with sufficient prompts you can recall a great deal, but they are no longer front of mind.

Recall is often discussed as though it was a self-contained event. On the contrary, it cannot be defined without a description of the prompt provided. From market research you get 'unprompted recall', a misleading term given that the lady with the clipboard is clearly testing you and the category name has been given: 'Tell me the names of any icecream you can remember.' 'Prompted recall' means the answer to a question like, 'Which of the ice-creams on this list have you heard of?'

Prompts can be a major element in an advertisement. The purpose is to get the claim recalled at the appropriate time. The pack shot, traditionally regarded by creatives as an interruption, is not just to explain which brand is being advertised. It is there because, seeing the pack at a later time, the viewer will remember the claim – you hope. It is depressing how seldom the pack itself is used for the same purpose, to remind the shopper about the claim.

There is another reason why effects occur well after the appearance of the advertisement. The viewer or reader has been affected at the time, the message has been taken on board, but there has simply been no opportunity to act on it. This of course happens routinely when the shopping trip is some days after ad exposure, or the need to buy in the category again (the end of the 'purchase cycle') is weeks later. But for some categories the actual purchase may be months or even years later: buying a car, moving house and so being in the market for hardware products, a change to another life stage – these may all be chances to act on what you were told long before.

Some old memories, important enough to be recycled often, stay fresh if a little garbled. But the prompt of writing a shopping list or seeing a confectionery counter may no longer be enough to bring back most advertising seen. So you need some method to allow for the decay of advertising's effects – the subject of Section 8.2. Since you do not know in advance what the rate of decay is, the method had better be flexible.

I write 'short-term' effects, meaning in days or weeks after exposure. At the same time, consumers clearly do retain some recollections of advertising for years. Is the long term just more of the short term, only further away? Is a short-term result necessary in order for the long term to exist? Many commentators answer 'yes' to these questions, and do not distinguish the two mechanisms. Some say they cannot see a qualitative difference; on the contrary, I see them as potentially quite separate.

If we were discussing memory only, their views may be correct. But memory is only a vehicle. What it carries can alter the effect we are thinking about.

Take the emotional appeals of the last section. Results from these may well be long lasting. 'That's the sort of thing for me,' or, 'yes, I used to have those when I was a kid – they're great', may be a reaction to the brand not quickly forgotten, or reducing fast in their appeal. You do not forget a friend in a hurry, if ever. But, 'thanks for reminding me', or, 'I'll get some tomorrow', is a different reaction and has not the same durability. The first is brand-building; the second nudges the brand up an existing repertoire. So you should consider the different ways advertising works as potentially decaying at different rates. Also of course, one may have a strong effect on behaviour, another a weak one.

Reinforcement helps the brand to retain a price premium for some time to come, and this can be the real benefit, while the reminder may hardly add to those prompts already present in the shopping trip. It is also possible that the reminder is the real job the advertisement is doing, and you get a good blip in a generally declining share. You need to allow for either, or for both, or (being realistic), for neither.

A final curiosity about time is that I have often seen the sales curve start to rise *before* the advertising burst begins. I can attribute this only to a trade effect, resulting in increased facings and display which are not fully picked up in the data meant to measure distribution.

5.9 Spell it Out

The ideas in our heads, or 'mental models', of how our own advertising works are too often taken for granted and left unexplained. Both the purpose and the 'how' of our communications should be spelled out explicitly:

You cannot be accountable unless you have set standards in advance.

Again, there are so many different ideas about what communications can do and this is a reason for being precise. If there is any misunderstanding in the team, the creative work may be inadequately briefed out, or misdirected, or inefficiently executed. It is also not too early to consider the method to be used in eventual evaluation. The team should know about this too. Without agreement about how it was meant to work, evaluation later will be hamstrung. These two simple additions – if not already there – of agreeing how the ad will work and how it will be evaluated – will do a lot to guide and to sharpen the process of creation.

The big distinction at this stage is whether the objectives in your mental model stop before behaviour – or whether what consumers *do* is included in what you expect to influence. The traditional or majority view, in what Paul Feldwick calls the second age of evaluation, still very prevalent today, is that you should stop at communication achievements. 'The received wisdom in every book I have seen before the 1970s is that sales are so remote from advertising and affected by so many different factors, that bottom-line sales response is unreadable. Therefore, all measurement is of something else ... Advertisers were consistently being told not to look for advertising/sales effects in any formal way.' This book argues that you should look precisely 'for advertising/sales effects' and in a 'formal way'.

Communication results should still be sought, but as diagnostics: *why* people acted as they did, and *how* it worked. This book does not dwell on advertisement evaluation, on the various forms of research about noticing advertisements and being aware of them (after Starch and Millward Brown), recognising and recalling them (Gallup and Burke), or changes in brand image. It concentrates on behaviour.

Because the details of persuasion and motivation are not investigated, this approach has been called a 'black box'. It is true I concentrate on input and output and do not attempt to get into the heads of consumers (which is anyway a process of dubious reliability). However, the inside of the box should not be completely dark. Think of the factors affecting behaviour (as described in Chapter 7) as levers at one end of the box. These include the type, amount, sales-effectiveness and timing of your communications, but also your price, the actions of your competitors, and so on. At the other end of the box is behaviour, usually purchase decisions of consumers. I do try to find out *how much* pulling a lever affects what people do, and also how the gears inside the box mean that one lever affects the results of others.

The simple view which started this chapter is that only one lever matters – advertising – and how much you pull it has a direct and simultaneous effect on what people buy. The only unknown is whether it causes a large or a small change. The real world is rather more complex, and Chapter 8 is less simple for that reason.

5.10 Advertisement Exposure

How your advertisements were exposed is an essential part of their evaluation. Standard methods of media research will be available. These methods depend on the audience definition, and this should be as close as possible to your real target. There may be some uncertainty introduced here, but this is not usually a serious problem.

Research cannot of course tell you exactly how your campaign was exposed; conventional definitions are provided with the standard sources. However precise media numbers look, remember that they are only panel or survey results, open to as much error as any part of the process you are trying to understand.

For example, how much competitors spent on their advertising – and spend is the basic measure – uses standard corrections between rate-card expenditure and actual spend. You can see how well these adjustments work when you compare your own actual spend with what it is reported to be.

For television, you get the most precise measure – the ratings for each spot, for which you also know the exact time. A television 'rating' means that one per cent of the audience were recorded as 'viewing'; a few of these were not actually present during the commercial transmission, others were paying no attention. Nevertheless, ratings are universally used for this work. One hundred ratings means that on average everyone in the audience 'viewed' once. This is on average one 'opportunity to see' or OTS, and ratings divided by 100 are often called the OTS in the burst or schedule. This is only an average, and you can obtain the distribution of those who 'saw' none, and those who saw at least one (were 'covered'). Within these, you can get those who saw exactly one, exactly two, and so on. Some analysts use this distribution in full, but here the average is used to give us a reasonable fix on the achievement. Thus the normal measure of TV exposure is a list, by weeks or months, of the ratings on the audience – 'the schedule'.

It is vital to be realistic about the amount of advertising or whatever your target is going to see. The amount of competition also needs to be known. It is easy in the sheltered and concentrated atmosphere of the office to enjoy grandiose ideas about how important communications are to the consumer, and about their effects. These ideas are sometimes out of proportion to your own efforts.

Example: Summary of the advertising exposed
In the example begun in Chapter 6, your brand in 1995 had 16 exposures of your 30-second commercial, plus a little press coverage – under 10 minutes a year. Competitors in total got 20 minutes.

You also know the length of all the commercials – and for competitors too. Rather than count simply the raw numbers of ratings, or OTS, you usually take into account this length. A conventional multiplier may be used, but it is better to convert each spot into its '30-second cost equivalent'. If a 60 costs twice a 30, then where you have one 60, you have two 30-second equivalents. In this way you allow for the presumed greater effectiveness of longer lengths – why else would time buyers pay more? A conventional factor in the UK for ten seconds is 0.57, and for twenty is 0.83. If you are using expenditure on television rather than ratings as your explainer, then you already use such modifiers.

You may sometimes use the fact that heavy viewers do see more of the campaign, and in some analyses you can separate these heavy viewers to find out whether they were affected more. If this is so, you add some conviction to the effect you attribute to advertising. The same can be done with other media. Bear in mind, however, that heavy viewers also differ in other ways – they see more of competitors' advertising for example. They may be different demographically and have different category and brand buying preferences and habits. You may have to allow for these before you can claim you have found an effect. Awareness is not a major theme in this book, but it is worth noting that people who see more of our advertising are often more aware of our brand, not because of the ads (this is the Rosser Reeves fallacy), but because our schedule has targeted our buyers, so they are aware for that reason.

Another conventional measure is used for newspapers and magazines: 'reading an issue'. For each insertion bought, you know the 'readership'. Within issue readers, some will not see the page carrying your advertisement, and the loss is likely to be larger than for the television measure. The time of the exposure is uncertain, unlike TV or radio (the latter is treated much like television). For magazines, the contact may be weeks or months after the insertion date. It may also be repeated. Hence, for press it is common practice to use in analysis only the expenditure figure, and to use as the normal measure a list by weeks or months of reported spend, accepting these uncertainties and expecting a less precise result with slower effects. More trouble can be taken: the readership of each individual publication may be used with an allowance for page traffic and later reading. This is rare.

Other media have their own conventions, but do not introduce radically different ideas.

When you have a pure TV campaign, it is best to use 30-second equivalent ratings in the nearest audience to your target as the measure. When TV is the major medium, it is best to convert the minor media expenditures to 'equivalent ratings' – the number which would be bought if TV had been used instead. Adding the real TV ratings, you preserve the greater accuracy of the major medium. When you have a mixed-media campaign in which there is no, or little, TV, then it is usually best to use recorded expenditure as the measure.

The precision of the data you use to measure sales and awareness and ad exposure is sometimes questioned. It is reassuring when eyeballing or modelling detects close connections between the three. I am impressed each time such different sources as a sales audit and a tracking study manage to be so in step with a TV ratings panel.

5.11 What the Analyst Needs

We have now looked at several important concepts: variety in different aspects of the situation; the unconscious level at which individual advertisements do much of their work; hence, the difficulty of observation, let alone measurement; the emotional values added; how hard it is to separate advertising from product and other factors; the need to deal with time difficulties; and the importance of the trade.

For the analyst who will have to deal largely with numbers, this chapter may seem imprecise and hardly usable. Some of it is quantified later on. Some of it has obvious implications when you come to interpret a tracking study. But the analyst is correct in seeing that you do have to deal with *behaviour* when you look for the accountability of advertising. The 'how' is less important then than the 'how much' (the opposite is true for the advertising researcher).

You cannot worry about individual responses; you have to deal with the big picture. But you might well segment people whose responses are very different: those exposed and those not exposed to the advertising, for example, either because of their habits or because you have run an experiment; those who never buy your brand and those who have it in their repertoire.

You do not know in advance in what way advertising works in a new situation. You have to acknowledge there is variety; you use a checklist of possible reactions, but you keep an open mind until the data informs you. The objectives of the advertising include getting the trust of the viewer or reader. There may still be calls to immediate action (pick up the phone), the communication of facts, making the brand the user's friend, adding value to the product, and/or impressing the retailer. These tasks are rarely the same for two campaigns together. There is just as much intuition and qualitative judgment needed at this stage as ever.

You must remember to treat the situation as a whole: not just advertising on the one hand and sales on the other. You expect measures for other factors to be more relevant: how good the product is, what you charge for it, and so on. People react to a whole proposition, not just to a commercial message. Other factors affect their choice and are ignored at your peril.

You look for effects in other fields than on your possible consumers. The chain of events, from making the product, getting it distributed and perhaps recommended – all of these may be affected too.

You must take previous advertising into account; you must allow for both short and long-term effects, for which the mechanisms and efficacy may not be the same; you do not know in advance how fast these effects decay.

Finally, you need to understand your media research numbers.

Part 2

6   Making it Happen

This case history is told as a dialogue between the manager and the analyst. The manager explains the background, what top management expects, and where quantification, forecasts and guidance will help. The analyst reports, in a way which is directed to the manager's needs, what the data have to say. No time is spent here on how these findings were produced – only the results are reported, with their applications.

This takes us through the following benefits from the techniques explained later: category description and forecasting, plots which show how the major brands make up the category and how they are moving – in sales share, in relative price, in distribution, and in advertising spend aggressiveness. Tracking data are simplified to make their meaning clearer. Plots demonstrate the effects of price and of distribution on brand share. Consumer Brand Equity is defined and plotted – a summary of how consumers value the brands in the category. An experiment is reported, with a way of getting more rapid and precise results than usual. Modelling is used to quantify effects, and brand budget data are added to show the effects of different scenarios on profit as well as on volume. The scheduling of the advertising is improved. An apparently impossible management request is successfully met with some changes to existing practice and beliefs.

The manager sees where most is to be gained from briefing and questioning the analyst. The analyst sees how the results really help.

This is the bridge between the first part of the book and the last. It shows by example how the marketer and the analyst agree what the questions are, and how the analyst responds. The case history illustrates how the previous chapters are applied for one particular brand. It also introduces the work the analyst does.

A single story cannot of course demonstrate every situation, or every way in which analysis can help. It has been constructed to show the most likely questions and how to answer them. It is based on real experiences, and except for the ease of interpretation, contains nothing unusual.

The case history is described by a series of conversations between the marketer and the analyst. The dialogue is supposed to take place towards the end of 1995 and early in 1996, when data for 1995 are mostly available or actually complete. At this stage, *how* the analyst gets the answers is not described. It is the *application* which is emphasised. Between the meetings, a great deal of work is done by the analyst. References are given in the text to later chapters where the methods are discussed more fully; this chapter is a prospectus for Chapters 7 to 9. Sufficient detail is given in the Tables section at the end of the book for the reader to try out some of the techniques recommended.

6.1 The Briefing

Marketer: Let's first run through where our brand, B, is now. Before we go forward, I need to know what benefits we have been getting from our activities, and what I can expect to get. Then I want your advice about forecasts.

It's common ground that our brand is having a good 1995. We are close to planned contribution at nearly £12 million. Tonnage sales are likely to be 7% up on 1994. I know we've had to hold prices to get that, and I've spent more on advertising than in 1994. I don't know how much may be due to each of these.

The people upstairs are happy. Their business priority is a minimum level of contribution. The £12 million target is sacred – we cannot fall below it. Once that is secure, everyone wants to see high volume.

Coming to the 1996 plan, the advertising budget is at risk because it seemed to cut into our profits this year, and some people resent that. Without it we might have made over £16 million. I'm not sure what real good it did us, and I may not be able to defend it next year. The boss might well be right: we could have bigger bonuses if we'd cut it.

Sales are claiming it was their promotions which counted, and they too may be right. Certainly they sold a lot of promoted packs. You'll remember that we have this value-adding idea, carefully designed to continue our advertising message, which is a lot more than a price cut. Of course, we do also cut prices at planned periods, just like everyone else.

Analyst: Do you want me to look at the category defined as all product types, or at standard and light separately? Are there any regional differences which you think matter?

Marketer: Well, we know it's much the same households buying all varieties, and I'm judged on the total, so let's start with the total category. We can always go back to another definition. And I'm happy to look at the national picture for the same reason. Sales can tell you about individual retailers, but again let's take the total.

Analyst: Which competitors worry you?

Marketer: We all know about Brand A; they are still the gold standard. They've been pushing up their TV spend, which is one of the reasons why I have too. I don't know what good it's done them, but I hear they are quite pleased with themselves.

Brand C used to frighten me, but we've put blue water between us now.

There are so many smaller brands, especially these new back-to-basics. The local specialists do good business. A lot of them are high quality, and they advertise too. But that may be too complex for a first cut – let's lump them together for a start.

Own label is a much more serious competitor. They aren't a cheap alternative any longer; their quality is now as good as ours, though we're still able to charge a quarter more than they do. They keep opening new stores and so gaining distribution.

Analyst: I'll look at own label then. And at A and C. The others I'll group for now.

Let's review the data I've got to look at.

Marketer: You know the consumer sales data we buy, which give us volume sales, prices and distribution. It's weekly back to the start of 1994; before then it was four-weekly, and I wouldn't go earlier than 1992 because the events of 1991 changed everything. I'm not too happy about the cover of our consumer sales source: it reports only 80% of our actual sales, but I'm ready to accept it as representative.

We've got the tracking data of course. The media people will update you on their own front. Sales will talk to you about promotions, which have been pretty regular. Accounts will give you all the internal data, but let's not worry about that until we've got a better idea about how the marketplace is working.

Analyst: What do you look at most in the tracking data?

Marketer: We know we've always done best on attribute F, 'for people I admire', but that doesn't seem to move much. Unaided brand awareness seems to move more and I think that's important. W, or 'worth the money' has started to move up, but I heard from a competitor the other day he doesn't pay much attention to that. We do worst on attribute K, 'know my problems', but I don't know if that's important.

Analyst: OK, I'll be back to you.

6.2 Total Category: Description *(more in Section 7.5)*

Analyst: Let's start with the total category and then go on to how it's made up. I'll come back on the detail about our brand later.

   The category is falling slightly: from 139,000 tonnes in 1994 to 134,000 in 1995, according to the retail research. 1994 now looks like the high year. Average prices dropped a little too: from £5.08 per kilo to £5.02. This is because own label continued to grow in volume and they are about 14% below the category average in price.

   Advertising in the category really shot up: from 3,800 TVRs in 1994 to an estimated 6,600 in 1995. Of course we more than doubled, from 750 to 1,570 TVRs, but the biggest advertiser is still Brand A, who almost doubled: from 1,300 to nearly 2,400 TVRs.

6.3 Category Modelling and Forecasting *(more in Section 8.5)*

Analyst: Let's now look in more detail at how the category total has moved according to our consumer sales source. Also, I have forecast the next two years, with the usual reservations about unexpected changes.

   Here are the plots of category volume (Figure 1) and price (Figure 2) with four years history and two years forecast.

   You can see that four-weekly sales have varied between about 9,000 and 13,000 tonnes; there have been sales peaks in April and in November; but from year to year, sales have been very steady.

Marketer: So the volume in 1996–97 looks like more of the same, with the seasonality we all know about. That seems reasonable to me.

Analyst: Prices to the consumer reached a peak of £5.12 per kilo in mid-1994. Since then there has been a decline which your people expect to continue.

Marketer: That's more complicated. I see you're showing the step-up everyone made, following Brand A, at the start of 1994. It didn't last though. Ever since the new cheap varieties came in everyone

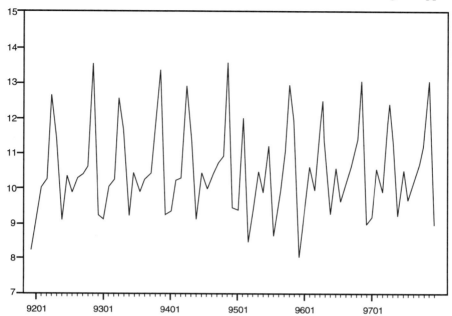

Figure 1 Category Volume, '000 tonnes
(1992–95 actual, 1996–97 forecast)

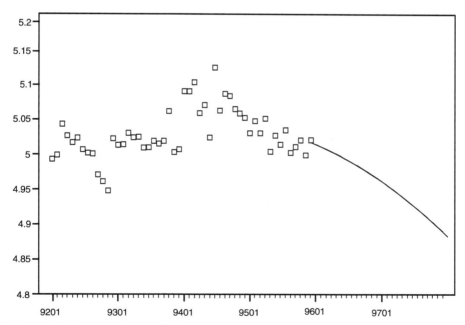

Figure 2 Category Price, £000 per tonne
(1992–95 actual, 1996–97 forecast)

has been chipping away at price. I see you're expecting that to go on and even accelerate. I'm afraid you are right. Life is going to get harder.

6.4 Splitting the Category *(more in Sections 7.4 and 7.5)*

Analyst: I've taken the years 1994 and 1995 separately. Let's look at the overall picture for volume sales and relative price first. This is the way the category is currently made up: *(more in Table 1)*

Category in 1995

Brand	Volume shares, %	Price relative to category = 100
A	17.3	122
B	14.7	107
C	6.7	110
Own label	31.1	86
Others	30.2	96

I've plotted this in Figure 3. This shows relative prices on the X-axis and volume share on the Y-axis. 'Relative price' means the brand's pounds per kilo shown as an index on the total category price; we are at 107, which is 7% above the average.

Look first at price. Brand A is easily the price leader, well to the right of everyone else. We're at about the same price as C. Own label is cheapest of course. The group of other brands is between own label and us on average, but there's quite a variety inside this group.

Now look at the volume shares, down the plot. Own label and Others in total are highest, or largest overall. They are about the same size – around 30%. Brand A is the largest of the three main brands, as well as being the price leader. We are second, ahead of Brand C.

A strong brand is to the right or high up on this plot. That is, it can either charge more than others who sell a similar volume – or it sells more at the same price.

So, how is each brand doing by that criterion? You can see that A is doing better than us in both ways: it's a very strong brand. We are doing better than C because we sell twice as much as them, at a similar price.

Marketer: Are own label selling so much just because they're cheap?

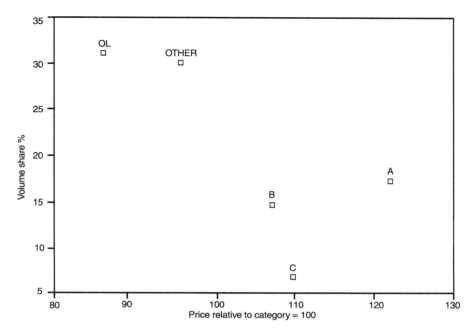

Figure 3 Do Cheaper Brands Sell More? Not Always
Do Brands at the Same Price Sell the Same
Volume? Not Necessarily

Analyst: That's an important point I'll come back to. I can't answer that question from this plot alone.

Now let's look at the plot which shows the movements from 1994 to 1995. Figure 4 has the same 1995 points as before, but I show 1994 too. To distinguish the years I've written the brands in lower-case letters for 1994. For example, in 1994 Brand A was relatively cheaper: little 'a' is to the left of capital 'A'. In 1995 the brand moved both to the right (it's relatively dearer), and slightly up (the volume share has risen).

Marketer: From what you said before, that means it's got stronger. But the movements of A, B and C seem to be all over the place.

Analyst: Yes, Brand A is doing exceptionally well: for the volume share to increase at the same time as price rose is quite an achievement.

We've put on a whole share point in 1995. But we've moved left as well as up. We've got our share gain with a small actual price drop, to retail purchasers, from £5.49 per kilo to £5.38, as

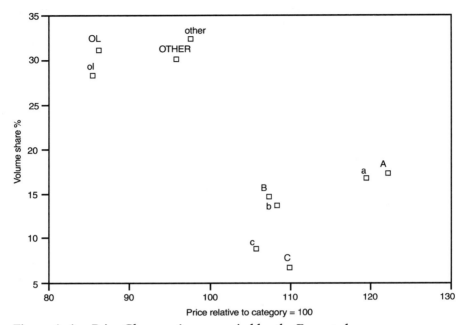

**Figure 4 Are Price Changes Accompanied by the Expected
Volume Changes? No**
Capital letters are for brands in 1995; lower case for 1994

you pointed out at our first meeting. This has translated into a
small relative price drop, from 8% above category average to 7%
above. Our price is now below C's.

We are not necessarily stronger: it looks as though sales have
reacted to the price reduction. I'll sort out later whether there is
only a price effect going on.

But C has moved to the right as well as down, just as we
moved to the left as well as up. Both of these volume share
changes look like reactions to price changes, at least in part. For
Brand C, maybe sales fell just because the brand got relatively
more expensive. We'll come back to all these movements again;
they are very important.

Marketer: Can we do plots like this against distribution?

Analyst: Indeed we can. I haven't included them here because there hasn't
been much change in the annual averages; all the major brands
have good distribution.

Now let's turn to advertising. Your investment in advertising was well up, from £1.6 to £3.7 million, as you said. Increased TV costs took some of that rise, and because the total increased so much, our share of voice went up from 19 to only 24%. That's not so unusual for a brand whose share of the value of the brands which advertised (excluding own label) is over 21%.

Marketer: So, we're not obviously over-spending?

Analyst: Well, Brand A has a 36% share of voice for a value share of 29%. And Others are spending heavily, with over 38% share of voice between them. Incidentally, this is a category with more small brands, taking a reasonable volume than is usual in my experience. We face a lot of competition.

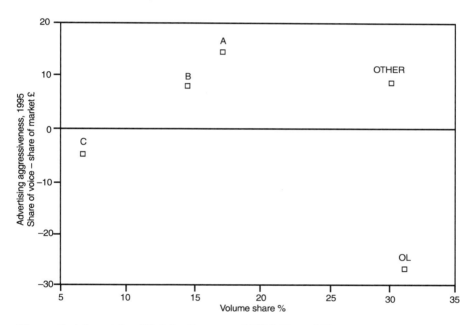

Figure 5 Advertising Weight Compared With Brand Size
(Jones diagram)

Look at Figure 5 (*more in 7.5.3*). The sizes of the brands are shown on the X-axis. I haven't plotted share of voice as such. Instead, on the Y-axis, I've plotted each brand's 'advertising aggressiveness', that is, how much its share of voice *exceeds* its value share of market. For example, A is the most aggressive at

+15 (36% share of advertising spend less its value share of 21%). But look at C. Its point is below the line, showing that its share of voice is below its value share; for a small brand, this is generally a sign of weakness. Of course, by this criterion own label has a negative value, as they do not advertise specifically in this category at all, but have a 27% value share.

The story in this plot is actually an unusual one. Normally we see big brands like A at the bottom right on this plot, with economies of scale. Here, advertising is being used very aggressively. This may be one of the reasons why A is growing. Brand C has dropped its adspend and we know what's happening to them. Their volume share fell from 9 to 7%, while ours of course grew.

The marketer and analyst agree there are some common sense arguments to be made in favour of the adspend, but the marketer gets a warning.

Analyst: Of course this is far from conclusive. I'm going to have to look at the data in more detail before I can tell you what all the evidence is.

Meanwhile, we should go back to price, and then have a look at distribution and promotions – and I have some comments on the tracking scores too.

Have a closer look at the volume–price plot (Figure 4). You know our relative price fell in 1995. But this rise in volume share looks to me out of proportion. Less than one per cent down in price could hardly have caused, on its own, seven per cent more sales. In our category that sort of price elasticity is unknown. I doubt whether price alone could have caused half of that. So we're doing something else right.

C is going in the opposite direction, which is also normal: price up and sales down. But this looks to me out of proportion too.

I must do some more work, but my overall conclusion so far is that it's equity change, as well as price, which is driving this category. 'Equity' means roughly how people value the brands – and that really matters. I'll come back to this.

Now, the last two points.

Our distribution and out-of-stocks levels have been pretty steady, compared with last year. The small changes can't have had a major influence on the improvement in 1995, but I'm going to have a closer look at the detail on this later.

Promotions too have been much the same as the previous year, so we won't see their effect just by looking across the two years. I'm due to come back to you on the way our brand responds over time to the marketing and sales activities.

6.5 Tracking Scores *(more in 7.5.5)*

Analyst: Let me take the tracking scores in two parts. First, the numbers we usually look at, for quite a few attributes, and principally about our brand, are not particularly easy to read:

Scores from the Tracking Study, 1995

Attribute	Our Brand B	Brand A	Brand C
A	30.7	47.8	20.9
F	58.9	61.3	54.6
G	49.3	47.1	41.7
H	44.9	44.1	40.1
J	16.1	15.9	16.9
K	7.4	9.2	8.3
W	21.1	15.1	19.8

You talked last time about 'for people I admire' (attribute F) and 'know my problems' (attribute K), but I don't think they are the main points. They are part of a set of attributes on all of which both Brand A and ourselves get rather similar top scores, but Brand C and own label do worse. I call such attributes 'general', and they're really a sort of halo due to how people see each brand in general terms *(more in Section 7.5.6)*.

Unaided brand awareness (attribute A) is very different and so is 'worth it' (attribute W).

I think being top of mind is critical in this category. Look at this plot (Figure 6) of volume shares and brand awareness. Again, I've put two years on the plot, so we can see movement. Lower case is for 1994 again, capital letters for 1995. The brand furthest to the right, with the highest brand awareness, is A. The awareness is increasing. And look at the sales movement, up the plot. That's going up as well.

Sales of the three brands are closely associated with awareness – for all of them there is a general diagonal movement. Higher awareness – higher sales (I'm not saying yet which causes which!). Own label is different; of course it relies more on

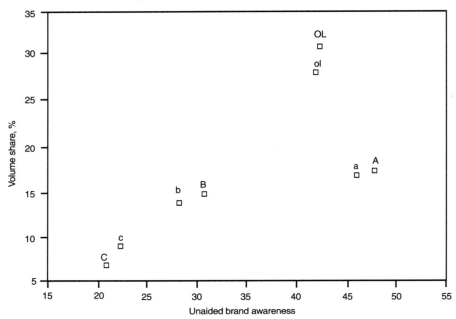

Figure 6 For Three Brands and Own Label, How are Share Movements and Brand Awareness Related?
Capital letters are for brands in 1995, lower case for 1994

store activity. Look at the changes from year to year. These lie on the same general line. For each brand, awareness increases or decreases with higher or lower sales.

Now look at Figure 7 for share of voice (on the X-axis) and brand awareness (on the Y-axis). Again, a close relationship, and again it is not only that the *average* positions show awareness high for high share of voice; the *changes* are also in line. First, we see the general positions of the brands – A is high on *both* share of voice *and* brand awareness, and so on. Second, A has raised its share of voice – its brand awareness has gone up. The same is true for us. For C, a drop in both.

I read this as awareness following share of voice, more than sales changes causing awareness changes. This can be debated, but I believe that here is one way our advertising works.

Another plot, which reinforces my belief that advertising really affects our brand awareness, is Figure 8. You can see the line for awareness clearly lifting when we advertise (*more in Sections 8.4.1–8.4.3*). In addition, awareness is generally growing slowly, which probably *is* due to our increasing volume.

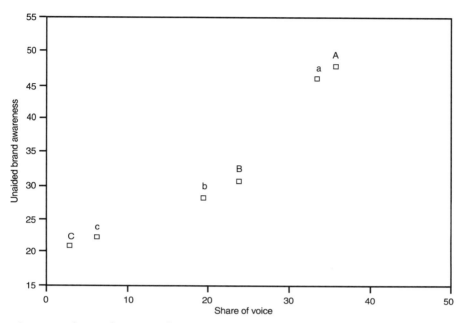

Figure 7 Share of Voice Influences Brand Awareness
Capital letters are for brands in 1995, lower case for 1994

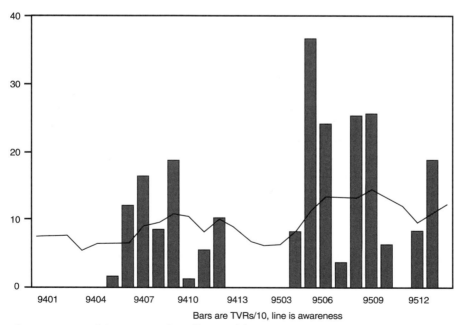

Figure 8 Brand Awareness is Influenced by TVRs

It's fair to hypothesise that the advertising works partly by reminder, and that this causes the housewife to be more aware of us and so moves us up in her purchasing repertoire. We know that in this category she likes rotating round a few chosen brands – advertising makes it likely that she changes to us. If this is so, I'd expect to see a short-term advertising effect directly on sales when I come to modelling.

Marketer: This is going to help me make the case for advertising, though the advertising–purchase–awareness debate is an old one. I can see implications for the creative brief as well. In Figures 6 and 7 it looks as though that is true for all the brands.

But what about 'worth it'? We do well on that.

Analyst: Yes, but Brand A doesn't and own label does best. It does differentiate between the brands and I think it's a complicated attribute. It doesn't seem to mean, 'Worth the high price you charge', which some people here think. It's more like, 'I'm pleased about your price', or, 'I get value for money', and it may be Brand A's weak point. Being the price leader, and at over 40% in price above own label, they may be on the edge of being too high.

Marketer: Rumour has it they are thinking of raising their prices twice next year; they are so pleased at the effect in 1995.

Analyst: Those consumers who find that is too much may switch to us, as the next brand down, but still with a high reputation. On the 'general' tracking scores we are level with Brand A, while own label is clearly lower.

6.6 Brand over Time *(more in 7.6.1)*

The marketer hears from the analyst about the four-weekly sales over the last two years.

Analyst: You're very familiar with the way our sales look at the retail level. Our ex-factory sales followed roughly the same pattern, because we've got the warehouse stocks levels right down, except of course that deliveries are about a quarter higher than the research source shows, for reasons we know.

What I'm going to show you is the way marketing seems to have influenced sales. To do this I'm going to look at share of category, rather than the actual tonnes we delivered. In this way the general trend and seasonality of the category are removed.

Marketer: What do they look like? The same as ours?

Analyst: Briefly, the total doesn't have the same trend as us, but our seasonalities are the same.

Our price, compared with the category, is the biggest reason for changes in our sales share.

You can see this in two ways. First, look at Figure 9, which is a plot of our sales share every four weeks, to which I've added, as a label at each period, the number for our average retail price (indexed on the category averaged at 100). You can see that at sales peaks like June 1994 and August 1995 we were at our lowest price, 104 and 103 – these were our focus periods – and the reverse is true for the troughs, when volume share fell to 11%.

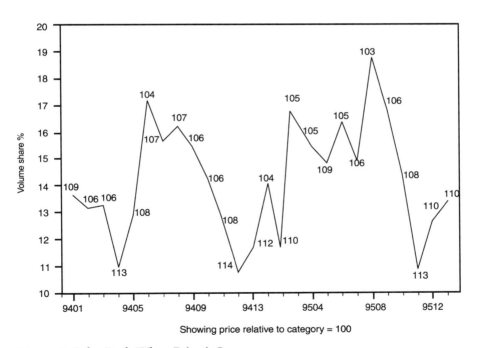

Figure 9 **Sales Peak When Price is Low**

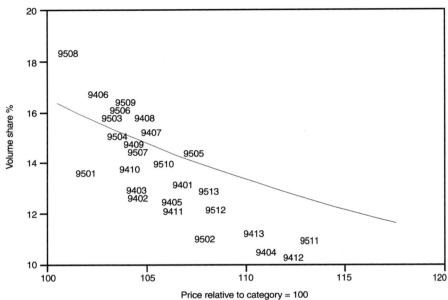

Figure 10 Low Price – High Sales

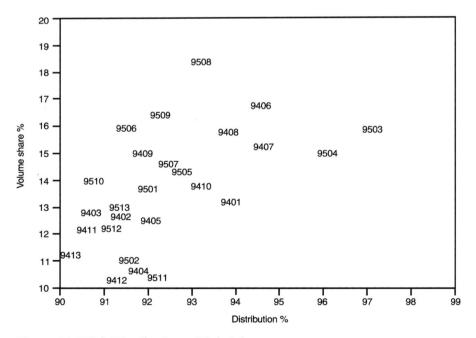

Figure 11 High Distribution – High Sales

This is when competitors promoted and retailers marked them down. All the peaks and troughs tell the same story.

Another way to see any relation between price and sales is Figure 10, where our position for relative price every four weeks is shown on the X-axis, from our lowest ever at 103 and our high at 114. (*Note to the reader: ignore for the moment the line which is explained in Chapter 9.*) On the Y-axis I've put our sales share, from our low of 11% to the high of 19%. There's a pretty clear relationship here: I could draw a line from top left to bottom right.

Marketer: But it's not very definite, is it? Here, where our price index is 105, we can be getting a share anywhere between 13 or 17%.

Well, this is about as good as it gets. There is always a lot else going on which might explain why you don't see an exact relationship. Distribution has an effect, for example. Figure 11 shows the relation between sales on the Y-axis again and distribution on the X-axis. This has even more scatter than Figure 10.

Analyst: Both these plots are giving the same sort of message. First, there is some connection between sales share and the factor, which is what we expect. Second, there is also a lot of variation within any one of the relationships. This isn't like an experiment in a laboratory. The situation gets more complex, because at the times when you had low price, like June 1994, you also got good distribution – and that's when you were running a promotion too. We're not going to be able to disentangle exactly the effects of these factors, though I will show you estimates of their average effects under the conditions we obtained.

6.7 Modelling: Weekly Brand Shares

Analyst: Even though price and distribution are related, they don't always come together in exactly the same way. Figure 12 shows the result of sorting this out. It's the plot of sales share over time, which we saw before in Figure 9.

It also gives a fit to our actual weekly sales share by a model using four of our activities. That is, I've written an equation, or estimate, for the effects on sales share of our price, promotions, distribution and advertising. The fit is the line; the actual sales are shown by the squares. I've been able to account for nearly all the variation in sales. You can see how close the actual shares

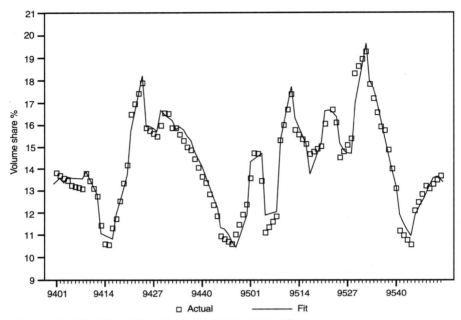

Figure 12 The Fit to Weekly Data 1994–95 is Close

are to those I calculated. (*Note to the reader: as already pointed out, the fits in this example are artificially good.*)

You can't tell from the last figure how much each of the four different explainers I used (price, promotions, distribution and advertising) contributed to my fit. The next plot (Figure 13 – *more in Section 8.6.2*) indicates roughly how much effect each of these factors had.

The X-axis is time again, the Y-axis is sales share points in the category share. The horizontal line across the plot stands for what the sales share would be if there were no promotions or advertising at all, and both relative price and distribution were at their lowest levels over these two years (these were 103 and 91 respectively). Our sales share would have been 13.6% in that case. That's the base I'm taking, and then I show how price, promotions and distribution subtracted or added sales to this line. For instance, our worst price week was at the end of November, 1994, when we were at 115. That lost us 4.8 share points compared with our base. Our best distribution week was at the end of March, 1995, when we hit 99%. The effect was to add 0.7 of a share point.

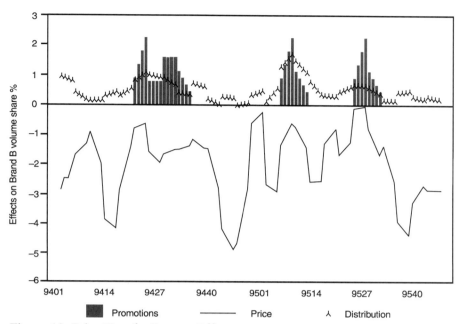

Figure 13 Price Has the Largest Effect:
Promotions and Distribution are Linked

Price has caused the biggest swings, as we saw in Figure 9 by the difference between our low volume shares of 11 or 12 and the highs of 17 or more. On average, it has cost us two share points below our base.

We ran our promotions at the same time as our price was low (you can see this from the plot), and we tended to get better distribution then (again, see the plot). We can't be certain how each of these factors really changed our sales share. Exact knowledge isn't given to analysts in this situation. The price effect is pretty clear, but promotions and distribution have been rather mixed up. And of course we only know about all this happening in the presence of our advertising. The factors don't separate as cleanly as I've made them seem to here. I have made my estimates by modelling but they aren't very precise. It looks as though the promotions can give us one or two share points, and distribution rather less, perhaps half a share point on average with the variations we've had above 91.

Marketer: So we can't really say what a pure price effect is? But you can tell me roughly what will happen if we do the same again?

Analyst: 'Roughly' is the word, but it's better than what we knew before. Let me give you the current estimates, after I've shown you what the advertising effects seem to be. There's one reaction to advertising which follows very soon after our ads appear. This is shown on Figure 14 by the little squares each week. There's another effect which is much slower-moving, and is shown by the line. Again, the Y-axis shows the share points contributed by advertising. On average, perhaps 0.8 of a share point from the short-term effect, and 0.9 long term.

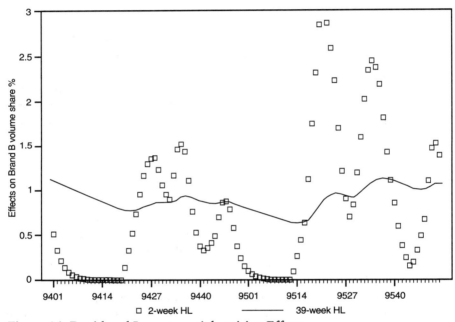

Figure 14 Rapid and Long-term Advertising Effects

But I want to look at the four-weekly data, which are all we have when we go back four years, before giving you my best guess.

At the moment, I'd comment on our marketing activities as follows:

1. What matters most is our average share. That's where we make our bread and butter. The variations round it are important, of course, but let's remember first our brand's *equity*, or the way purchasers and consumers value it, and the *price* they are prepared to pay. After all, we are 7% more expensive than the average, and 24% more than own label. We know from qualita-

tive consumer research how people talk about us. We do well in the tracking study.

Our main strength shows in this way. It's the habit which some people have got into, of buying us fairly regularly. That's the benefit of branding. We have a good idea where all this comes from. They are long-term effects and they come from a variety of sources. Perceived product quality is one of course, though the lab tells us we're at parity in lots of ways. The number of our variants probably adds, though we don't get any extra sales when we launch a new one. The researchers say the packaging isn't remarkable.

Advertising must have been a major contribution, judging by the way focus groups replay with approval what we've been saying, as well as by the modelling. There's a clue too in the way our equity has some association with our advertising weight.

2. *Changes in price relative to the category* certainly matter, and I have an estimate of our price elasticity, but we have to bear in mind that the overall price level is more important – that's where we make most of our profit.

Marketer: Do you mean it's not really worthwhile to promote on price occasionally?

Analyst: I'll come back to that. I'm just saying that the effects of the changes aren't as important as being able to sustain a premium.

3. Our *promotions*, and the small increases we get in *distribution,* are both linked with price, so I'm not sure yet where I'd rank these two.

4. *Advertising*'s direct short-term effects may be a little larger than the last two activities – I'd say it can help us get up to three share points. I have an advertising elasticity estimate too.

Advertising also has a long-term direct effect on share, as well as helping us to support our overall price. I'm not ready yet to put a value on all that, but we'll come to it later.

Competitors' advertising doesn't have a clear direct effect on our sales, because it's tended to be fairly uniform. I'm sure it does pull us down, but I don't have a number for this yet.

Marketer: My reaction to all this is that we do need firm estimates of the two elasticities. I accept that we won't really separate promotion effects from price, but I need a point of view about them. Our distribution has been near the top limit for some time, so I'm not surprised you're getting a fuzzy picture about its effects. I see that I must separate the numbers you're going to give me, about what you call the direct effects of advertising, from the general argument that it helps us in other ways. I hope the numbers are going to be good though, as I can't rely on the arguments based on tracking data when I debate with the finance director.

6.8 Modelling: Four-Weekly Brand Shares

This section is about a four-year four-week model, agreed elasticities, and a first view of where to go for volume and profit.

Analyst: I've now modelled our sales share over four years, and compared the results with the detail of the last two years, and I've firmed up the estimates of the effects of our activities.

This gives us a first calculation of the sort of volume and profit effects we are getting from each of them. These aren't yet the recommendations for 1996 and beyond, that'll be for our next meeting.

The overall explanation of these four years again gives us a very close fit to what actually happened. This is the same sort of

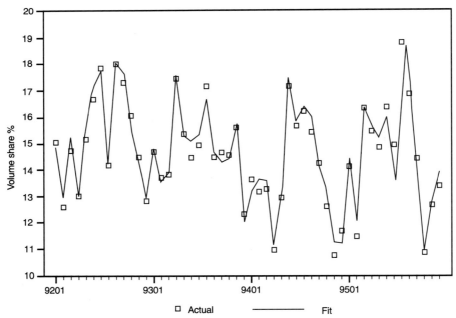

Figure 15 The Fit to Four-Weekly Data 1992–95 is Close

plot as Figure 12; the X-axis is now four-weekly and we cover twice as many years.

6.9 The Sizes of the Effects

Analyst: I am now confident that we have an adequate fix on the effects of our main marketing tools: average price relative to competitors, the way we alter this temporarily at focus periods and offer extra value by our promotions, advertising, and our relations with retailers which get us the distribution and displays. The findings are much the same as I showed you earlier, when I analysed two years of weekly data.

Marketer: What are the sizes of the effects?

Analyst: I could show you a plot very like Figure 13. But this time I will talk you through them. I have to warn you that they are only our best estimates about the past. We can't rely on exactly these results in future. They aren't forecasts which apply to anything we might do next year; for instance I haven't built in the category forecasts yet. I also haven't put costs or profit in. They are just to give you a feel for the importance of each activity.

Our *promotions* bring in about 250 tonnes each time we run them.

With 100 rating points on *television*, we get a short-term effect, over in a month or two, of about 90 tonnes. There is also a longer-term addition of 100 tonnes, but this takes a couple of years to be complete.

A *price* difference, from the highest to the lowest relative price we experience, is worth about 100 tonnes in the same week.

Distribution varies little, but we see changes worth about 30 tonnes a week.

6.10 Elasticities

Marketer: But do you think we're making money with each of these activities, or have I been buying volume?

Analyst: We know something about that for price and for advertising, because we now have elasticities for them measured in the marketplace. For price this is around –3, though as I've explained this may be a little too high, since promotions and additional distribution are mixed up with it. I've talked to the finance people and looked at the current budget for 1995. From this, I see that we need an elasticity of –2.2 to breakeven. Because 3 is a bigger number than 2.2, we could drop the price and get a good short-term sales increase, more than enough to compensate for the lower price. Crudely, yes, you have been buying volume, but I'll be more precise later.

Marketer: That may be so, and I'd like to go into this. But I don't want to start a price war, or risk losing my good pricing position.

Analyst: That's a good point and this isn't yet the time to talk strategy. I'm only reporting the facts at present.

For advertising I measured a short-term elasticity of +0.05 or 0.06. I think we'd have to be at 0.09 or more for it to be worthwhile spending more on advertising from the point of a short-term return. So we don't get back our investment immediately. This isn't unusual, and we get other benefits from advertising.

Another way of putting it is to talk about the effect from 100 ratings. The 90 tonnes short-term return is worth £170k extra profit, at our marginal revenue this year of £1,790 per tonne. But we're paying more than that for the ratings: £235k.

Marketer: So if I'd spent less on advertising we would have made more profit?

Analyst: That is so, if you are thinking of a few months only. But there are also the 100 tonnes we get over the long term, worth another £190k. That takes us into a good profit. In this plot I show how I think our base has moved. It's not constant, though it has moved only a little compared with the variation from one four-weeks to another, which I also show. These small changes can build up, and in the long run are of great importance.

The X-axis is four weeks again, and the Y-axis is volume share points. The squares show the short-term effect, the line is what we call a 'floating base'. That means it will sink if we do nothing to support it; but it can also float up, as it did in the last half of 1995. This is a delayed result of your increased spend on advertising that year.

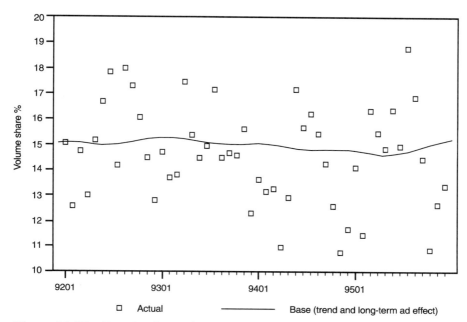

**Figure 16 The Base Varies Only a Little but
Explains the 1992–94 Decline**

Marketer: I've got problems with all this. First, your 0.05 short-term ad elasticity sounds very small. How can I be getting any money back with that? The price elasticity of –3, or whatever it is, must be a better route.

Analyst: You're quite right, 0.05 *sounds* very little, and *is* a smaller actual number than three. But you mustn't compare the two directly. We're talking about what happens when we increase the adspend by one per cent, and even in 1995 that is a change in expenditure of under £40k.

The price change, on the other hand, affects all our sales. If a one per cent drop didn't increase sales, we'd be talking about a much larger revenue loss of over £900k.

Also, we know now that short-term gains aren't all that advertising does for us. We'll talk about that later too.

Marketer: Now you've talked about two fits. I can see they are going to be different, because one is based on two years data in weeks, and one on four years data, four-weekly. Figures 14 and 16 both show similar quick rises and falls in share as a result of the advertising bursts and I understand that. But what about the wavy lines, which you've called the long-term effects. Are they the same? And why two fits anyway?

Analyst: The weekly data give us the best fix on short-term effects. Four weeks are not going to be much good for that when the effect is mostly over in three or four weeks. But for the long term I think it's more convincing to look at a long run of data, and so the four-year information is preferred. The lines were produced by different methods. (*Note to the reader: this is mostly to demonstrate the two techniques.*) In fact the results are much the same.

6.11 Consumer Brand Equity *(see Section 8.7 and Table 10)*

Marketer: How would you sum up the value of the brand to consumers? Do you think we're gaining ground or losing it? What affects this value?

Analyst: The number I'll use to sum it up is called Consumer Brand Equity. It's the volume share we would get on a level playing field, that is, if the distributions and the prices of all the brands were the same. It removes the benefits of low price and of high distribution, which may be only temporary.

We can work this out for each of the brands in the category. Figure 17 describes how they are doing. The current value is shown on the X-axis: for instance Brand A, at the right, is shown at nearly 29 share points. That's about what it might sell (hypothetically, of course), if its relative price fell from 22% above average to the average price. This plot puts own label between us and Brand A. Its equity is well below the actual volume share of 31% because a lot of those sales are simply because of its low price. Brand A is the clear leader in equity, mainly because it is able to charge such a high price.

On the Y-axis is the percentage change from the 1994 equity. Own label is growing fastest, at nearly 11% above the 1994 figure, and A is next fastest. Own label, Brand A and ourselves are in fact all growing in equity. So the answer to your first question is that we are third in equity, and growing, but not as fast as own label or A. We're getting used to seeing C falling behind.

As for what's related to this growth, we can look at the likely factors: advertising and promotions. Other factors of course play a major part: product quality, the number of our variants, and our

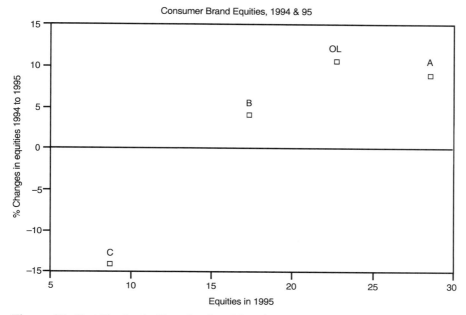

Figure 17 Our Equity is Growing but Not the Fastest

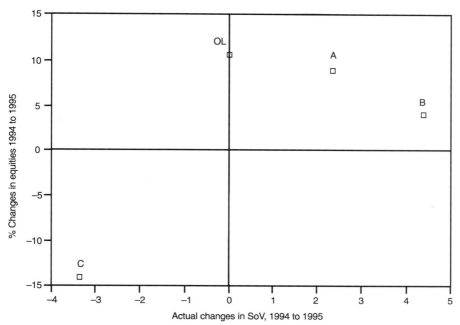

Figure 18 Increased Adspend is Associated with
Improved Equity

packaging – but these haven't changed much recently. There are two ways we can investigate this. The first is to look at changes *across* the brands, the second is to look at changes *within* our own brand.

Figure 18 shows that movements in equity *are* related to advertising weight changes. The X-axis shows that our increase in share of voice was the greatest. Own label of course had zero share of voice in both years. The Y-axis gives the percentage rise (or fall, in the case of C) in equities.

This is something we find quite often, and which applies in most categories: *changes* in equity seem to be related to *changes* in share of voice. The two brands improving here, A and B, are those which increased advertising share. C lost in both. Own label managed the highest growth without directly advertising its product in this category, but of course stores have different sorts of publicity. As I said before, we don't expect the equity to be directly related to current share of voice, as so many other factors contribute to it.

Marketer: But we're not seeing consistency here, are we? Brand A increased advertising weight less than us, in proportion, but their equity increased more.

Analyst: I agree. This is one of the places where the quality of the activity shows through the numbers. We're seeing how well each brand's copy adds to its base, or regular, sales. The plot shows only spend, but we learn also that we don't seem to have as effective copy. You may want to talk to the agency about that.

I've also worked out our own Consumer Brand Equity separately for each four weeks. Figure 19 is a plot of our equity over two years. The period numbers give the actual positions. This shows we had a peak in mid-1994, and then further growth to the autumn of 1995. A lot of this is explained by the timing of our advertising, which peaked around then and was higher this year. Our copy can't be that bad! It's just that it could be better.

Equity growth was also related to the timing of promotions which I can tell you is very unusual. I know this because I fitted or explained our equity by our recent advertising and by promotions. The fit is shown by the line on Figure 19. This is not as close as previous fits I showed you. *(Note to the reader – but typical of real data.)* You'll agree the fit captures the main movements. Other factors which I've not been able to include are responsible for the discrepancies.

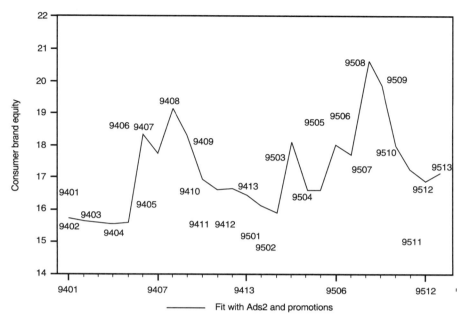

Figure 19 Equity is Variable – Advertising and
Promotions Explain a Lot of the Variation

Marketer: So this tells us the promotions really do add value, and aren't just buying volume? That's very satisfying, because we pride ourselves on making them more than price cuts. We'd worked out for ourselves that our competitors are losing a lot of money on their price promotions. Ours certainly produce the extra sales. And you're saying that advertising demonstrably adds to the underlying strength of the brand, though perhaps not as well as it might.

6.12 Budget Allocation over Time (BAT)

Analyst: I mentioned the timing of the advertising, particularly our summer peak. The schedule looks reasonable at first sight because sales are high in June, and also September looks a good time, at the shoulder of the industry sales peak. These have been major factors in our media planning.

As well as the seasonality of sales, or the number of purchases in the category being made each month, we should take into account the cost of TV time in different months. Sometimes

I have to say the opposite – decisions are dominated by TV cost criteria, and the size of the category at different times of the year is ignored. The trick is to consider both.

In Figure 20 the Y-axis height for each week is given by dividing the *value index* of each week (based on category sales volume) by the *cost index* (what we pay for TV time). Obviously we should look for high value (which we do), but also for low costs. This shows us that January is a good month to spend TV money – it's a peak on the figure – but it is a month we neglect, and so is August. When we come to schedule next year we should also take into account the way the advertising effects decay over time; this plot is just an indication of the good times to advertise.

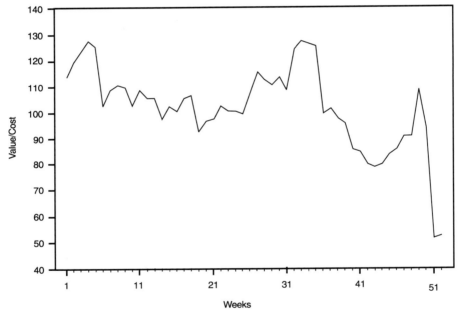

Figure 20 Good and Bad Weeks to Buy TV:
Value Index/Cost Index

But that isn't all we should think about. Our practice of buying bursts means there are weeks on end when customers are in the shops making decisions in our category, without having seen one of our ads for a long time. We really should think about the recent exposures to advertising being more valuable than those long ago. Plus, our habit of bursting means we ensure that they see several ads close together, if they see any at all. It's likely that the second exposure, the third, and so on are having less effect than the first one they saw.

Marketer: But how can we bear in mind all of these factors together – value and cost and recency and the effects of one or two or three ads close together? I'm not clear how you're asking me to change our scheduling strategy and I don't think I'm ready for that.

Analyst: It is possible to consider all of the factors simultaneously by being explicit about how we think each of them works. In some cases we can check this out with relevant data. I won't go into detail here (*see Section 8.9*). But we can put a number on the effectiveness of our current plan: it's 84, compared with 100 for a schedule which lays the TVRs down each week in proportion to our value over cost. And we can do better than that, while at the same time making sure that the plan is realistic and buyable. We can't do much better than a rather continuous schedule when we think about our short-term advertising effect. For the slower effects we'd do better to increase the spend early in the year. We'll come to a compromise between these two when we look at our 1996 plan later. But for now, I think we can see a way to add between £400k and £700k to the worth of our TV budget; so I hope you change your mind about considering a new schedule.

6.13 An Area Experiment

Marketer: Those are very tempting figures and we will look at this more closely. Perhaps we should test out such a major shift of policy before we move. Which reminds me to ask about the copy test you designed for us. Do you have the final report yet?

Analyst: Here it is. You remember we had very mixed results from the development and pre-test research on the new copy; we decided to run the new ad in 10% of the country.

Marketer: But the actual sales figures in the area don't look very different yet. I've had this year's volume plotted on the same scale as last year's and there's some improvement, but a lot of noise. Anyway, sales are up in other regions too.

Analyst: There's another way of looking at it. If we look at *share* instead of volume, we should allow for the trend and seasonality in the category. And rather than using the data from the test area alone, we should take into account more carefully that data about our overall growth in the rest of the country. It's the *ratio* of our share in the test area to share in the rest of the country that gives us a better reading, that is, a measure which has less irrelevant movement.

Our test area has always had a slightly higher share for our brand than the average. That doesn't matter for the test – it's a *change* in the ratio for the last six months we are looking for. And the weekly variation in the ratio is smaller than for the volume sales in the test area you were looking at. So the measure is more precise and gives us a better chance of seeing the ad effect.

Marketer: There doesn't seem to be anything very clear going on though.

Analyst: There's one more thing we can do. You know that our sales are considerably affected by our relative price. Some of the changes you see in the ratio are because we aren't at the same relative price in our test area as we are elsewhere. Local brands and local outlets are significant enough for their pricing changes and their promotions to have a different effect on our share here, from those which relative price has elsewhere.

We can measure what this relative price has been locally, compared with the rest of the country. The *ratio* of these relative prices affects the ratio of our sales share, just as relative price affects share itself. Here is a fit I've calculated for 18 months before the test started, showing that price was responsible for quite a lot of the variation in the share ratio. We need to allow for this during the test, since we can expect it to have a similar effect. The amount of natural variation left is smaller so we will detect any ad effect earlier. I've projected this fit by price forward to show what we expected during the test.

Marketer: It looks to me as though we have fallen below the line you have drawn.

Analyst: Exactly. We should have seen some rise in the sales–share ratio in the test area, from our slightly better pricing there, compared with the bigger attacks we've had on price in the rest of the country. But we haven't seen it; instead, there's this decline. Over the last 26 weeks, when we'd expect the new ad to have made an impression, our ratio has been significantly lower than it should have been.

Marketer: So the view that we'd gone over the top with that commercial was probably right. I'm glad we didn't run it nationally. And it's good that we know this result so quickly – certainly a lot faster than if we'd used only the area sales figures, and you're saying more precisely too.

6.14 The Recommended Plan

Analyst: Now's the time to pull together everything we know. We have learned quite a lot about the different factors we control. Let's summarise that and then go on to make some predictions about next year, so that you can decide on your marketing plan and clear it with your boss.

Our special sort of promotions have a good effect on equity as well as being popular with Sales and with retailers. I'm sure we should go on running them.

Price changes – by competitors as well as ourselves – are producing the biggest changes in volume. We have to decide both on our list prices and what we'll spend on price promoting. We expect A to increase prices again, but because of the growing small brands, overall prices will fall. We think we could drop prices and increase volume economically, but you have to think about this strategically.

We've agreed we can and should push up brand awareness, and that advertising can do this. The existing campaign is the one we'll continue. We've seen good effects on equity, and we have direct effects both short and long term – but uneconomic in the short term, which gives us a problem. I'm sure we should consider scheduling more continuously. We know how TV costs are expected to grow. We can confidently expect A to raise adspend, since we've seen the good results they've had.

We needn't bother too much about Brand C, and Others aren't expected to do anything new, though the lowest-priced of them and own label will probably continue to grow.

We have forecasts of the category size and price. I've talked to Accounts, so I know how we expect our own costs to change.

What we now have to do is to combine these forecasts with what we know about how the marketplace works. Then we can consider how you might meet your business objectives.

Marketer: Let's review the 1996 plan.

I'm being pushed for £14.5 million profit and that's the priority. The volume growth, which was over 7% this year, needn't be more than 4% and 25,000 tonnes will be satisfactory.

I want to put the price up a bit, but I don't want to do anything dramatic. If A lifts his price, that might be enough to benefit me. But I have to remember the low-priced competition. I'd like to average below £4k a tonne to retailers, so let's say an average of £3.98k.

The factory have got the variable cost down a bit, and they really can't cut any more.

We'll use the same sort of promotions plan, because that added to equity as well as to sales, according to your analysis.

There was a lot of criticism of the £3.7 million on TV, so I've been asked for a TV plan spending about £3 million. They say TV costs will be 10% up, so this will give about 1,150 TVRs, a quarter down on last year. As I said before, I'm not ready to change the schedule. The small spend on print will go up a bit, but I can live with that since I like the look of the new magazine ads.

This is what my budget looks like. It gives a bit more profit than I'm asked for.

Proposed budget for 1996

	£000
Revenue from 25,000 tonnes at £3,980 per tonne	99,500
Variable cost at £2,130 per tonne	− 53,250
Gross margin at £1,850 per tonne	46,250
Fixed cost, including advertising production	26,400
Adspend (TV £3060k, print £320k)	3,380
Promotions, including production	1,680
Profit or contribution	14,790
	46,250

Is this a good plan? Could I do better?

Analyst: The first question is, do we really expect 25,000 tonnes from your marketplace activities. It sounds as though that figure came out of the air. On the face of it, the answer must be no!

To your admittedly small price increase, which we expect the retailers to pass on, you have to add our forecast that the category is getting cheaper on average. The net is that your relative price of 107 will be up to 109.3. If we use a price elasticity of −2.8, this means your volume will fall by 6%.

With advertising, which is your other major change, you are losing 25% of the 1995 TVRs. The short-term ad elasticity of 0.049 means volume will go down 1.2%, ignoring any long-term effects.

So together you will drop over 7%. That looks bad, given that you have budgeted a gain! On profit, I'm afraid it looks bad, too.

There is, however, a further point. We have to bring in the long-term effect of 1995 and earlier advertising. We haven't allowed explicitly for any competitors' advertising effect in our model, but we have a constant decay which stands for their efforts, more than countered at present by a long-term effect of our advertising. You remember that in the second half of 1995 we saw an upward turn in the base. This will continue to benefit us in 1996. I estimate it will give a lift of nearly the same size as the harm done by the higher price and reducing the TVRs.

Marketer: So I'm almost rescued by the long-term advertising effect, and that comes from the 1995 spend I've been criticised for! But it's the same old story – I've been given an impossible task. Is that really so? Is there any way I can rescue the plan?

Analyst: Well, I've looked at some alternative pricing and adspend strategies, and I've been talking to the accountants, and I think you are right: it is an impossible task. At least, it is nearly impossible on volume, and also on profit, if you don't change your view about advertising and about some established practices. You could go back upstairs and agree a new plan with lower profit, that is, if you don't want to risk a price war.

Marketer: There are no options there. I'm not going to turn in less profit than asked and I'm not going to endanger the price structure of the category by starting a war we can't win against own label and the cheap brands. What do you suggest? What's this 'view about advertising' and 'established practices'?

Analyst: There's a hard part and an easy part about advertising. The hard part is that they see it upstairs as a cost. You said it 'seemed to eat into profits', and you 'could have got bigger bonuses if you'd cut it', without giving it credit for the way it returns your investment.

You need to convince yourself and your boss that the picture we've now got of the short and long-term returns is more likely to be right than his idea of being an unaccountable expense. We do have qualitative evidence of the way consumers talk about the brand which we know is based on the advertising. We know people like the ads, but that's not the main point – it's the way they value the brand, and the way we see this in the numbers as well as in the qualitative reports.

We now have a good idea of how volume improves, about how Consumer Brand Equity responds, to our main marketing activities – price changes, advertising and promotions. We have numbers about this which are at least as good as the forecasts you get from the factory about alternative product formulation sales, or from the accountants about interest charges. What we must do now is convince top management that the work which your marketing people and the accountants have done together is a better way to support decisions than the way we've made them in the past.

Marketer: I accept that. What's the easy part?

Analyst: We really can improve the scheduling of our advertising – and I can put a number on that too. We have been using some very expensive months, and our policy of bursting at seasonal sales peaks is not optimal, especially now we know more about the short and long-term advertising effects. When we talked about this before I was looking at the historical data, but I have now worked out a new schedule for 1996 with the media people. This will actually get more ratings than the previous policy, but that isn't the criterion they want to hear about upstairs. It will push up sales too, without extra cost.

Marketer: You're right, that's the language they understand. This is the time to decide. Well, let's see the alternatives with all those arguments built in. What would happen if we did have the reduced ratings we've been thinking about, what a little more spend on advertising might do, and what the new scheduling will deliver. If the basis is agreed with the accountants, that makes me more confident about suggesting a new strategy.

Analyst: *(more in Section 9.9)* Let's agree to keep the price at £3,980 a tonne. The argument is all about the TV part of your media spend. Management asked for this to come down to £3,060k, compared with the £3,700k last year. You know that at 1996 costs, that means a 25% drop in your TVRs.

With print, which we won't disturb, that makes £3,380k on media. Production is already counted in fixed costs.

I have looked at alternatives, and rather than a drop on 1995 ratings, I think you need an increase. And we will spend it in a more efficient way. I want you to ask for £4,080k, and this will give you 1,675 ratings, rather than the 1,060 which you would have got with the suggested plan and the old schedule. You really do need the new schedule and its greater sales-effectiveness.

Here's the plan you should take upstairs and a summary of the arguments for it. You already have all the back-up analyses we've been discussing.

Recommended budget for 1996

£000

	£000
Revenue from 25,240 tonnes at £3,980 per tonne	100,452
Variable cost at £2,130 per tonne	− 53,761
Gross margin at £1,850 per tonne	46,691
Fixed costs, including advertising production	26,400
Adspend (TV £3,760k, print £320k)	4,080
Promotions, including production	1,680
Profit or contribution	14,531
	46,691

This higher spend in 1996 will also pay off in 1997: I can show you an estimate which lets advertising spend fall back below the 1995 level, but gets volume up to 26,500 tonnes and a much higher profit that year. The point is that if you want such a big jump in profit in 1996 you can't get it by cutting adspend.

Marketer: I follow your arguments. Your explanations of history show me you know what you are talking about, and common sense says you should be right. I don't see any better way of doing it. That will be my recommendation.

6.15 Conclusion

So ends the case history. Both the marketing and finance departments have worked on the new plan, so it is pre-sold to the financial director and is that much more likely to be agreed by top management. Scenarios with different prices and different amounts and timing of advertising have been evaluated. There are forecasts for profit as well as for volume. The timing of the profit stream is spelled out, so the consequences beyond the current quarter or year are clear – and the benefits or drawbacks from previous and alternative decisions. The mechanics of getting the money in, and paying it out, are all included, so that monthly cash flows and profit forecasts are in the form which the accountants and management are used to.

The analyst has sent off a more confident marketer to make a good business case in the language such cases are argued. The explanations given for what has been happening in the competitive marketplace – drawn from knowledge of competitors as well as of ourselves – have convinced management that marketing has a grip on events, and that the past has been understood, that the forecasts are as good as they can get, that the plan is viable. No better alternative is available. Benchmarking opportunities and action standards are on offer. Advertising has been made accountable.

Part 3

7 Description

The book now starts to explain how the analyst – or anyone else – can produce the results quoted in the case history of Chapter 6. The examples given are not restricted to that case, but many others are given, either from real-life, published stories, or as simple explanations which make the techniques easier to understand. In this chapter there are no complex calculations. The purpose is to collect methodically and then to re-present the basic data about the brand and its competitors in order to see what is going on. Hence, stress is laid on plots and graphs.

First, the brand audit is described in detail. Then, the way the simple and necessary data is collected and arranged. This is examined in a logical sequence: from category totals, to the way the category is made up of the major brands, and finally the detail of a brand's movements over time.

7.1 Outline

It is usually obvious what data should be used to measure the effects of advertising and other communications, and so make them accountable. The task has been agreed already: to get enquiries or leads of good quality, to get direct orders, to preserve or improve sales volume, to maintain the price as acceptable, to communicate specific information – and so on. Whatever criteria are defined, the first job is to get data about them. It is also clear that you must get data about the advertising itself and how much of it reached your target.

It is less obvious what *other* factors influence the achievement of the task. These should also be measured so that you can, if possible, allow for them when you attribute some effects to communications. This list must be written too. It is a common error, and one to be avoided at all costs, to estimate the effect of advertising in a specious but over-simplified way: by the direct comparison of sales and advertising data alone, without discussing possible other causes.

In some situations data is pitifully scarce: your own sales, your own revenue, but little else. Make estimates if you can do no better, and see what these imply. The importance of the likely real findings may persuade management to release money to find out more facts. Even small surveys, or estimates made by trade surveys, are far more productive than abandoning hope.

Every brand situation is similar in these ways: the brand is available to purchasers, but not in perfect distribution; it is against competition; there are reasons for choosing it or for preferring others; so much is sold at such a price and perhaps with incentives of some kind. In what follows, a particular set of data describes this process. You will have your own equivalent of this set, and your own technical terms.

The work now considered is the selection, organisation, interpretation and evaluation of the data you have, so that the implications of the facts are as clear as possible – even obvious. The analyst has to look at and think about this data in as many ways as are likely to lay its secrets bare. This is the stage of detective work: sifting clues and reconstructing events. Then the analyst moves to advocacy, describing and defending a view of what happened.

Averages and ratios are calculated in this chapter, but nothing more elaborate is attempted. These, and tables of data, may be enough to make the findings clear. It is in Chapter 8 that we come to the more complex techniques. But numbers may not be the easiest way to look at the data and in what follows heavy use is made of plots.

7.2 Types of Data – and a Warning

This is not a book about market research; it is about using the results of research, so detail about data sources is not discussed. In any case, your own sources will be well-known to you.

There are three sorts of research findings you are concerned with. The first is basically *counting*. The second is about what people think and say, which has been *turned into numbers*. The third is essentially *qualitative* (like the second) but has not been reduced to numbers; it is left as words, though usually in summarised form.

There are many things to count in marketing: the units sold; the money exchanged; your branches in the High Street; shops stocking your brand; how many people used a coupon or joined your database; what proportion of shelf space a retailer allots us; how many representatives or agents you have; how many sets were tuned to the TV station when it carried your commercial; and many more. Most of your information arrives in this form.

When people are interviewed, for example in a tracking study, they answer questions, many in numerical form. They mention your brand or claim to have heard of it, to buy it, or use it. They give it scores for various qualities: it is durable, or tasty, or good value for money. They would buy it at this price; not at that one. They are or are not aware of the contents of commercials and say whether they would or would not like to see them again. The answers appear in a printout as neat percentages; these conceal many possible difficulties and need interpretation.

Some answers in surveys are left in the respondents' words. They may then be coded: so many of them showed by their answers they had seen the commercial you are interested in; so many used the word 'refreshing' or 'sporty', and so on. Or they are left as verbatims: 'I thought the drink was much too sweet' or, 'The pension salesman really pressured us.' The answers that are coded can be treated as numbers; the rest go into the 'qualitative' group.

This includes reports of interviews and focus groups. Verbatims are a great help here, but a report is essentially the view of a researcher – skilled and accurate, we hope – reporting all the clues given in a face-to-face or group situation about informants' true feelings. Attending the groups, and watching videos of them, communicate the experience in a different way. A similar sort of data comes from the field force: reports about their meetings with retailers or purchasers.

Qualitative sources are not made much of here, though their help in interpreting the numbers and in guiding management decisions can be invaluable. I am going to concentrate on quantitative results.

This book does not pursue questions about the reliability and comprehensiveness of the data. There are always problems about whether some sorts of people are adequately represented, about the coverage of the real world which is provided by Nielsen, IRI and other suppliers – and what adjustments this implies – about the weighting techniques and averaging which smooth out the real world and so on.

A warning is appropriate about checking data and presenting the numbers to best effect. Ideally, the analyst gets data in electronic form and from a well-proven system. It is virtually untouched by human hand and the chances of errors in the data are small. This does not mean the data have not been 'tidied' in some way, as everyone who has worked in a research agency will understand – there were missing records and a hundred and one other problems, which someone had to sort out. Once the data is published, such tinkering is forgotten; it has become the official record.

At the other extreme, the analyst works with data entered in a hurry by hand from a poor photocopy of a garbled fax. Even when conditions are not quite as bad as that, it is inevitable with this kind of work, where data comes from several different sources, that it needs checking. To err is human.

Some errors can lead to a loss of confidence in the data and in the analyst, which can undermine a whole project. It is therefore essential that the data and its use are as error-free as is practical. Some hints to ensure this now follow.

(a) Direct checks

If there is a natural check in the data, use it. For example, if you have the individual brands or groups of brands *and* the category total, then enter all of these. Then write a check column which is the entered category figure less the sum of the brands – which should of course be zero. Note that it is easier to inspect a column of zeros than to compare the two totals.

A classical method is for two different people to enter the data separately – or do this yourself on two different days – and then calculate the differences.

(b) Check totals

For example, if you have a two-way table for which the row totals are used for one purpose, the column totals for another, check that the sum of the row totals, minus the sum of the column totals, is zero.

(c) Plots

If there is a sensible value to be obtained from the data, calculate it and plot it. For example, if you enter volume sales and value sales, calculate price as value/volume, and plot this. Some swings are to be expected, but most catastrophic errors produce absurd results which are all too visible.

(d) Likely errors – and corrections

As in any typing, the likely errors are repetition (so the series 1, 2, 3, 3, 5 is suspect), and reversing the digits (172 instead of 127), as well as missing out numbers altogether, or confusing two columns or two rows.

The difference or plot method is likely to tell you where the error is, and of course the correction should be obtained from the master copy. If this is impossible, or the entry is genuinely missing, then enter the number which is suggested by the surrounding entries. In the series in the paragraph above it is obvious enough that it should read 1, 2, 3, 4, 5 – but you could also calculate the '4' as the mean of '3' and '5'.

(e) Automate

Much of the work is repetitive. For example, you may have to group weekly data into four or five-week months – and you have to do this over many brands, or several regions. Create a 'master' sheet or other process, such as a macro, to do the work. Check this thoroughly. One way to do so is to enter very simple data – perhaps, make every entry 1. Apply the process, so that you expect the result to be a string of 4s and 5s at the appropriate months.

When you are sure of the process, then you have only to copy or combine in each set of raw data to get the required result.

It is all too easy to confuse the names of columns or plots. You have ten plots to produce for Scotland, say, and then another ten for Granada. The plots are made once and for all, and checked as above – but what about the title? You do not want to retitle each plot by hand, and perhaps forget to do so for one of them. Instead, arrange the titling process so that it picks up the name of the region once only – and ideally from a cell in the data that you combine in.

(f) Easy to read

Do not confuse rounding the data (dropping the decimals, for example), with formatting (keeping the decimals in the background in full, but showing in the table only the whole number). You can lose so much information in rounding that the data become unusable – a rise from 2.5 to 3.4 is serious, but 3 to 3 looks like no change.

When you format, try to have the minimum number of digits varying. For example, show 119 and 121, not 118.76539 and 120.60741. The first pair can be 'seen', the second pair cannot. This is why the analyst reported 750 and 1,570 TVRs in Section 6.2, not 747 and 1,574.

If you present a table of formatted data, ensure that it passes obvious checks. For example, showing percentages which should add to 100, like 14.4, 25.4 and 60.2, do not just make the table:

$$
\begin{array}{r}
14 \\
25 \\
60 \\
\hline
100
\end{array}
$$

Either say '*data rounded*', or change the number to which the proportionate change is least. Make it:

$$
\begin{array}{r}
14 \\
26 \\
60 \\
\hline
100
\end{array}
$$

because the 0.6 correction is relatively smaller on 25.4 than on 14.4.

If you do not use one of these methods it will probably be the chief executive who says, 'the percentages do not add up', to which there is no harmless answer.

(g) False impressions of accuracy – or of variation
If you are working from a sample of 47 examples, do not report ten cases as 21.277%, which looks as though the result is very precise. But do not round too severely and say '20%'. Better, 'in ten cases ...'.

Do not plot a decline over time from 74 to 71 on a scale which shows 75 to 70 – the fall on this chart looks like 4 to 1, or to a quarter of the starting height. If the proportion of the decline matters, use the scale 75 to zero so that the decline is only 4% (3 on 74).

7.3 Carrying out a Brand Audit

The analyst is occasionally asked to assess the data on the brand for one of the purposes described in Chapter 3. That is, the reason may be a general review of the brand's strengths and weaknesses, to assist management in every area, so covering the widest range of data, or, to assess the brand's position in its category.

These are the two purposes for which the following very wide list of numerical data may be used. What follows is a checklist to help you when reviewing your data for a brand audit. Presentation of the results is not difficult and is not covered here. Nor is a full brand audit included in the case history, since so much of an audit is taken up by items which are very specific to each application – for example, laboratory tests of quality. But many of the analyses described later find their place in a brand audit, and many of the comments made here are relevant also to accountability.

An audit may also aim to estimate the return made on the marketing investment by calculating a Brand Equity. A method to do this is described in the next chapter. An audit for brand valuation on the balance sheet is not described.

7.3.1 Brand Audit: Definitions

Before listing the dimensions you may use, there are comments which apply to all of them.

The brand is almost always thought of in relation to competitors, and so within a category. The definition of the category is critical. It is a management decision. The analysis of panel data may help here, showing which other brands your own buyers choose as alternatives. It may also be sensible to split a category up into sectors – plain and milk chocolate, malt and blended whiskies, credit and debit cards, originals and light or slimming variants, and so on. You may analyse either a category or a sector, and you do each in exactly the same way.

The effect of the decision may be to see yourself as a small fish in a large pool – or do you define your competitors in a more limited way, so improving your relative position? Do you compete with all cars, all lagers, all holidays? Or in the luxury car sector, the premium lager sector, the long-haul holiday sector?

If you make a mistake in the category definition, and ignore brands which have an effect on yours, or include brands whose progress is irrelevant to yours, you can be led to unfortunate errors.

Example: A non-competing brand
The category has been defined to include a new, low-priced entrant which is making rapid progress. You ignore the fact that it appeals to a completely different target, which does not buy your brand – and vice versa.

You interpret the numbers as showing growth in the category accompanied by a reduction in the average price. Hence your brand appears to have falling share and rising relative price. Indeed, you can show a convincing relation between the two.

You react by cutting price in order to maintain share, and are then surprised to find the action has had no effect on your percentage of the total volume. Your volume has been unaffected throughout, but your profits have suffered as a result of your mistake.

When you talk about 'customers', who exactly do you mean? You already know you will consider separately the *trade* purchasers of the brand, the retailers and middlemen, and its *ultimate*, off-the-shelf purchasers (from retailers) and users in the home. The latter need very precise definition, and advertising agency planners will go into this detail.

Once you have this definition, consider whether the standard data collected on so-called 'consumers' are genuinely about the target. For example, financial products like a building society account or a pension are bought only rarely and under special circumstances. Normally, the buyer about to make a decision tries, however imperfectly, to consider it quite carefully, and may collect information for the purpose. Is the target this informed purchaser, or the mass of the population, currently uninterested and even less well-informed? If the latter, the scores in the survey may mislead us about the real purchasers. Some special analysis may be needed to reduce the universe surveyed to those who are relevant.

A general point is that some measures which *look* as if they measure brand 'strength' independently of the size of the brand (consumer views, loyalty), are in fact heavily dependent on the brand's size. Larger brands tend to do well on dimensions which are in effect different ways of measuring perceived size. This is an example of the 'halo' effect discussed in Section 7.5.6. However, the results sometimes tell us more than this, and the differences may be revealing. It is recommended that volume or market share is borne in mind when considering such scores. The question you should ask is: '*For its size*, is this brand scoring high or low?'

It is a sign of a strong brand that it has a brand essence (introduced in Section 2.3), which is easy to define and in which the four quadrants are consistent – these are: the functions of the brand, the ways it differs from competitors, its image and personality, and its source of authority. Carrying out a brand essence study can be an important part of a brand audit, and involves several of the different dimensions described below, as well as the views of brand management.

Note that workers in this field use a variety of words to talk about relatively few ideas. Those who offer operational definitions (some do not even bother to do so), give methods which are at least subtly different. The reasons are that the concepts are in common use but no one has yet successfully standardised the measures. Notorious examples are 'brand loyalty' and 'brand equity'. The commercial advantage of research companies seems to depend on being different. So be warned that you are entering a verbal quagmire.

Finally, you should always look at trends as well as absolute levels. The purpose of the exercise is to improve your future position, so you need to know which way you are heading. The comment that trends should be looked at is not repeated below each time, but always applies.

The rest of this section expands on the following list of possible dimensions from which a selection can be made in any particular case, dependent on the availability of data. The list is also of possibilities for deciding how well a brand is doing.

Is the brand in a healthy category?

Survey data about the target:
– salience or awareness
– penetration
– various ways to segment the target
– image, including quality.

Laboratory, or other objective measures, about the product.

Trade:
– terms of doing business
– listing, display
– trade surveys, recommendations to purchase.

Consumer behaviour:
- volume sales
- value sales
- price, elasticity, per cent of sales on deal
- penetration
- loyalty.

Value to the company:
- revenue
- profit
- marketing investments by type.

Note that loyalty, awareness, perceived quality and other associations have been picked as four of the five headings for brand equity by David Aaker. Here, they are just part of the consumer component of a brand audit. He lists intellectual and legal properties as the fifth heading: trademarks and so on.

Tim Ambler defines brand equity in a way which embraces more of our brand audit dimensions: 'The aggregation of all accumulated habits and attitudes in the extended minds of consumers, distribution channels and influence agents, that will enhance future profits and long-term cash flow.'

7.3.2 Brand Audit: Category Characteristics

It can be part of the evaluation of a brand – especially when making comparisons across brands – that it belongs in *a healthy category*. Is the category large? Ten per cent of a big or valuable category can obviously be worth more than twenty per cent of a smaller or less valuable category. Is it in growth or decline? Are category prices under pressure, or are they moving up in response to improvements and innovation?

7.3.3 Brand Audit: Survey Data

You are trying to measure whether purchasers are particularly close to the brand and trust it above others.

You first have to establish brand *salience or awareness* – taking care about the prompts given to informants, for example, how is the category described to them? Do you distinguish between first mentions and others? Is a brand list shown?

You also need to know if they claim to have *ever bought* it, are lapsed users, bought or used in the last six months, and so on. Within these people, you may create segments by claimed loyalty or buying behaviour, share of category requirements, and so on.

Brand image may be defined in a general way – overall rating? For me? Seen as good quality? Good value for money? Liking? Different from competitors? What sort of person would it be …? Or by associations and descriptions specific to the category – a pleasure to drive? Children like the taste? Or by items you have planned to communicate in your brand essence? Again, the number and order of the brands checked, and the list of dimensions or attributes asked about, will affect responses.

7.3.4 Brand Audit: Laboratory Evaluation

Note that as well as consumer *opinions* about the product, which tell you about perceived quality, you should take into account *laboratory* or other impartial measures about genuine quality or competitive advantage. For financial products, league tables of performance meet this need. After all, product development is a major responsibility of marketing, and having a superior product is a starting point for brand success – many would say a prerequisite. Imitations follow faster these days, but that is no reason not to be first with an improvement.

7.3.5 Brand Audit: Trade Behaviour

Trade terms: the level of trade discounts, etc given or required; relations with retailers, however measured.

Listing (meaning, does the retailer agree to carry the brand), *display*, shelf space allowed, and so on.

Surveys of *retailer opinion*, and the behaviour of staff involved in selling – on the forecourt or behind the bank counter or wherever recommendations by staff are relevant.

7.3.6 Brand Audit: Consumer Behaviour

Volume bought, with care taken about the data source – does this cover the real total? This is usually expressed as share of category and ranking by size in the category.

Sterling taken over the counter by retailers.

These two may be combined into a *price* dimension – relative to the category, or to an unbranded or store label product, where these are reasonable comparisons. Price is usually measured by check-out records, or in-store audit or panel data; it may also be collected, less reliably, in a survey. Price actually paid may be compared with other products and extended to a price elasticity. A low elasticity when competitors make price offers, and your relative price increases, is a measure of loyalty or of the durability of the brand's relationship with purchasers. The per cent of the brand by volume sold on a deal is another way of measuring price strength (the more sold on promotion, the weaker the brand).

Penetration, or the proportion who bought at all in a specified period, may be measured in panel data as well as claimed in a survey.

Loyalty – such as share of category needs among those who have bought at all in a specified period. This measure is particularly close to brand size. Again, it may also be asked about in a survey as one of the image measures. Note that in some circumstances it may be the retention rate which is thought valuable – in other circumstances it is the *new* sales.

> *Example: Loyalty to ketchup brands*
> The data used for this example is described in Section 8.13. In the comparison between Heinz and Hunts Ketchup, obvious differences were in the sizes of the brands (37% and 28% respectively), and prices (Heinz 30% above Hunts). Even more dramatic was the result of classifying each shopper by the share of the category purchases she made with each brand. Then, what proportion of the total sales of the brand were accounted for by shoppers who always bought the brand? By shoppers who gave it 90% or more of their purchases? 80% or more? And so on. By this process Heinz soon reached half of its sales, which came from shoppers who gave it 80% or more of their purchase. Thus loyal shoppers were very important to Heinz. The same calculation for Hunts showed that half of its sales came from shoppers who gave it only 40% of their purchases. Thus Hunts had to take into account that much of its sales came from promiscuous shoppers, very likely to buy other ketchups.

7.3.7 Brand Audit: Value to the Company

Revenue, especially in proportion to costs and capital employed.

Profit (with careful definition of the costs allowed for). This may be as a 'profit stream', with attention being paid to its consistency as well as size and trend. It may be in proportion to turnover or capital employed – 'return on sales', or 'on assets'. It may be expressed as 'economic value added', that is, in relation to costs.

Share price is an often-used way of measuring how well the whole company is doing, and in the case of one-brand firms (or those perceived to be so), this may reflect how the City sees the brand. It may legitimately be a definition of forecast shareholder return. It is not just the equivalent of a forecast profit stream, as some people seem to believe, since it allows for the perceived risk for brands in the sector. Great care should be taken to judge whether this is a reasonable measure of the brand's inherent worth, since other considerations influence the City view – category expectations, quality of management, takeover opportunities, forecasts of the economy, fashion, accidents like exchange rates, and so on.

Sometimes the *communications or marketing investments* are counted as a measure of brand strength. Certainly they are a critical part of the evaluation process and you of course check them out. If brand-building, they are correctly perceived as a plus. If they are price-cutting, but presented to the City as 'marketing', viewing them as contributing to strength is incorrect. It is arguable whether in themselves they are outputs (showing the brand is strong), or inputs (whose results you are evaluating). It depends on your point of view and the exact purpose for which the audit is done.

7.4 Your Data for Regular Work

So much for the broad and occasional review which you may be asked to carry out. From now on, I concentrate on the smaller set of data which is regularly used and which is the subject of the rest of this book.

There are four main types of data you will use:

Sales, whether in counts of transactions, meals sold, packets or cans bought, policies signed, or pints drunk. Sales are also counted in sterling and there may be a record of whether a coupon or other promotion was used – two for one, a free draw for a holiday or whatever. From the two sorts of data (volume and value) you get the average price paid – pence per can, thousands of pounds per car, and so on.

More than the average *actual* price, the average *relative* price is often used. This means, relative to the category average indexed at 100 (occasionally, to the rest of the category, or to the brand leader). The sum to be done is:

$$100 \times \left(\frac{brand\ value\ sales}{brand\ volume\ sales} \right) \Big/ \left(\frac{category\ value\ sales}{category\ volume\ sales} \right)$$

This comes to the same as:

$$100 \times \left(\frac{brand\ value\ sales}{category\ value\ sales} \right) \Big/ \left(\frac{brand\ volume\ sales}{category\ volume\ sales} \right)$$

in other words, 100 times value share over volume share, a form which is easy to use as these shares are usually already calculated.

Distribution is both a general term, meaning how accessible your brand is to its purchasers and how does it flow to its outlets, and also has a specific meaning: what per cent of outlets of a certain type have agreed to list your brand, weighted by size of store (there are also complexities of the distribution of different pack sizes and so on). We talk about numbers of petrol pumps or forecourts, how many feet of shelf your brand gets, what proportion of stores actually have your brand in stock, forward stocks (actually on the shelf, not merely in the storeroom), how many independent financial advisers are in touch with your offices, how long your address list of repeat customers is, and so on.

You will certainly have *media research* numbers for the exposure of your paid-for communications: how many people read the publications you use, attendance at sports events you sponsor, how many ratings on television – and also figures for the cover (see one of your spots at least) – and so on. If not exposure data (read, see, hear), for other channels of communication, you know at least how much you spent and when.

Finally you have *survey research data*, at least as some one-off reports, but preferably as before-and-after surveys, and ideally as a continuous monitor or *tracking study*. This source will give various forms of awareness, of scores for attributes, and so on.

It is the analysis of these four sorts of data which this chapter and the next discuss in detail: sales, distribution, media exposure and tracking data.

7.4.1 Regular Work: Holding and Showing the Data

Naturally your data suppliers (audit, panel or survey research agency) provide their results in a format you have agreed with them: printed report, on-line, on disc, and so on. It may sit on a shelf or occupy a sophisticated management information system.

It arrives in great detail, ready for all the interrogations to which you and your market research colleagues will subject it from time to time. You may profile your customers, segment them in various ways, investigate both their behaviour and media exposure simultaneously. This book does not describe the techniques necessary for exceptional work: it is about the mainstream analysis on which management relies every day.

Whatever its other uses, I recommend that key or headline numbers, those in which management are most interested, are extracted into a small database. Exceptionally, this could be as simple as a page or two in a Filofax, but more likely it is on a disc, or in a few files in your company system. The essentials are:

- you have agreed with your manager that these are the numbers he relies on as his best guidance
- you receive them regularly and update the database.

You need a system to hold your database and to help you present the data. The description which follows is based on an actual purpose-built method. The main use of the system is to create automatically the plots which experience shows are most often useful.

Plots are chosen as the main way to show the data because in this way the main features are more self-evident than when tables of numbers only are examined. Of course the numbers are indispensable: only from them can you get at averages, combine variables, and do more complex work. But plots allow us to study associations – with time and between variables – to judge the stability or variability of the data, to see exceptions easily, and much more.

In a spreadsheet you can set up once and for all every plot you are likely to require (with a suitable macro to ensure that data files of different lengths are properly plotted and the axes are properly labelled to guard against misattribution). If the data are held in a standard way, and then combined into this sheet, all the plots are filled. The trouble taken to prepare all these plots is quickly repaid. A macro walks the user through all the plots and prints out only those selected. It is better and faster to look through ten plots and find the one which is unusually revealing than to have to make new plots each time, and perhaps not bother to make one which turns out to be important on this occasion.

It is convenient to have a system which labels your plots in three ways: with the name of the run (eg Brand X and advertised competitors, 1996–97), with a description of the axes and type of plot (eg share of the Z sector in 1997 and percentage change since 1996), and with space for you to add a comment on the implications of the plot (eg brand leader losing share while X and Y are gaining).

7.4.2 Regular Work: Raw Data

We now go through the process which ends in these plots, starting with the raw data. In your own case the key data will require its own definitions. To explain the method here, a particular set of words is used. Please adapt this to your own situation. The time period here is weeks but four-weeks and months and in some countries bi-months are also normal. Often the periods will be mixed (as in the case history in this book). This will be because the sources are not, or used not to be, able to supply in the periods you really want. Accounting periods or TV costs may be in months, marketplace data in weeks or four-weeks – conversions and grouping or de-grouping will be necessary. The general rule is to store data at the shortest time period – you can always group it later.

The answer to the frequent question – how far back into the past should you go? – depends on the following considerations: How much data is available? And what data is relevant? There is little point in including data under conditions which can no longer be obtained. Have you got enough data points to indicate regularities, exceptions, seasonality, and so on, and for doing decent modelling, if that is one of the uses of the database? For a quick answer, two years of weekly data and four years of monthly data are desirable.

The sales data may be split into sales regions or TV regions, by retailer accounts, and so on, as well as for pack sizes and variants. The data about people will be broken down by demographics, and perhaps by buying and viewing behaviour. You consider first the national total picture as the one responsible for total profit. Segments may be looked at later.

Because little is said about segmentation (except for a comment on the most common way, by regions, in Section 7.7, and on loyalty, in Section 8.13.2), do not conclude that it is unimportant. On the contrary, choosing the right groups to examine is often the key to understanding what is going on in the marketplace. Groups may behave completely differently. Price and volume relationships within a single supermarket chain may be far clearer than over all outlets; they may also be vital information for the sales force. Removing light buyers in the category, or people who never buy your brand, may lead to a key finding. Please do not forget that this can be done for all the analyses described later.

By this stage you should have taken a decision about the category or sector you are going to analyse. This was discussed in Section 7.3.1. You must also decide which competitors you must examine individually – the largest? those advertised? your closest competitors? You should group some others – stores' brands, or own labels, are likely to be such a combination. You usually group the smaller competitors as others, or the rest. How the category is made up partly determines this, but remember that defining too many individual brands or groups of brands at this stage over-complicates tables and plots; defining too few means that something which you should know about may be going on inside a group but escapes your notice. Ten or so items is a sensible number. Twenty is a maximum. There are only five in the case history, but that is to simplify the exposition.

Finally you have come down to the specification of the key data, which are normally, for each brand or group of brands:

- *volume* sales (units, litres, kilograms, …)
- *value* sales (sterling)

- average *price* (such as pounds per kilogram, from the two numbers above; sometimes price but not value is given in the original data, so you have to reconstruct total value sales)
- *distribution* (eg the weighted per cent of stores stocking, advertising weight, eg *TV ratings*. Thirty-second cost equivalents should be used. Remember, in the UK this currently means weighting 10-second spots by 0.57, and 20-seconds by 0.80, because the rate card suggests this is how buyers value these lengths
- *scores* from the tracking study, chosen for their relevance for this work, ie usually meaning they do differ across brands or for one brand over time (like distribution, scores are hardly meaningful for groups of brands).

7.4.3 Regular Work: Category Totals

You now have your raw data. From it you construct by addition, if you do not already have it, the category total volumes and values. Hence the average category price.

Often, you know that your data source under-represents the total sales of the category. It can do so severely, covering for example only three-quarters of all sales. This may be because it does not cover all the outlet types, especially retail chains which do not sell their data, and innovative and minor ways of retailing, or because the weighting is incorrect for your brand. You may deduce this because your own deliveries over a year or so are not reflected accurately by the audit or panel total; you may have agreed this is so with your research supplier. To describe the category size realistically, an adjustment factor should be included in your work.

Data on the category deserve separate study from how the brands are doing within it. What are its overall trends and seasonality? How are prices moving in comparison with relevant economic indices? Can you reasonably forecast volume sales and prices, bearing in mind everything else you know about the category and the economy? These are questions we return to in Section 8.5.

As well as its size, value and trends, it is necessary to be aware of the *type* of category you operate in. For groceries, a review of 50 categories gives us a structure which may be helpful.

The two dimensions suggested are, first, what proportion of volume sales are of *own label*, and second, what proportion by the *three largest brands*. The reasons these are important are as follows.

There is a battle between manufacturers' brands, which traditionally (but not invariably) created and developed categories, and the retailers through which the majority of these brands are sold. Retailers are themselves brands, and are able to spread their perceived benefits (such as quality, freshness, caring for the consumer, and especially perceived lower prices), over all the products which carry their label. Thus they can 'brand' more economically than the manufacturer. Since they do not care where they buy products, provided the quality and price is what they seek, they can play off one supplier against another, while many manufacturers exist to sell only one factory's output. The retailer controls the selling price to the consumer and, above all, controls access to the shelf and other displays. So once the retailer has reached critical mass his position is very powerful. Many manufacturers regard the retailer, and particularly own label, as their biggest problem. Much thought goes into finding strategies to cope with this competitor.

Outside groceries, the situation once seemed less threatening, but the move of retailers into financial products and petrol brought home the true dangers to manufacturers. Even if it is not the large retailers taking these actions, other newcomers enter categories at rock-bottom prices, spending nothing to develop or sustain them, and targeting the most profitable sectors. Telecommunications have experienced this strategy. Traditional retailers themselves have suffered a little in this way. Thus there are 'tertiary' brands, priced below both manufacturers' brands and own label, and these may be as threatening as is own label itself. In response, retailers have in some cases created 'budget own labels' at similar low prices.

In a 1993 analysis of 50 grocery categories, the average prices, relative to the category average at 100, were as below. Since then, 'budget' own labels have grown, at the same prices as tertiaries, taking mainly from stores' own label. Some of the differences in price may be due to real qualities, others show the benefits of branding, yet others are the result of a different budget structure with lower costs. The average percentage volume shares of each type are also shown.

Averages in 50 Grocery Categories, 1993

	Price	Volume share
Brand leader	115	30
Top three brands	108	53
Other manufacturers' brands	111	20
Own label	79	23
Tertiaries	65	4

In many categories the situation is more dramatic than this, with own label completely dominating the picture. In some, the brand leader offers a price below the category average: this is part of the reason for its success. In general, the types of category are very diverse.

When you add the volume shares of the top three brands and of own label, and get less than 80% of the volume sold, the consumer gets a wide choice: these are called *variety categories*. About half of all categories seem to be of this type but they account for 80% of grocery turnover. They include the large, heavily-advertised markets and are the most active. Own label is relatively the cheapest here.

The rest of the categories split into roughly equal thirds. One, called *top three*, is dominated by the top three brands at over 75% of volume – averaging in fact 87%. Own label and tertiaries have found it difficult or uneconomic to break in.

Where the own label share is over 40%, it actually averages 61% and clearly dominates. These tend to be for staple products which manufacturers have failed to brand successfully. Tertiaries are common.

The remainder, or *head-to-head* group, is where own label and manufacturers are struggling for mastery. The battle is largely over price: own label's relative price can be 75 or lower.

The successful strategic positions which this analysis suggests are as follows:

(a) Product innovation may keep you ahead, or even create a new category in which you are obvious leader. You are then likely to be able to justify a price premium, either by a product advantage or an emotional benefit.
(b) However, price can get too far ahead – but how far is too far? Quite a few brands do well at 50% ahead of the category average.
(c) There is also a genuine strategy of low price – combining acceptable quality with a price that's hard to beat.
(d) Once own label and tertiaries get above 40% share by volume you have an increasingly difficult problem in their outlets, especially if you are a minor brand. No one can tell these days when an own label will attack or a price war break out.

7.4.4 Regular Work: Brand Files

You make a file for each brand, for which the entries in the first column are the week numbers, while the other columns hold:

- per cent share of category volume
- per cent share of category value
- relative price
- distribution
- ratings
- tracking scores.

This brand file will be used to describe how the brand is doing against the background of the category average. You will be able to look at competitors in this way as well as your own brands.

7.4.5 Regular Work: Splitting the Category

Before we start this description, return to the raw data and think about the way the brands make it up. You want to look at all the brands you have decided to study. This means simplification of some kind. For this purpose it is not necessary to keep all the individual weeks' data and you work with *averages* over a selected period. The most recent 52-week total is often chosen, or the most recent calendar year – or some other convenient period, such as over the time since a major competitor launched.

You can usually cope with at least two separate periods on your plots, which indicates movement. The year before the most recent period is often chosen, so we talk about year one (meaning the more distant), and year two (the more recent). Sometimes you should make a summary with more years than two. Sometimes it should be parts of years – the weeks round Christmas, for example.

If you are using two years then you make from the brand files a summary for each brand and each year:

- volume total
- value total
- ratings total
- average distribution
- average scores.

Using the category total volumes and values you then make a 'category' file which describes it by summaries of the individual brands which constitute it. Remember that the same process may be used for what is a sector in some larger category; in fact, all categories nest inside some bigger group and can themselves be segmented in some way.

If you have two years or periods the category file is in two parts. Each brand takes a row in the file (conveniently in the order of volume size in year two), while the top rows of the file form year one and the lower rows form year two. The brand names are the entries in the first column, and a useful convention is to write these in lower case for year one, upper case in year two. Thus in plots showing both years (described later), you can distinguish the first from the second.

The category file holds in the second and later columns:

- per cent share of category volume
- per cent share of category value
- relative price
- share of voice (eg of ratings)
- share of voice – share of value
- average distribution
- average scores.

Example of a category file

In Table 1, supplemented by Table 3 (see the Appendix for tables), there is an example of the result of the process just described. The brands of interest are called here A, B (your brand) and C. Own label is looked at as a group, and the remainder of the category is called 'others'. In practice you may have to study more brands, and you may well split up 'others' – for example separating 'tertiaries' with prices below own label.

From the volume and value data by brand you calculate annual totals and derive volume share and value share. Value share divided by volume share gives us the relative price of the brand as a ratio, which we multiply by 100 to give a more convenient number: Brand B's relative price as a ratio in 1994 was 1.08, but this is usually written as 108: its price was 8% above the category average.

This category is clearly a 'variety' one, with the large (but declining) share taken by 'others' giving consumers considerable choice.

Distribution less out-of-stocks is averaged for each brand over the year. Here distribution is defined as 'the weighted per cent of stores with any one of your varieties listed'. It is of course possible to be more complex, and to consider separately different varieties, flavours and sizes. For own label the definition is clear: 'any own label listed', but for the group of others such a definition does not make sense and a distribution measure is not attempted.

If the category were very severely seasonal (the volume peak in November in this category, at 25% above the annual average, is not too serious), you should strictly weight the distribution over the year by the category volume each period. In some categories brands appear on the shelves only or mainly at certain times – eg Easter eggs and some toys.

Share of voice comes from adding whatever media measure is used for the category, and percentaging the brand's share of this. In a television category this means ratings equivalents – standardising by rate card cost the different lengths of commercial used. For other media, rate card spend may be all you have. For a mixture where TV is significant, calculate 'ratings equivalents' for other media from the rate card costs. Where television is minor, take rate card spend for TV too.

The last column in Table 1 – share of voice less value share – represents the advertising aggressiveness of each brand. It is zero if its advertising to sales ratio is average for the category.

This completes the construction of the data files you will use for analysis. To summarise, they consist of:

- raw data files, which you update regularly
- total of the category, which you also update
- category file, showing how the category divides between the brands, constructed occasionally, and when you have decided which longer periods to group, such as a year
- brand files, for the detail within each brand, regularly updated.

Before you start analysis, it is good practice to record the details of what you have decided, but which may not show within the individual files. Someone may later have to use your files – it may be you, and it is not always easy to be certain what decisions you made.

The data sources and definitions should be stated: the country, the outlet types, the category and brand groups, the period dates, the units for volume and for money, and the sorts of advertising. Category totals should be recorded, since many of the later definitions are relative to these. You need any conversion constants used, total volumes, total sterling, average prices, and totals for advertising. Even the full brand names are worth recording, since these may be abbreviated in the tables, in order to fit onto plots. For cars, white goods, and similar products, record the names of marques or manufacturers as well as the model name. Of course the locations and names of the original and of the derived files must also be kept, plus who requested them and who made them.

7.5 Category Data

You have now collected the necessary data and organised it in a convenient way. It is time to put it to use. First, you *look* at the data. The system outlined below allows you to do this thoroughly yet expeditiously. You should carry out this inspection with the brand's business and marketing objectives in mind. Are you doing well? This may mean with a high volume share? With high revenue? With a growing share? Who else is doing well? Most importantly, why? Even with a small data set there is so much to inspect that you need specific questions in your head in order to make the job manageable.

You begin with the category total, to understand your marketplace. We move on to how the category is made up of brand totals, to get an overview of all the brands and to see your brand in context. We finish by looking at selected brands in detail.

7.5.1 Category Data: Totals

As already explained, you may be looking at a whole category, or at part of it which we call a sector. There are four items of data each week: volume sales, value sales, average price derived from these two, and total ratings for all the brands in the category, and it is the analysis of these we discuss here. Occasionally there may also be numbers of interest about the distribution for the category as a whole, such as the total space in groceries (shelf footage, chiller cabinet capacity) allotted to the category.

In Chapter 8 you put numbers on the relationships between these numbers. Here you are just inspecting the data. The first obvious plots are for each of the four main variables over time. Two of these were given in Chapter 6: Figure 1 showed volume and Figure 2 price. For a mature category, the major movements in volume, value and price are likely to be seasonal, with perhaps a small trend. For growing or declining categories the trend in volume and value will be more important, but seasonality cannot be neglected.

For price, the promotion of major brands will have an influence, and of course price wars if they have broken out. A scatter plot of volume sales against price may be revealing, emphasising perhaps Christmas promotions or how the industry deals with seasonality.

Advertising weight is likely to be quite variable and may indicate peaks and gaps you should bear in mind in scheduling.

7.5.2 Category Data: Brands Make Up the Category

When you constructed the data set, you started with brand detail and then made the category file, which contains all the brands (some in groups) but simplifies the complexity down to a few averages. To view the data you work in reverse order. You have reviewed the category total, now you look at how the brands make up the total. The main questions are: Does your brand seem to be behaving in the way you expected? What is its volume share? How is this moving? Why? And how are your major competitors moving and why?

Brand shares are best shown in two ways. First, a histogram for year two, the most recent data – I assume here that the file covers year one and year two. Histograms represent size in a dramatic way – by the height of the bars. The order of the brands should be as stated above – by volume size – so that your ranking is also shown and the diagram is easy to read.

Second, make a scatter plot for which the X-axis is brand share (in year two), the Y-axis is the percentage *change* in brand share (year one to year two), and the data labels are the brand names (when there are many brands and the names are long, abbreviate them). This plot shows which brands are growing and their rate of growth or decline. A similar plot for Consumer Brand Equity was given in Figure 17.

These two plots answer the first two questions about your volume (with further detail to come when you look at your brand file).

Show a histogram for value shares as well, since managers over-concentrate on volume as a criterion. It is wise to give them a reminder about the share of consumer spending which the different brands achieve.

7.5.3 Category Data: Price, Distribution, Advertising

The other variables in your database are possible explainers or diagnostics, and you start with histograms for all of these too. It is worth doing scatter plots, similar to those for volume, for relative price, for distribution and for share of voice, to show actuals and changes.

So much for description of the variables. It is the relation between them, and between changes in one and in another, that we turn to next. This is achieved by scatter plots, which use more than one variable.

Take price as an example (similar work should be done for distribution and for share of voice). The relation of volume share to relative price can be of two sorts. First, is it the cheaper brands which sell more? Second, when a brand drops its price, does its volume share improve and by how much? The first is about the average position, the second about changes and price elasticity, a very different subject though sadly often confused with the first.

A scatter plot for all the brands, using the averages for year two, should show relative price on the X-axis and volume share on the Y-axis (there is an example in Figure 3). This is one of the most important plots in marketing. You expect a general decrease of brand size as you move from cheaper (larger?) brands to more expensive (smaller?) ones. But it is usually *not* the case that all the cheaper brands sell more, nor that the relationship is a simple one. A strong brand, one which is valued by its purchasers, will outsell a weaker competitor at the same price. In the figure, Brand B outsells C. Alternatively, it will be able to charge more and may sell a similar amount or more. Brand A charges more than B, and also sells more. In other words, strong brands tend to be relatively high, or to the right, or both, on this plot.

Since volume sales, once you know costs, determine outgoings, and volume times price determines revenue, the position of a brand on this plot also indicates its profit. It is possible to draw lines of equal profit on the graph, which help in planning where you want to be (there is an example in Section 9.5).

At present, you use this plot simply to record the relative positions of the brands. Chapter 8, when we come to modelling, shows how the 'strength' of brands, or their positions on this plot, can be turned into numbers: Consumer Brand Equities.

A second plot should show both year two positions (the brand name in capitals, as noted above) and year one (the name in lower case), *see Figure 4*. Usually the movement of the brands from one period to the next is fairly small: the two points for a brand are close. Nevertheless, the direction in which the brand moves is critical.

Finally, calculate the percentage changes in relative price and in volume share, again for all the brands. This is done in Table 4. Plot the changes in price on the X-axis, changes in volume share on the Y-axis. The plot holds similar information to the movement described in the previous plot. Is relative price going up or down? Is the volume change in the expected direction for this change? That is, it is often the case that a *price drop* means *more volume* is sold (the relative price fall may be due to a competitor's price rise, not to any change on your part). A *price increase* usually means *less volume* is sold. On this plot, most points could be in the first and third quadrant; life is easier for the analyst when they fall approximately on a straight line. There is in fact other evidence that price elasticities within a category are roughly equal when equities do not change much. The proviso is critical: in fact, you recognise a change in equity precisely by the relationship with a price change being untypical, as is now explained.

For brands following a simple relationship with the activity, you could be seeing only the effects of price changes and price promotions. But there may well be some exceptional brands in the second and fourth quadrants, or nearer the horizontal, than other brands. A relative *price increase* accompanied by *volume increase* is very desirable but not so common. It indicates an increase in the strength or equity of the brand. Something good is happening to cause this effect. At present you do not know what the something else is, but you are on notice to look out for it. Conversely, when a brand which has reduced relative price nevertheless falls in volume then something is going wrong.

Exactly the same arguments hold for distribution and for similar plots for volume and distribution. When you look at these, you may well see suggested explanations for earlier anomalies. Perhaps a brand did not change in price but grew in volume – was it a distribution change which caused this? We are getting close to the need for multivariate work, again deferred to Chapter 8. But many of the effects are visible in these sorts of plots, which a statistical analysis later quantifies.

Share of voice rarely explains sales as clearly as price and distribution do. Similar plots for share of voice may however be revealing. It is a quantity which should also be calculated only over quite long periods – a year, or six months when advertising is heavy. It then reasonably represents advertising pressure. Over short periods it is much too variable and ignores the decay of advertising effects. Share of adstock is then preferable (this term is explained in Chapter 8).

There is an additional graph for share of voice which well represents the aggressiveness of the brands' media spend. This plots on the X-axis the volume share, and on the Y-axis the share of voice *minus* the value share. This new variable indicates whether the brand is spending above or below the category average advertising-to-sales ratio.

This can be seen by supposing the share of voice *equals* the value share. Thus

$$\left(\frac{brand\ advertising}{category\ advertising} \right) = \left(\frac{brand\ sales\ value}{category\ sales\ value} \right)$$

This comes to the same as

$$\left(\frac{brand\ advertising}{brand\ sales\ value} \right) = \left(\frac{category\ advertising}{category\ sales\ value} \right)$$

In many categories, the brands on this plot fall from high-left (small brands which are trying to grow), to bottom-right (large brands with economies of scale); there are also the unadvertised or barely-advertised brands on a line falling below the X-axis. Figure 5 is an example. This plot, which I have called the Jones diagram after its inventor John Philip Jones, is most interesting when some companies do *not* follow the norm, for example large brands who advertise above the average advertising-to-sales ratio, indicating an exceptionally militant stance.

You have now looked at three of the factors which may affect a brand's average volume share: its price, its distribution and its weight of advertising support. In some cases, there may be other factors, such as product improvement or promotional spend, which have major impacts on sales. Data for these should be collected and the appropriate plots kept up to date.

7.5.4 Category Data: Brand Strategies

It is sometimes useful to compare the strategies on price, distribution and share of voice which the different brands have adopted. To see these, plot scatter diagrams of pairs of them – for example price on the X-axis, distribution on the Y-axis. Do all the brands which have poor distribution also have a high price, for example?

Another reason for these plots is to see whether two variables, which at a later stage you may be using as explainers in modelling, are in fact associated. If so, modelling may throw up one of the factors only as the reason for high sales, when in fact both – or even the other – are the true cause. You are warned by knowing that such associations exist. An example is given in Section 7.6.2.

Another way to look at the relations between explainers is as follows. Take a scatter plot showing the brands by, for example, price and volume. Instead of the data label showing the brand name, substitute a label showing the share of voice, or perhaps the distribution. Does this additional information help to explain outliers or anomalies? For example, are brands with high equity (towards the top-right on the price/volume plot), those with high share of voice? What you are doing is attempting to see the multidimensionality of the situation, rather than being restricted to over-simple solutions. 'Three-dimensioned' plots do the same job.

7.5.5 Category Data: Tracking Study Scores

Next you look at tracking study scores, of which you may have already chosen two or three key measures. Or, you may be doing a preliminary scan, in order to decide which *are* the key measures, since it is a separate job to sort out how the tracking scores relate to each other and to a possible 'halo' effect, which is covered below. Typical scores are measured for advertising and brand awareness, 'worth the money', 'good quality' and 'for me'. We now investigate how they are related to sales and to advertising.

The obvious place to start is with scatter plots, for year two, with the scores on the X-axis and volume sales on the Y-axis: these can be followed by plots showing two years, or showing the changes in the scores and in volume.

What are the relations between sales and the scores? Is it true that the better brands (large, or growing) have high or increasing scores? If so, there is evidence that scoring high there is indeed desirable. This was found in Figure 6. You may be able to see *why* moves in sales are taking place, and creative strategies may be confirmed in this way. Other scores may show no such association, or even no discrimination between brands, and are therefore less important. It may at first sight be surprising that scores, which the manufacturer has paid to get, actually move very little or are not related to consumer behaviour, but this is often the case, as items are left in questionnaires just in case they may be useful, or for consistency, or simply because they were once thought desirable.

Other useful plots are between shares of voice and the tracking scores. Is a higher rate of advertising associated with high or growing consumer evaluation of the brand? Often it is weight of advertising and not creative content which determines how a brand is scored, which means that the tracking study is not simply a copy evaluation.

7.5.6 Category Data: Rearrangement of a Scores Table

A table of tracking study or image scores consists of column headings which are the names of brands, typically half a dozen or so, and row headings which are attributes or statements, perhaps a dozen to twenty. So you have a tall, thin table of entries which are the average scores given to each brand on each attribute. Here it is assumed all the scores are high for a good attribute; if some are worded so that high means 'bad', reverse such scores.

You can read this table down the columns to get a picture of a single brand. Or you can read it across a row to see how the brands compare for a single attribute. But this is laborious and wasteful. Informants simplify their task when they contribute to such a table and we will now uncover how they do so. They tend to think of *all* the brands in the category as having or not having each attribute, and so mark every brand high or low on that score. They also tend to think of some brands as 'for me' or 'desirable', and mark these up on all or many of the attributes. This is known as the 'halo' effect.

You can simplify the table in the following way, as recommended by Andrew Ehrenberg. The process can of course be computerised and our program is called the Ehrenberg Rearrangement. First, average the scores down the table at the foot of each column, and across the table at the end of each row. Then rearrange the columns so that the highest average is on the left. Next, rearrange the rows so that the highest is on top. The brands are now in the order of their average scores, and so are the attributes. Format the data as recommended in Section 7.2 so that only two significant figures are shown – this makes for readability.

For each entry in the table, you calculate the expected entry from the marginal averages. This means, 'expected' if the only information the informant used was, first, the column averages, which represent her overall evaluations of the brands as 'for me' and, second, the row averages, or her overall evaluations of the attributes as 'relevant to the category', or 'what a desirable brand is like'. To get this 'expected', you multiply the relevant row and column averages and divide by the overall table average.

Now work out the observed score in each box of the table *minus* the expected score and write out a new table with 'observed minus expected' in each position. Finally – and this is optional – work out:

$$(\text{observed} - \text{expected})^2 / \text{expected}$$

for each position, sum the result across the columns, and show this sum as an 'index' at the end of each row.

You read the new table as follows. Informants have an overall view or evaluation of each brand, summarised by its column average. They have also told us how they regard each attribute, as relevant for this group of brands, summarised by its row average. This is usually most of what they are telling us.

However, some of the 'observed minus expected' entries may be large. If large and positive, then *this brand* is specially well-thought of on *this attribute* – more so than the averages would lead you to expect. If it is large and negative, then it is particularly badly thought of. If these exceptions are common in the row, or specially large, their sum of squares at the end of the row is large. This exceptional information does not exist in rows where the index is small; all you need conclude for such attributes is that the overall evaluation is sufficient. In rows where the index is large, there is significant extra learning.

You have now reduced the table to a list of the brands in order of their overall evaluation, plus a few characteristics on which they are outstanding – either plus or minus. This review of tracking study scores is worth doing occasionally. It will help you choose which scores are worth examining regularly, those where there are useful differences between brands. It will also help you to choose a 'halo' or 'for me' key score for each brand: the average for suitable individual scores where there is little difference between attributes.

Example of rearranging a scores table
In Table 2, the figures given first are typical of the way tracking scores are thought about: your Brand B comes first, as the one important to you, the attributes are in questionnaire order, and the data are given to one decimal place. Such a presentation makes it hard to see what is going on. You might conclude that you do particularly well on attribute F and badly on K but that is about all that leaps to the eye.

In part B, the averages of the rows and columns have been used to rearrange them and the scores have been formatted to whole numbers.

On average we are only just behind the leader, Brand A. Attributes F, G and so on are those all the brands do well at. All are low at K.

When we take the differences from expected, in part C as explained above, three numbers stand out in the new table: +12 and –9 for attribute A, and –5 for attribute W. The index, also explained above, picks out these attributes as those where the differences between brands are largest; the rest may as well be averaged as a general score for each brand, due to the halo effect.

The final result is in part D. We have reduced the information to nine numbers.

On attribute A, brand awareness, the brand leader does much the best. We are in the middle. The volume shares of the brands are 17, 15 and 9% so the results are not unexpected, except that Brand A is clearly more front of mind than its actual sales warrant.

Surprisingly, Brand A does not do at all well on 'worth it'. It is at the highest relative price (112) while your brand and C are at 107 and 101. Being the price leader has had this worrying effect and Brand A probably has some justifying to do, but that is not your problem.

On the 'general' scores there is little to choose between the brands.

7.6 Brand Detail

Consider a single brand, with all its weekly changes. Strictly, the brand is not in isolation, as it is brand *shares* and *relative* prices you look at. Normally, you pay attention to only a few brands in detail – your own of course, and one or two key competitors. You review all the brands when you use the category file, and when one comes to your attention you then call up its brand file.

7.6.1 Brand Detail: Volume Share Over Time

The critical plot is the brand's volume share over time. This is what you need to explain, and in particular what part communications played in its general level, and its ups and downs. To do this you have to see how other explainers affected it, especially price and distribution. You must remember it is rare that advertising is the major explainer; almost never is it the only reason for change. Therefore you have to look for other, and probably more important, explainers.

It often helps to maintain a historical plot of your brand share on which relevant events are marked up: promotions, product or packaging changes, the date of Easter, and so on. You are reminded by this annotated plot about reasons for outliers when we later come to fitting or modelling the data.

There are several ways you can show the relation between say, price and volume. The first is to plot price on the same timescale and look at both the volume plot and the price plot. This is made easier if the price plot is looked at from the back (turn the top over, not the side), and against the light. Using an overhead foil as an overlay is neater. You can then see the *high* prices as *lows* on the plot, which is how you expect price to affect volume. So you look for simultaneous highs and lows in both plots.

Another way is to add price as a data label above the volume plot. You then examine times when volume changes took place, to see whether price altered then. This was used in Figure 9.

A third way is a scatter plot, with price on the X-axis, volume on the Y-axis; as data labels it is advisable to use the week numbers. An example is Figure 10. In this plot, as in the others, you must be careful to note the *actual spread* of relative prices. When plots are automatically laid out, they always fill the sheet. So a range between relative prices of 103 to 105 *looks* the same as for 103 to 150. But the first range is so small that you are unlikely to see any price effect, while the second is substantial and you certainly expect a result.

When inspecting such a scatter plot, remember there is often more going on than the overall relationship. It is sometimes helpful to use as the data label another variable, such as distribution. Or, plot a line joining the points for successive weeks.

Example: Two simultaneous effects
No general relation between price and volume was visible in the scatter plot in this example: the points simply formed a cloud. Once the line joining successive points was drawn, it was clear there was a trend from top right to bottom left. As prices had been reduced, volume share simultaneously fell. This indicates a slow and general loss of equity. But short term, there were swings bottom left to top right and back. These reflected periods when equity did not change much but prices moved violently as we or competitors promoted. At these times we saw the normal price–volume relationship.

In all these (and with similar plots for value and for distribution – *see Figure 11*), we look out for *trends* in the data as well as the relation with price. We look for *outliers*, for times when *other measured factors* (eg price, or distribution) changed, and associations with these changes. We note non-price promotions, in-store activities, major activities by competitors, distribution gains and losses, and so on. We are not quantifying such associations here, but picking them out, so that when you come to modelling you know what to look for.

Promotions must always be identified on plots like Figure 10. When they are pure price promotions, they are usually indistinguishable from the scatter round the line suggested by the other points. When they offer something more, when they give some value rather than cut-price, you hope to see them above this line. Major price reductions (two for one, for example), lie well to the left. It is particularly important to decide whether they are also high (deliver extra sales in proportion or more). All too often, they are not as high as the general relation suggests they might be. Then they are being used for purchases which would have been made anyway, and probably cost us money.

Never forget that an association, or positive correlation, between sales and another factor, does not *prove* that the factor caused increased sales. We are dealing with data 'as it falls', not with the result of an experiment, and in such a case many of the associations are not causative. Every course in statistics warns against this error – that because a relationship between A and B has been found, we have not proved that A caused B. Sometimes the reverse is true, sometimes C caused both A and B, sometimes it is coincidence. This is a hard lesson for the analyst who is eager to get results, but scepticism can prevent a nasty tumble.

Example: A third factor
The annual plan was for price cuts in certain months, supported by advertising. Analysis by months showed high sales in these times, and of course high ad-spend. The two were related, but because the pricing plan caused both. It may be that the two possible causes can be disentangled, but this is not done by the simple relation between advertising and sales.

In another plan, advertising was scheduled for times when price was not cut – for example to even out deliveries over the year, or because the price cuts were intended to bring in new users who were not influenced by advertising. This time, price had a larger effect on sales than the short-term effect of advertising. Hence the times of advertising were when sales were low, so the simple relation between advertising and sales was negative.

7.6.2 Brand Detail: Other Plots Over Time

As with the category data, the value share should be plotted. This will also show, when compared with the volume plot, associations between price and volume. If volume is being kept stable by reducing price, for example, the value share will be in decline.

Advertising data – or information on other communications – are best shown on a bar chart. This makes clear its intermittent nature (on-air or off-air); in Chapter 8 I describe how the effects of advertising which persist after its appearance can be represented by adstock.

Again, plot one explainer against another (eg price and adstock, price and distribution), in order to ascertain whether one varied with the other.

Example: Distribution fall, price fall
The plot of volume against price showed little effect. It could have been argued that the brand simply had low price elasticity and a small, exclusive group of loyal buyers: price had been reduced but this had not brought in extra sales. The plot against distribution also showed little change. Apparently distribution was not critical.

The conclusions were false: both price and distribution actually mattered. This could have been discovered in two ways.

First, inspecting the dates on the scatter plots, or drawing the connecting line, showed a trend. This is always a danger when you are trying to infer an effect. You are on safer ground when sales have both risen as price fell and re-duced when price increased again.

Second, the plot of distribution against price showed a clear relationship: the two explainers were confounded. This might mean only one was the real cause for both the other variables changing, or, as in this case, simultaneity. That is, the brand manager had cut prices in order to compensate for falling distribution and to maintain the volume on which he was being judged.

Tracking scores are probably not available weekly. It may be necessary to show these as four-weekly averages on a weekly scale, or as rolling averages, and then amalgamate sales for this comparison into the same intervals. Scatter plots of volume against these scores may be revealing.

7.6.3 Brand Detail: The Size of an Effect

In this part of the book we are not modelling, or doing anything complex. But from the sort of descriptive material discussed here, it is often possible to give a number for the size of the communications effect. This means you make a judgment about what would have happened without communications, and subtract this from what you actually saw. All estimates of the size of the effect are comparisons. A few simple examples below suggest short-term or rapid results. More complex and realistic examples are in Section 7.8.3.

Example 1
Sales volume averaged 10,000 units a week before your campaign, but 12,000 during the campaign. You estimate the effect at 20% improvement.

Simple and common as this example is, it contains an important lesson. There is the implicit assumption that sales would have continued at 10,000 without the communications. But, could something else have caused this change? For example, did you also run a promotion? If the increase happened pre-Christmas, could this be a time-of-sales increase?

You can strengthen or support the estimate by explicitly measuring and reporting possible disturbing factors and showing, for example, that no promotion was run (argument by elimination). Another way is to quote qualitative research, which might show increasing reasons for purchase being exactly those which your campaign was designed to stimulate.

You may also need to show that, although sales varied somewhat up and down before the campaign, it is statistically improbable that such variation could have produced the 12,000 observed. We are treating the campaign as an 'experiment' of the type analysed in Chapter 8.

Example 2
If you had comparable data from last year, you might be able to show there was no surge in sales share pre-Christmas, unlike this year. The assumption is now that sales this year would have followed the same pattern as last year.

Example 3
Sales share averaged 10% before your campaign, but 12% during the campaign. You estimate the effect at 20% improvement. The assumption is that you would have followed the same pattern as your competitors.

Example 4
Rather than compare yourself with all others in the category, you may make a selection. This might be necessary, for example, if own label sales were rising sharply so your overall share did not increase. But you might assume that you would have followed the same pattern as other branded manufacturers, or as others of your own brands, or as you did in another country.

Example 5
You may have figures for stock sold in to retailers, rather than volume bought from retailers by the final consumer. You may also get the views of those who did the selling.

   It can happen that they credit additional sales to the effect of a consumer campaign on the retailer, often one due to start soon (again, you sometimes see a sales rise before advertising for this reason: extra shelf space, display and sometimes new packaging are the mechanism).

In the last example, the sales people are saying that sales would have been lower without the promise of the advertising. Normally, sales staff favour trade deals at the expense of advertising, so endorsement of this type probably underestimates the communications effect.

7.7 Regional and Other Analyses

So far, data has been national. It may be necessary to report data for different regions, either because there are regionally-varying brand preferences (arising from history, distribution, and so on), or regional marketing differences. The data may similarly be broken down by outlet type, or individual store group, or by brand details like packing or flavour. Regions are used here as an example.

   Two sorts of plots can be constructed with regional data. The first shows *the individual regions* on a bar or scatter plot about the variables (volume, price, distribution, advertising). This is to demonstrate the differences between the regions: you have a good share in Scotland, but poor in the South, in London you are relatively expensive, in the West you are cheap. The second way treats *a single region* in exactly the same way as you did the whole country.

   The first allows you to ask what differences there actually are, for the category or more likely for your brand, across regions. A sales volume per head sales difference for the *brand* may be due, for example, to a similar *category* difference; on the other hand, it may be because you have a higher relative price or poorer distribution in the region.

7.8 Campaign Evaluation

7.8.1 Campaign Evaluation: Introduction

Now suppose that you have been assigned to work on the evaluation of a communications campaign. In other words, we are not discussing here *planning* the evaluation at the time the campaign is being designed, though that is very desirable and is summarised in Section 7.8.5. The requirements of that job are self-evident from the description which follows. This is about the question: what did this campaign achieve in the marketplace? This section is a self-contained description which does not get into detail about methods, nor into financial evaluation. It gives many examples of actual evaluations.

There is a difference of emphasis between 'being accountable' and 'campaign evaluation' which means that they are not really synonyms. They are very close, and often used interchangeably, but 'being accountable' is the bigger subject. Campaign evaluation need not go into business objectives with the same care – it can start at communication objectives. It may end with conclusions about the campaign, not with the improvement of future plans. It may not combine in the budget data, but stop at the marketplace findings; it may concentrate on *how* the effects were produced, because it is more for internal use in the marketing department than to convince people outside the department. Nevertheless, there is a great deal to be learned from the set of 'ideal' campaign evaluation sections in the series *Advertising Works*.

Suppose that you have already completed the database work described above so you are aware of the findings from this numerical analysis. You know how the brand behaved and you have a good idea why – and also what was *not* responsible. But that is not a formal campaign evaluation. The questions now are: What more should you do? And how do you turn the results into an evaluation report?

When you are asked to carry out a 'campaign' evaluation, you are not concerned only with communications. The question is really about the brand. First, you have to understand all facets of its marketing and their effects, in order to eliminate these from your enquiries about what communications do. Second, findings on other marketing activities, or about competitors and the category as a whole, are just as valuable to management.

You should review two areas other than your database before you start work. First, what information is held which is additional to this data? This certainly includes qualitative results which are not held in continuous form. There will be information about the product, reports on the trade and your relations with them, which are wider than just distribution and promotions. Second, check again on how it was originally believed that the communications were to work, since this will tell you what mental model to look out for.

So you should list *all* the measures and other information available about the trade and marketplace, not just those in the database. These will split into:

- *media exposure* to the target (mailings, promotions, phone calls as well as traditional media) – and remember that 'target' means trade buyers as well as marketplace buyers and users;
- *evaluations by the target of these messages*, in pre-tests and after exposure, including qualitative work;
- *evaluations by the target of the brand* in the context of the category, again including qualitative data;
- *behaviour*, largely covered by your database analysis;
- *other factors* which may affect sales shares: product changes, editorial comment, and factors affecting the category, whatever these may be (new house starts, inflation, and so on).

7.8.2 Campaign Evaluation: Methods

You then look for those connections between these measures which are suggested by the mental model assumed when the campaign was planned. Although this will not have laid down specific equations, it tells you what to look for. If the expected mechanisms are not visible, you must try to find out why.

For example, suppose communications are to change attitudes and this should lead to trial. Then you examine what attitudes have changed and whether this can be linked to communications. You see whether the people who have changed attitudes subsequently tried the brand (note that trial for other reasons is likely to be *followed by* attitude change!).

Or suppose recent ad exposures are meant to increase sales; at the same time you know that price affects sales too. Then you look simultaneously at the relations over time between sales, recent ad exposures and price in the way this chapter and the next one describe.

From a review of the 157 papers published in *Advertising Works*, Volumes 1 to 8, there is a list of the most common methods, so those most likely to be relevant to you. Do not look at these papers as a record of elitist achievement; rather, they are a toolbox which you plunder at your convenience.

A striking fact about the case histories is the *number* of different analyses carried out. It is in this way you create conviction – successful evaluations never stop at a single measure looked at in one way only. In the average evaluation, there were *two* different analyses of sales and *two* of other consumer reactions, supported by *one* measurement of a direct reaction to the communications.

Most of the effort goes on sales measures, but these are backed up by evidence of consumers' reactions in the marketplace. Finally, corroboration is provided by research into the advertising itself.

For your purpose, total priority is given to sales or other desirable behaviour. This is how communications are generally made accountable – by estimating the bottom-line return. You want to know the *size* of the benefit which communications brought, hard though this is to measure. Everything else is there to add authenticity and conviction to your estimate of this benefit.

One of the arguments already mentioned and often used – by elimination – deserves expansion. Suppose the brand is doing better than before – by some criterion such as profit or volume share. Various reasons might account for this improvement. Examples are a development in the product itself, a change in price, better distribution, and so on. But a review of these possibilities may show that they could *not* have accounted for the change. By elimination, all that is left as a reason for improvement is the advertising. This works as a method only when there *was* no change in the factors. Modelling is the way to disentangle them when they did change.

The main methods are now listed under three headings and then in order of the frequency with which they were used.

A. Marketplace Behaviour

Direct reporting of changes in:

- Sales, share or rate of sale, from audit or panel data
- Argument by elimination
- Sales, company data
- Support of own staff and sales people
- Direct response
- Distribution gains and other retailer effects.

Advertised vs. non-advertised area and other tests

- Sales, share or rate of sale, from audit data or panel
- Sales, company data.

Longer and broader effects

- Effects visible over a long period
- Support of price.

There are also reports of modelling, which is the subject of the next chapter.

B. Consumer Research

Direct reporting of changes in:

- Brand awareness, attitude and image
- Claimed brand usage.

Links between campaign and results:

- Ad awareness and brand usage
- Brand usage etc in line with strategy
- Usage profile in line with strategy.

C. Advertising Research

- Advertising standout
- Qualitative communication pre-tests or marketplace checks
- Quantitative communication pre-tests or marketplace checks
- Verbatims.

7.8.3 Campaign Evaluation: Examples

You will find examples of the techniques in all volumes of *Advertising Works*, and you should get hold of some recent volumes.

They are best read in the context of the evaluation as a whole: How was the campaign expected to work? How did this particular method fit into the general picture? and so on. What follows is no substitute for the full papers, but merely indicates the variety of situations faced and techniques used. They are summaries, chosen mostly from the latest volume at the time of writing (1995, Volume 8) and from the main prize winners. The references to the methods quoted (and to other useful examples) are by the volume number followed by the paper number (given in the contents list and at the head of each paper).

A. Marketplace Behaviour

Sales, share or rate of sale, from audit or panel (8/1, 8/6, 8/11) simply gives facts about the brands' performance. It may be unreasonable to attribute all good news to the communications used. You need some evidence that communications can take the credit. This may come simply from timing – the argument by elimination (nothing else changed) being taken for granted.

BMW
Sales data shared across the motor industry allowed BMW to show that its market share almost trebled between 1980 and 1994.

Boddingtons
Sales of canned Boddingtons, compared with all canned bitter, are measured by an independent audit firm. Over two years, Boddington's share grew from 5% to nearly 14%, overtaking the previous brand leader, John Smiths.

Peperami
Sales in grocers, measured by an audit company, were 55% up, when the advertising broke, on the previous month. In the six months after the campaign started, sales were 35% up on the previous six months.

Using the argument by elimination explicitly (8/2, 8/4, 8/6, 8/10) makes the case much stronger.

Cadbury's Roses, Boddington's Bitter and *Hall's Soothers* all argue that the gains in sales observed could not have been caused by changes in the product or in the price.
   In addition Roses eliminate packaging, Boddington's rule out promotions (this is in the core accounts), while Hall's Soothers again argue against packaging but also against sampling, competitive advertising and the effect of a flu epidemic.

Sales, using company data (8/1, 8/6, 8/11) have potentially the same weakness as audited sales, that other possible causes have not been eliminated. But because people inside the firm or close to it are involved, there may be ways of bolstering the case: reports from salespeople about *why* the change took place, and *why* the trade behaved as it did. Even if the evidence is anecdotal, it can add considerable reassurance.

Boddingtons
A list of 959 'core accounts' was drawn up – pubs which had bought the brand every month for the last three years. Distribution therefore becomes a constant. Boddingtons Bitter grew its share from 51% to 66% of all the cask ales sold by Whitbread to these accounts.

Peperami
Deliveries to retailers grew 52% in the first quarter of the campaign, 20% in the next quarter.

Support of your own staff and salespeople (7/1, 7/18) again calls for direct checks on how communications helped.

The National Dairy Council advertised doorstep milk deliveries in order to slow down the switch by housewives to supermarket milk.

Scottish Amicable sell pensions, endowments, and so on mainly in the 'independent' sector, where brokers make recommendations to purchasers. Brokers strongly refute the direct effect of advertising on themselves, but are inclined to recommend names which customers are ready to accept. The role for advertising was to increase consumers' awareness and predisposition to purchase Scottish Amicable and hence brokers' readiness to recommend it.

Direct response (7/13, 7/20, 8/18) is the classic field for effectiveness measurement. It is sometimes necessary to allow for other effects than those which the campaign ostensibly aimed at, to provide additional support for the investment – in the example below, could the anti-smoking campaign have affected people who did not telephone?

The Health Education Board for Scotland has an anti-smoking programme. It offered a free telephone helpline, launched and promoted initially solely through advertising. A booklet 'You can stop smoking' was available only to telephone callers. 79,000 booklets were given out in the first year, the average weekly call rate being 4,300 when TV advertising was running and 1,500 when it was not.

Direct Line Insurance is primarily a direct response advertiser which in 1989 used only print advertising, but it added TV in January 1990. In the next three months, telephone enquiries for quotations increased between 24% and 54% over the same months of the previous year.

Distribution gains and other retailer effects (6/3, 7/18, 8/6, 8/11) may or may not be immediately relevant for your purpose. It is more likely they were the means by which sales gains were created than objectives in their own right.

Boddingtons Canned Bitter nearly doubled its distribution over three years of advertising.

Peperami
The campaign coincided with the siting of additional stands on the deli counter in every major multiple – the first time this had been negotiated and feeding directly off the advertising.

Area and other tests on sales, from audit data or panel (1/7, 2/4, 7/11, 7/13) are often a strong way of showing 'what would have happened without advertising'.

Gini is a fruit-flavoured, carbonated soft drink bought by Cadbury Schweppes in 1989. This was not advertised in Tyne Tees, which appears to be a typical area in other respects. Some marketing activities undertaken in the re-positioning of Gini were national – trade and consumer promotions – and were not expected to influence sales in Tyne Tees in a different way. In Tyne Tees the brand share gain was less than half that of the advertised areas.

BT wanted to increase the penetration of its network services and identified Call Waiting as the most widely appealing. Direct mail was used on targeted households, those with high phone bills. Radio and press advertising was considered as a back-up, aimed at parents with teenaged children. A regional test was planned for London, where all three media were used. As a control, 25,000 target households in Edinburgh were mailed, but received no other promotion.
Responses to the mailing in London were 9%, but in Scotland 4%. In addition a large number of responses were received in London to the other media.

Area and other tests on sales, using company data (7/14, 8/1), can be very simple but compelling, especially where other things are clearly equal.

BMW
The UK campaign was not run in France, Italy or Germany. Sales grew here at a higher rate than in other European markets. Britain is the only market in which the brand has become as strong as it is in Germany.

Whipsnade Wild Animal Park lies in the middle of the overlap of the London, Central and Anglia regions. Surveys establish the proportions of visitors by TV region and measure also advertising awareness and claimed influence of advertising. Advertising spend, in all three regions in 1990, switched to London and Anglia only in 1991.
The share of visitors at end of May from London and Anglia grew from 71% in 1990 to 88% in 1991. The Central share fell from 20% to 12%. Awareness and claimed influence swung similarly.

Econometric modelling of sales, share or response (7/2, 7/4, 8/4, 8/6, 8/11) are relevant to Chapter 8 but included here for completeness:

Cadbury's Roses audit sales data at the Christmas sales peak was extracted for nine TV areas and the years 1983 to 1982. A regression equation was calculated which allowed for a regional effect, a price effect, weight of advertising and underlying growth not attributable to advertising (incentives to retailers, new pack sizes, and so on). The equation explained 70% of the variation in the data and allowed the calculation that 37,000 tonnes sold were generated by advertising.

Boddingtons rate of sale (see above) was regressed on four explanatory variables: price, seasonality, competitive advertising and Boddingtons' advertising. Advertising was represented by adstock, the weighted sum of previous advertising ratings at each bi-month. Thus it was possible to calculate the advertising contribution to rate of sale and hence to sales volume.

Peperami volume sales increase mentioned previously can be split (by calculation of the effect of other factors), into a 27% lift directly due to advertising and 8% due to extra distribution and store sitings (themselves related to the campaign).

Effects visible over a long period (7/4, 7/5, 7/6, 8/1, 8/2), are the most difficult to measure but probably the most important objective of communications. It is the dearest wish of advertising and other agencies to have a long-lasting effect on the brand by creating a new position, a new image. The major difficulty is that we are now talking about communications in its role of creating or sustaining a brand, as opposed to a product. This is not the job of communications alone. Everything, including the standing of the parent company itself, the quality of the product, the range of services, flavours or sizes offered, acceptance by the trade, the price position, the treatment of complaints and attitudes of counter staff – all of these contribute to branding. Separating out the effect of communications can look nearly impossible. But people have succeeded in tackling this problem convincingly.

Volkswagen Golf
Twenty-seven other cars' sales histories were studied, and in general showed two years of increasing share followed by five years of decline until a new model was launched. The Golf did not follow this pattern, but share continued to grow from 1985 to 1989.

BMW, *British Airways*, *Andrex* and *Oxo* papers all describe consistent but refreshed campaigns which helped create and maintain successful brands over many years.

Support of price (8/1, 8/2, 8/9) is a powerful way of demonstrating the effectiveness of branding. This important subject is expanded in Section 9.7.1.

> *Clarks Shoes* decided that:'The primary role for advertising was to justify a significant price premium for the new branded product … using advertising to simply sell more of a product is not always the only (or even the best), way to increase profit.'
>
> In 1992–93 children's trainers prices dropped sharply. Of 16 brands audited, only two were able to increase their price (Nike and Adidas), while Clarks went from selling own label trainers at £19.32 to CICA at £25.99. There was no real difference between the previous own label product and the new CICA in 1992; in 1993 several models with a higher specification were introduced but these accounted for less than 10% of total volume.
>
> Despite this large price increase, overall sales of Clarks trainers were not only maintained but increased.

> *BMW*
> 'The strength of the brand allowed price increases even during the recession, unlike the market as a whole.'

B. Consumer Research

You now start on measures which are more diagnostic and supportive, adding conviction that communications were the cause of what you see.

Brand awareness, attitude and image (8/1, 8/6, 8/11) are the classical tools.

> *BMW*
> The image overall is stronger in Britain (where the campaign being evaluated ran exclusively) than in other countries: scores averaged 50.4 here, 49.9 in Germany, and 38.1 in France. The detail of the British scores showed BMW above Mercedes, Audi, and so on for items such as 'make well-engineered cars', 'make stylish cars', and 'make cars which are stylish to drive'.

> *Boddingtons*
> Six per cent said it was the 'brand liked best' before the campaign, 18% said this after.

Claimed brand usage (8/6, 8/11) may be the only way you can measure sales, in which case it must be an acceptable goal. In other cases, as below, it is the best way to identify regional or other demographic differences. You must always be on your guard for people making statements in interviews which for one reason or another are not strictly accurate.

Boddingtons
The task was to grow volume outside Granada (its home area). Pre-advertising 11% of bitter drinkers outside Granada claimed to have ever drunk it, and 4% to have drunk it regularly. After the campaign these figures were 79% and 14%.

Peperami
Children were asked how much they would like to eat various snack brands, before and after the advertising. The mean score increased by 21%. For mothers, the mean score for likelihood to purchase rose by 26%, while among those aware of the advertising it increased 40%.

Ad awareness and brand usage measures combined (8/11, 8/14), are a convincing way of showing where the benefits come from. Claims made in communications and then replayed as reasons for using the brand are specially convincing.

The Edinburgh Club (for health and fitness)
New members were asked where they had heard of the club and why they joined. The two major sources were a friend's recommendation and the advertisements for the club. In the reasons for joining were aspects of the club likely to have come from the advertising: 'non-intimidating members' scored 38% and 'atmosphere' 29%.

Brand usage etc changing in line with strategy (8/1, 8/7) is an extension of the same idea: linking exposure to communications with subsequent beliefs and behaviour.

BMW
An objective of the advertising was to associate the values of top-end models with more affordable models. In the event, it was the higher proportion of the 3 Series which contributed most to volume sales increases.

Usage profile changing in line with strategy (7/2, 8/13) is another way of demonstrating the required link.

Cadbury's Boost
The aim was to achieve greatest growth among 16 to 24-year-olds. This was achieved by raising penetration (claiming to eat nowadays), and frequency (once a fortnight or more), in this group, so that a real change took place in the demographic profile.

C. Advertising Research

Advertising standout (8/1, 8/6, 8/11, 8/12) is sometimes treated as an objective, but can be a false trail on its own. As confirmation that the communications achieved part of their task, these measures are acceptable, but evidence of behavioural change is needed before communications can be properly evaluated.

Peperami
Prompted ad awareness of the advertising among 7 to 14-year-olds with the previous advertising was 12% (the leader among snacks was Milky Way at 52%). With the new advertising, Pepperami reached 62%, now the leader on this measure, ahead of the next highest, Monster Munch at 48%.

Wonderbra
One of the objectives of the campaign was to increase the power and reach of the advertising through the generation of editorial coverage. Maximum publicity and exposure had to be generated with a limited budget. £330,000 was spent on media. It was estimated that the cost of the airtime/column inches of editorial coverage would have been nearly £18 million. Examples are:
      'The current Wonderbra ads are hard to miss.' The *Financial Times*, 10/3/94
      'Congratulations to Wonderbra on their eye-catching ads.' The *Guardian*, 17/2/94

Qualitative communication pre-tests or marketplace checks (8/2, 8/4) are again evidence that communications are capable of carrying the message, rather than of effectiveness of the message.

Cadbury's Roses
Research on the 1979 campaign showed that consumers recognised that Roses had created a new and motivating role for the brand:
      'It's just a little thank you. Appreciation.'
      'I think the message was, if you wanted to give a little gift, buy Roses.'

Quantitative communication pre-tests or marketplace checks (7/6, 8/1, 8/3, 8/11) are not basically different from the item above.

Boddingtons
In the national survey, only 19% said it was 'a pint with a creamy head' before the campaign, but 49% after it. Seven per cent said the brand 'had good advertising' before the campaign, but 39% after it.

Verbatims (8/2, 8/4, 8/6) add similar conviction.

British Airways
These are extracts from consumer research, describing progress to becoming 'the world's favourite airline':
      'We have seen enough of aeroplanes in ads ... this is different ... it grabbed my attention.' 1983
      'Oh no, I don't think they should change that ... it's become their trademark.' 1991

7.8.4 Campaign Evaluation: Reporting

Do not try to prepare a report on your own and then announce it to an astonished world. Go through the main points beforehand with the manager. This will not only show you what needs more explanation or argument than you thought, you will learn also which conclusions need emphasis because they bear on current concerns.

You do not need to be as elaborate as the papers in *Advertising Works*. It is unlikely that as carefully-written a text is required, only enough to say clearly what you have done and what you have concluded. You are writing a report, not a paper. On the other hand, the data section can be fuller and you will probably use your database analysis system for this.

The headings for your report will probably be:

- Administrative details (campaign dates, costs, etc)
- Campaign brief or objectives (and business and marketing objectives where relevant)
- How the communications were expected to work
- Measures used, including other factors affecting results
- Summary of analyses
- Conclusions and recommendations.

It is likely that this will all be handed out at a presentation which needs only a few key charts.

After reporting your findings, the job is not quite over.

First, make sure that all the data you used is stored and accessible, as well as your routine database. The work will have to be done again, perhaps by you, and you will not want to start the collection and organisation of data a second time.

Second, you have now decided what the key measures are: those which management need to know and which explain most. It is sensible to arrange for this small set of numbers to be updated regularly in future. They should be plotted and annotated about exceptional events – a competitor's promotion, your own product improvement, and so on. A good brand history is the best start to the next evaluation and, more importantly, this monitoring will be an aid to management.

If you have modelled successfully, for example explaining a lot of the variation in sales share by your relative price and distribution, the new data can be used to check the model and perhaps to update it. Thus you will be able to say which changes are as expected, and whether an explanation which worked in the past is still applicable, or whether some new factor needs to be taken into account.

A final word: evaluate your own evaluation! Was the team clear enough about objectives and how the advertising was expected to work? If not, can your planning process be improved? Did you have all the measures you really needed? If not, should you lobby to get them in future? Are your analysis methods adequate? If not, can you learn more before the next call on your skills?

After you have reported, and also done all that is possible to prepare for the next evaluation, then you can congratulate yourself on a job well done!

7.8.5 Campaign Evaluation: Planning Ahead

As pointed out above, this section has so far been about drawing conclusions from existing data. There is a better time to start: when the campaign is being planned. You are now not restricted to the measures already there. You may be able to add questions to a survey, organise a new survey, get measures before the campaign breaks ... These help diagnostics. Better, you may be able to cover sales in a more thorough way than before. New types of outlet may have become important, but you are not sure what happens there. Or the money which could not previously be spared now becomes available in order to get a decent measure for your campaign investment.

You can also alert the team, as they work on the campaign, about the way they will be assessed. Knowing this concentrates the mind and often makes creative work sharper and more relevant.

Making clear to management, before the event, what is possible in the way of accountability will also make their expectations realistic. Managers should be aware what good practice in campaign evaluation is. It is at this stage, when manifest attempts are being made to be accountable, that a manager convinces his superiors that he believes he should be held to account. This is a better position in the budget meeting than, 'of course, we know it can't be done.'

Further, the goals which are set should be those which are measurable. This does not mean you are reduced to those which are easiest to measure – like a score in a tracking study – but are not genuine objectives. It means efforts should be made to measure behaviour in some form – assuming that is your goal. If it is only from a sample of shops, only intermittent, only over part of your product range – it will still be an informative number.

7.9 Conclusions from this Chapter

Surprisingly often, companies do not keep selected and accessible records of history, which would help them with many of the decisions they have to make. It is always better to consult the recent past before forecasting. This chapter has described how to select and hold the most important data.

Routine analysis of this database can be tedious unless the methods are set up and easy to use. An outline has been given of how to achieve this.

Next, you have to interpret the tables and plots, and speculate about the forces which are causing your brand's sales to rise or fall. The analyst's job is to organise and present the data to support a reasonable explanation of how the marketplace works.

8   Modelling

This chapter continues to explain how the analyst produces the results of Chapter 6. I now move into more elaborate uses of the data, to disentangle more complex situations and to provide numerical estimates of the sizes of the effects of marketing activities. How to allow for the decay of advertising effects over time is shown; also how to represent, when necessary, the effects of marketing activities by an equation which is then fitted to the real data. There are sections on allocating advertising budgets over the year, on the design and analysis of experiments, and on an unusual data source, where both sales and media behaviour are reported by the same individual.

8.1 Outline

There are many ways you may estimate, after a campaign has finished, the effects of your communications. They all have one thing in common. The effect is defined as it was towards the end of the last chapter: the difference between what *actually* happened and what *would have happened* without the communication.

For some effects, it is easy to say that *nothing* would have happened *without* the communication. If you send out a press release and then study the coverage you get on TV and in the Press, you know that without the release you would have got no mentions.

Sales would hardly ever immediately fall to zero without the communication: you cannot count all your sales as a credit. Nor can you assume that communications have changed nothing, and give it no credit. The answer is somewhere between these two, and at first you do not know where. In fact you cannot expect a truly exact measurement of the size of the effect; usually you aim to estimate and then convince, not to prove.

When you do succeed in establishing, with reasonable precision, a volume effect on your brand, it may be necessary to check whether this was at the expense of other parts of your business, such as other brands (were you cannibalising?), or the price you were able to charge (were you 'buying' sales?).

There are three main ways to proceed. First, there may be some simple comparison, in which you assume that another available measure is what would have happened without communications. For example, you compare the brand's actual sales with the average in the category, or for selected competitors or others of your brands; or what happened last year; or what happened in other countries. This approach is very common and was covered in the previous chapter.

The second way is to allow explicitly for other factors which may have affected the outcome and to estimate their effects as well as what communication achieved. This means mathematical modelling. You are *calculating* what would have happened without advertising.

This process should not be so complex that a manager cannot grasp it when it is properly carried out and explained. A disadvantage of some modern econometric techniques is that the people who should use the results do *not* understand the processes, so do not trust them, so do not use them. To explain as well as to calculate is part of the job of the analyst and is given considerable emphasis later. Re-presentation of the findings, making them simple and believable, is as important as finding them in the first place. These are essential skills, because the results will *not* be used unless they are understood and trusted.

Third, you may set up an experiment.

Both these last two approaches are described in this chapter in detail, with several of the applications – evaluation, forecasting, and decision-making – to which modelling naturally leads.

Regression is a major part of the approach. Dangerous attitudes to regression include:

- dismay at the perceived complexity and difficulties, so rejection of multivariate analysis in all its forms;
- over-enthusiasm and ignorance of the dangers of applying the standard methods, since it is all too easy these days to use the packages available on most office PCs; the manual and textbook are boring, but the results look exciting;
- aiming at the maximum reduction of variance, using large numbers of explainers and dummy variables; embracing the latest ways to relate explainers and the objective variable, hence the indiscriminate use of modern econometrics, neural networks, fuzzy logic, and so on, with a minimum of attention to the meaning of the explanation.

Some statisticians find it worrying that regression is applied to marketing data at all. Variables which the strict theory requires to be independent turn out not to be so. Terms in the time series depend on earlier values. Factors like price cuts and advertising are used at the same time so that the effects are hard, and occasionally impossible, to disentangle. The underlying models are not really understood by the people who use them, and they tend to extrapolate beyond their experience. Some managers find it hard to believe the view, which statisticians seem to take, about the independent way two different explainers operate.

Hence, both untrained managers and highly trained professionals find reasons to suspect this technique. We are back in the science or craft debate described in Section 1.5, but with both sides apparently against us. I recommend taking the best from each side in this debate – with a pinch of salt. Managers should add judgment, or override unreal conclusions. Professionals are over-cautious and unhelpful – but their worries must be listened to.

My view is that we must evaluate the alternatives to considered numerical analysis. To do no analysis at all, and rely on intuition seems to me to be dereliction of duty. Over-simple analyses, for example those which consider only one explainer at a time, can be much more misleading. Are sales up when we advertise? Then attribute all the improvement to the campaign, and ignore that we also used a coupon, were at a low price, and so on. We do need some kind of protection from these errors.

The criteria which a statistician might strictly require are usually not met in our sort of data (independence of the explainers being the most important). This does not in fact introduce *bias* into the estimates you produce, which matters much more than that the *precision* is less than the regression output table suggests. Your job is often to make the best guess you can for, say, advertising elasticity (this is explained in Section 8.6.1). It may well be that the limits of the estimate you make are quite wide; wider perhaps than the reported test suggests; so wide indeed, that it is, in the technical phrase, 'statistically non-significant' – which means only that you should not bet with much confidence that it is even positive (we are pretty sure, from general experience, that it is not negative, but it could effectively be zero).

So my take-out from these arguments is to use the results of regression with caution, but still use them. I do not claim that marketers enjoy the certainties, such as they are, of the laboratory. If you have better data (from an experiment with individual stores, for example), use that in preference. If the suggested results of a regression offend common sense, reject them. But if you have no better guidance and the findings look sensible – it is foolish not to make them part of your decision-making.

As for the dismay of partly trained managers faced with the sort of presentations they have not seen since they were at business school, this is understandable. I am not suggesting that people without some expertise do this work, only that the expertise is hired or acquired. I do suggest it is not so hard, and this book teaches it.

Finally, only a simple and robust form of regression is recommended here. 'Ordinary least squares' is the technical description. There are reasons for choosing to restrict myself to such an approach, for not using some of the 'optimisers' now available, for not piling all sorts of possible explainers into the regression, for not adding dummy variables to 'explain' all the outliers and so on. The first reason is that we are concerned most with those factors which have large effects, preferably those which are visible in the data when it is well-presented. A small effect is by definition not of much interest, so that subtle methods of teasing it out can be wasted effort. The second reason is that the findings have to be understood to be used, and I am interested in action at the end of the process. Only simple models are employed because, as is shown below, they are easy to explain. Explaining a neural network model, and the possibility that it may be different the next time you apply it to your data, is not simple. That technique also ignores a great deal of prior knowledge which you possess about how things work. As an exploratory tool for the analyst – fine. As the recommended general approach – not here.

Modelling should always be preceded by discussion and agreement on a mental model – how do you expect the factors to affect the objective variable? It is the effect of these factors which you want to study and quantify. There is an alternative: the fishing expedition. This means that many possible explainers are input into a regression, without much thought. I have seen 70 possible variables used, which sounds exhaustive until you hear that no decay in advertising effects were included, only current TVRs for the brand and for many of its individual competitors. A very good fit is usually found when so many explainers are included. But this is not the real objective. It is to use common sense in examining the catch. Is price versus a particular competitor more useful than the price relative to the category, or to the rest of the category? If you include promotion periods as explainers, may you legitimately also use price at all? After a fishing expedition, much should be thrown back. It is only one stage in finding a robust, understandable model.

If the models described here do not explain nearly all the variation in the objective variable (technically, they do not have high R-squareds), the conclusion is only that there is more going on than accounted for by the explainers used. In marketing there are many 'other factors' – including human nature and genuinely random decision-making. The objective is to estimate reasonable coefficients for the few you are most interested in – 'reasonable' meaning acceptable to common sense and in line with other experience. Ideally the coefficients should have 'good t-values' – this is explained later.

8.2 Adstock

8.2.1 Adstock: The Decay of Advertising Effects

Advertising can be recalled after it has been seen and can have effects over subsequent weeks and months. You need a system to model this, to provide a sort of 'present net value', or 'current pressure' from past advertising. The recommended way is an adstock model.

An alternative, which was often used and still persists, is to suppose that advertising works only in the period in which it is seen. In some cases, this is so. But many people have analysed sales with this assumption and concluded that advertising has no effect, simply because they have been using an incorrect mental model of how it works. They had not transformed the advertising variable to an appropriate form.

To understand advertising decay think of some weight of advertising, say 100 TVRs in a particular week (other periods of time can be used, such as four weeks or a month).

If the effects of this exposure of advertising were instantaneous, they could be represented as produced by 100 units of 'pressure' from television advertising in that week. Suppose the effect were to move some index (sales share, a tracking study score or whatever), from say 10 to 11. I can say there is a linear relationship: 100 units of pressure produces one more index point. The index starts at 10, when there is no pressure. Then the 'model' says the index takes the value $10 + s.p_t$ where (a) p_t (pressure at time t) is zero at all times except during this week, when it is 100 and (b) the coefficient 's', or the slope of the relationship, is easily seen to be in this case $1 / 100$. Thus the index is 10 in the weeks without advertising, but when in the week of advertising it is $10 + (1 / 100).100 = 11$. The slope represents the effectiveness of this advertising in producing the specified response.

More generally, our problems are to find (a) what p_t is, when the effects last some weeks, and then (b) how to estimate the slope s.

It is a fact that pressure from advertising generally decays over time by some constant ratio. It is as if we lost a steady proportion of our memories of it each week. This is called 'geometric' decay.

Example: Geometric decay
Suppose the ratio were 0.5 per week and the pressure started at 100 in week 1. Then in weeks 2, 3, ... the pressure would be 50, 25 and so on. Adding up the pressure over weeks 1, 2, 3 and so on gives $100 + 50 + 25 + ...$

A geometric series is easily summed. Suppose the ratio is represented by the symbol f: here, this is called the fade parameter. Sometimes it is called the decay rate, though it tells us how much is left rather than what is lost. It is always less than one. Write the total you have to find as

$$t = 100 + 100.f + 100.f^2 + \dots$$

then, multiplying both sides by f you have

$$t.f = 100.f + 100.f^2 + \dots$$

Subtracting the second line from the first you get

$$t.(1 - f) = 100, \text{ or } t = 100 / (1 - f)$$

In this example, f had the value 0.5 so the total is $100 / (1 - 0.5)$ or 200.

The total takes different values, depending on the value of f. It is more convenient to make the sum of the pressure, over all subsequent weeks, take the same value, whatever f is. This 'same' value is going to be the original TVR figure. Thus you are 'spreading the pressure' from the 100 TVRs over subsequent weeks as a set of numbers which add up to the same 100.

All you need do is define 'pressure' as multiples of the original TVRs which are the series $1, f, f^2, \dots$ but multiplied by the constant $(1 - f)$, since this corrects for the sum of the series which is $1 / (1 - f)$.

Example: Summing a geometric series
For example, take a new value of f, such as 0.3. The constant $1 - f$ is 0.7. The series is 1, 0.3, 0.09, ... So from your 100 TVRs we calculate the pressure to be 70, 21, 6, ... where 21, for example, comes from 100 TVRs, times 0.7 (constant), times 0.3. This series indeed adds to your original 100.

The meaning of the parameter f is not easily grasped. What does it *mean* to say that the fade or decay parameter is 0.5 or 0.3? Also, if you used a different period length, you would need a different parameter to convey the same rate of decay. Fading to 0.3 of the starting value every four weeks is the same as fading to 0.74 of the starting value every week for four weeks in succession (0.74 x 0.74 x 0.74 x 0.74 = 0.3). There is however a related idea which *does* have a simple meaning and which does *not* depend on period length. This is the *half life* of the advertising, by analogy with radioactive decay, which is also geometric.

How long does it take, for half the total effect to be felt, if the effect each week is in proportion to $1, f, f^2, \dots$? To answer this you need the sum of this series up to the time h. This is easily found by the same device as above, and is $(1 - f^h) / (1 - f)$.

So the half life is when this expression is half of $1 / (1 - f)$, or when f^h equals one half. This can be written: the half life is at

$$h = \log \{0.5\} / \log \{f\}$$

Given f, this determines the half life h. Conversely, given a half life h, you can find the fade parameter as 10 to the power log {0.5} / h. This is when logs are taken to the base 10. If ln{ } means that logs are 'natural', or taken to the base e, then the fade parameter is exp{ ln{0.5} / h }.

For example, your previous f parameters of 0.5 and 0.3 correspond to half lives of one week and 0.58 weeks. If you want a half life of two weeks, f should be 0.71.

You now have a way to define the rate of decay and to relate this to the parameter used in calculating individual terms. You also have a way to spread the pressure, from advertising at any weight, over later weeks. You can therefore create this pressure from any schedule, by adding the pressure arising from each week's ratings.

8.2.2 Adstock: The Formulae

I am now ready to define adstock. The method above is not exact, for the reason explained below. Before giving the formulae, the ideas are explained in words. 'Week' below stands for other periods, like four weeks or a month; if you are working in days then the method above is satisfactory.

When you are looking *back* to see what the advertising pressure in this week is due to:

the adstock in any week is the weighted sum of recent ratings.

You can also look *forward*, to see what pressure will be produced by the ratings this week:

adstocks in following weeks are a rearrangement of the ratings this week, allowing for the decay of advertising effects.

The units for adstock are the same as for the original schedule of transmissions, for example 30-second housewife ratings per week. Total adstocks for a schedule are the same number as total ratings in the schedule – but they are spread over a longer time. You expect the effects which advertising ratings produce over time to be proportional to adstocks (hence, 'pressure'), not to the original ratings. You also expect adstock to decline at a steady rate, unless there is more advertising: in each week following the one the transmission took place, adstock is a constant proportion of its value in the previous week – but there is one exception to this statement, which is explained below, and that is what happens in the actual week of transmission.

The reason why adstocks are defined differently from the system in the previous section is as follows. That method counts the effect in the first week (when the advertising actually appears) as one, compared with its smaller effect in the next week as f. This cannot actually be so in the week in which the ad is seen, since the moment in the week at which an individual is exposed to the advertising may be before or after the moment at which she makes a purchase decision or is interviewed to determine awareness. Seeing advertising on a Thursday cannot affect a sale or an interview on Tuesday. It is equally likely that one took place before the other. Hence the effect in the first week can only be one half that assumed in the system explained above.

The result of introducing this realism is only that the detail changes. Note that anyway all the detail is looked after by a computer macro or program. Given the ratings schedule and a couple of other numbers, the calculation of adstock is automatic. Hence it is not necessary to work through all these formulae each time, only to program the process given in Section 8.2.4.

The constant used to multiply the terms of the series 0.5, f, f^2, ... is no longer $(1 - f)$ but $2 \times (1 - f) / (1 + f)$. The half life h is now related to f by $h \log(f) = \log\{(1 + f) / 4\}$.

In fact you can calculate how long it takes to reach the proportion p of the total effect, for any p between 0 and 1:

$$\log\{(1 - p)(1 + f) / 2\} / \log\{f\}$$

Given f you can now calculate the half life. Unfortunately there is no easy way to solve the equations for f, given h and p.

One practical way to find f when you are given the half life is to write a table, or make a plot, for f given various half lives. Table 5 does this for you. In such a table you can include another calculation: how long it takes before 90% – in other words nearly all – the effects are over. For example:

Half life, weeks	Time to 90% of effect	Fade parameter f, for weekly data
0.5	9 days	0.072
1	3 weeks	0.333
2	7 weeks	0.640
3	12 weeks	0.761
4	4 months	0.822
6	6 months	0.882
10	10 months	0.930
20	20 months	0.965

Such a table, or a plot made from it, gives us quickly an estimate for the fade parameter, given the half life. Note, as a handy approximation, that the time to have felt 90% of the effect is about four times the half life – except at very short half lives, say under two weeks.

Half a week for the half life means almost immediate results; one or two weeks is quick; three to six weeks has often been found to fit well; ten weeks and over is too slow to be called a short-term effect. The longer term is discussed further on in this chapter.

Example: What does adstock look like?
Figure 21 shows a plot of two different adstocks, calculated with two different half lives, resulting from 100 TVRs over one week. A week is the unit in the plot, so the 100 TVRs are shown as a bar, one unit wide and with the height of 100.

With a two-week half life, half the effect is over after two weeks. Hence the area under the higher line at units one and two is equal to that of a bar one unit wide and with height 50. The area at units three, four, and so on totals the same again. The effect is over quite soon.

With a six-week half life, the line starts at a lower height, but it decays more slowly. This time it is the heights at one, two, … six units which add up to half the total.

8.2.3 Adstock: Other Period Lengths

Suppose that the periods by which the data is held are not weeks – say they are four weeks. What changes? First, it will be harder to detect short-term effects in the dependent variable, that is, sales or a survey measure. They will be averaged out in the numbers you see, so your methods will be less sensitive.

Second, if the ratings are also held in four weeks, you again lose detail and your adstocks will be less accurate. Suppose you are told only that there were 100 ratings at some time in the four weeks. It makes a difference, especially at short half lives, whether these ratings were all in the first week

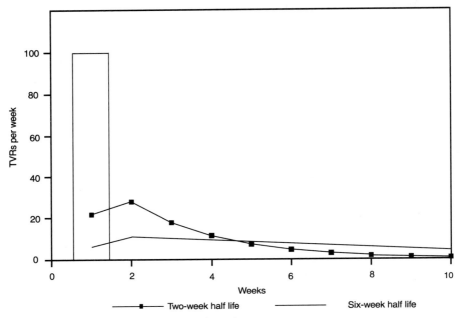

**Figure 21 100 TVRs in One Week and
Two Resulting Adstocks**

or in the last. But with grouped ratings data, you can never know this. Hence, even if the *dependent* variable cannot be broken out into weeks, it is still worth using weekly *ratings*, calculating weekly adstocks, and then cumulating these into the longer intervals.

Third, if you are forced to work with four-week ratings, it is easier to understand the decay if you continue to define half lives as so many weeks, and not so many four-weeks. The other arguments apply as before, simply substituting 'period' for 'week', whatever the period may be. But the fade parameter, which has to be applied to the four-week data, is not calculated in the same way. The table in the last section, of f for various half lives, no longer applies.

If you state the half life in weeks, for purposes of calculation you must divide it by the period length so that it too is in period units. If the period is now four weeks, a six-week half life is 1.5 periods long, for example. There is more on this in Table 5.

Finally, the period length used affects the estimated half life in ways not fully understood. The smaller the period, the shorter the half life that fits best. Thus the three to six weeks often found for weekly data may come down to between one (or even less) and two weeks with data analysed by days.

8.2.4 Adstock: Practical Calculation

In practice, you have to calculate adstocks for a given half life and from a schedule of advertising which is a list of TVRs (or equivalents in other media) over weeks. Now that we have the formulae, I describe the practical method.

It is usual to start this calculation at a week in the schedule a year or so before the periods for which you want to use the adstocks. Additionally, you have to take into account the rate of advertising even before this. You need these earlier numbers since advertising at this time could affect adstock at the time you are interested in. It is better to make an estimate, if you do not have records, than to assume there was no advertising. Of course, if there was no earlier campaign, then the previous rate of advertising was in fact zero.

The 'previous rate of advertising' is given exactly by the adstock in the week just before the period of calculation. This is of course rarely available, as it requires another set of sums. In practice, you estimate it. For example, suppose you had 50, 50, 50, 0, 0, 0 in the six weeks beforehand. Typically, you say that the previous rate is 150 / 6 = 30, though it would be less for a very short half life, more if previous TVRs had been heavier and the half life was long. This uncertainty is why you start the adstock calculation a year before the period analysed, so the assumption made about the previous rate has less influence.

You must also pay attention to what copy was running earlier: is it the same or very similar to the copy whose effect you are assessing? If it was very different you can create adstocks separately for the two campaigns, and then do your analysis with two separate variables, one for each campaign.

So you find f from the half life as described above, and record the 'previous rate' of TVRs per week.

Let 'column 1' be the column which holds the TVRs in rows 1, 2, ... The starting row above this, 'row 0', will be used to start off the recursive calculations. Create two more columns for calculations and a fourth which will hold the resulting adstocks, p_t in row t.

Enter starting values in row 0. In column 2 write

$$(1 - f) / (1 + f).\text{previous rate}$$

and in column 3 write 2.f.previous rate / (1 + f).

Fill column 2 from row 1 with:

$$(1 - f) / (1 + f) \text{ times the corresponding TVRs in column 1.}$$

Fill column 3 from row 1 with:

> f x twice the entry in column 2 for the row above
> + f times the entry in column 3 for the row above.

Finally fill column 4 from row 1 with the sum of the entries in columns 2 and 3.

These formulae should be written into a spreadsheet or program so that adstocks are created automatically or with a single command once the half life, previous rate and TVRs are entered.

An example is now given which the reader can follow through, since the data are given at the end of the book. This assistance is available for several of the techniques described.

Example of adstock calculation
The ratings for your brand in 1994–95 are shown in Table 6, as are details of the calculation. The previous rate was 26 TVRs a week and the half life is four weeks.

First you calculate the fade parameter: to six decimals it is 0.821468. Then you complete the starting values in columns 2 and 3. Since there are no TVRs between 9401 and 9419, adstock then is simply the previous rate decayed by multiples of the fade parameter. In 9420, there are 17 TVRs which contribute to column 2 and the full calculation starts.

Figure 22 shows the schedule as a bar chart. The adstock calculated in the table is the central solid line in the figure. Also shown are the adstocks for a two-week half life (rising faster and decaying more quickly) and for a thirteen-week half life.

At two weeks, the line follows the bar chart quite closely. At thirteen weeks, it smoothes it out but still has a clear relationship with the bars.

8.2.5 Adstock: Direct Use

As well as their application in modelling, adstocks have a direct use. They represent, as we know, the 'pressure' at any week from the schedule, and they smooth out the peaks shown by the bar chart of ratings. When you plot on the same chart this bar chart and the corresponding adstocks, you observe two facts.

First, because it is a sort of moving average, adstock represents, better than the bar chart, the overall weight of advertising. It shows how advertising pressure changes over time. When the rate of advertising is increasing or decreasing over time, this is sometimes hard to pick out from the forest of the bar chart, since it means comparing both the heights and the frequency of the bars. The adstock line more clearly trends up or down, at least when half lives are reasonably long, say six weeks or more. It is very

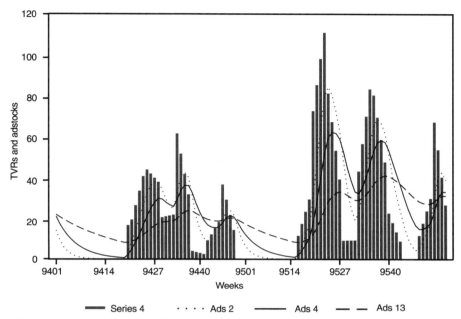

Figure 22 Schedule of TVRs and Three Resulting
          Adstocks

clear in Figure 22, from the thirteen-week adstock line, that the pressure from advertising is higher in 1995 than in 1994.

Second, the adstock plot makes clear when a gap in the schedule has got so long that very little effect or pressure is left. This may be used by a TV planner who is looking for continuous pressure, to see when the troughs are serious so buys should be moved from the peaks in order to fill up them up.

8.3 Fitting the Linear Adstock Model

We are now ready to see how well the linear adstock model fits or explains observed data. The simplest objective variable is a score like brand or advertising awareness measured in a tracking study. Such observations are often well-explained by adstock, plus perhaps a trend term. In practice the fit is for a single campaign, or even a single commercial, since you expect steps up or down as the treatments change.

In choosing awareness as the first example of an objective variable, I am not saying it is the most important. Certainly it is practical and helpful to use an adstock model to analyse and to predict awareness, if this is a chosen objective. Sometimes it is a legitimate aim. But sales will be the objective looked at later. It is used as an example here because it is often undisturbed by other factors so it is easy to model. Changing it is just one of the effects of advertising, and changes in sales rarely follow simply from changes in awareness. The half life you find for awareness therefore may not be the half life which fits sales.

In an ideal world, awareness would be reported weekly, but four weeks is more common (the sample size may be too small to report weekly). The four-week data should be reported for discrete periods, not as a rolling average which introduces another time shift.

As pointed out above, when you have data for the dependent variable for longer periods than a week, adstock should still be calculated for weeks, and then summed over the other periods. This is more accurate than working with four-week TVRs, which lose the detail of *when* in the four weeks the ratings appeared.

What half life should you use? With a sophisticated fitting procedure like Marquardt, the fade parameter f, like the slope s, can be estimated directly. Most people use ordinary least squares, and this is what I recommend. For this sort of variable, a half life of five or six weeks is normal. Or, you could look at the periods without advertising and see what the ratios of successive observations are: these are estimates of f, but disturbed by a trend if this is present. Hence, as always, you should plot the data over time; you look for the presence of a trend and the shapes of the declines which follow the blips.

Having made a guess at half life, say six weeks, you make a set of adstocks for various half lives, perhaps four to eight weeks. You will then choose the half life for which the adstocks fit best ('fit' is used in an exact sense which is described below).

In practice you need a computer program to do the work. It should calculate several adstocks, one for each half life. It should also provide a trend term (1, 2, ...). It is then usually convenient to move the data set into a proper multivariate regression package. You can choose which adstock fits best by trying each of them out, with or without a trend term; or a stepwise procedure (available in a general statistical package), will quickly tell us which to use.

The procedure for choosing a half life, and taking a view on the significance of the coefficients for advertising effectiveness and trend, are both the same as those used in more complex modelling, so the following advice applies throughout. The 'best fit' is, by definition, the choice of parameters which gives the largest R-squared. There are however decisions to be made about whether to include all the possible explainers, and about using prior information.

Statistical courses often advise that 'non-significant' coefficients mean that the variable concerned should not be used. You need to think hard about whether to follow this advice when looking at the t-value. This is the statistic, produced by the regression program, by which you judge how well-determined is the coefficient referred to – suppose this is for an adstock variable. You can look up a table, or the computer package does this for us, to find out the probability that a coefficient this much different from zero, or more so, could have arisen by chance (were the coefficient actually zero). If this probability is small (conventionally, one chance in 20 or less), then the coefficient is 'statistically significant', meaning it is very likely to be non-zero.

This is much too rough an argument for this situation. First, you know that ad effects are unlikely to be negative (it may happen, I have never seen it myself). So when you look at a t-value it is only the one-sided probability which is relevant (different from zero in the sense of being larger), though packages give the two-sided value (different from zero in the sense of either being larger, or negative and of a greater absolute value). When you have a reasonably large number of observations (above 20, say), the table tells us that a t-value larger than about 2 to 2.1 is 'significant'; hence it is conventional to 'accept' the coefficient if the t-value is 2 or more. With a one-sided test the figure is not 2, but 1.7. If you use one chance in ten as the probability, than 1.3 is the test to use.

Second, you should not automatically reject, say an advertising effect, simply because a conventional probability level is not reached: this is saying only that the effect is not well-determined by this data; there is uncertainty about its actual size; it is even possible it might be nil. You often have other information (previous analyses, from other brands, or qualitative), which assures us it is likely to be real though it may be small; the noise in the data means you do not know it exactly. It is therefore reasonable to report the estimated size of the effect and the fact that you do not have a precise estimate. It is still the best estimate you have.

Next, including or excluding another explainer, like a trend term, can make a big difference to the apparent effect of a term like adstock. Suppose your adstock has been increasing over time *and* price has been trending down; that is, there is a correlation between the two variables. It makes a big difference to the estimate for the size of the advertising effect whether or not you include an estimate of the price effect. Without a price term, the regression will exaggerate the size of the advertising coefficient, attributing to advertising some of the growth really due to price. But if you include both terms, the regression will give you an unbiased estimate of the size of the advertising effect. However, the values given in the table you use to test significance (t values) are now dubious. This is because classical statistics assumes that such explainers are independent, and in this case they are not – and the dependent variable has some autocorrelation too.

In this work, you are not in the business of accepting or rejecting hypotheses. Nor should you say with resignation that the classical assumptions do not apply. Your job is to make the best estimates you can.

Finally, the regression for your brand may be only one of a series of regressions, in which other brands are being modelled too. It is normally preferable to use a single half life for all the brands, since the coefficients for the effects will then be directly comparable (changing the half life means the coefficient alters). So you may look at a plot of the R-squareds for each half life fitted, across all the brands, and make a judgment about the common half life to choose. Millward Brown's awareness index is based on a rather similar system with the equivalent of a half life of around five or six weeks for all brands and all countries. This is a statement about the rate of losing memories, with a particular prompt, at 12–14% per week (f is 0.86 and 0.88 at half lives of five and six weeks).

'Judgment' is a key word throughout. You look at the fits for various half lives, with and without a trend term, even for a single brand. You note the R-squareds – you would like them to be high, meaning that most of the variation has been accounted for. We note the t-values for the coefficients – high again, meaning that the coefficients are determined with reasonable precision, and are not of the wrong sign. We usually know whether we expect positive or negative values – for advertising effects, positive; for price, negative; which is the reason why a one-sided test is appropriate if we are going to quote confidence limits. We hope that the coefficients themselves do not change much, as other terms enter or leave the equation, and with values which your common sense and experience can accept. Also, bear in mind the use to which your findings will be put. Thus, deciding what to recommend is far from a mechanical step.

Example of adstock modelling
Table 7 gives the unaided awareness for your brand for four-week periods in 1994–95. The TVRs at these times were in Table 6, where the adstocks were calculated for four-weeks half life.

Note that the data in this example – and the others in this book – have been constructed to give clear results. They are based on actual cases, but the analyses are easier to interpret than many in real life.

Before doing any calculations, you must look at the data. Figure 8 in Chapter 6 shows the tracking score and the TVRs. You see a relationship – awareness generally rises during the advertising bursts. You cannot disentangle by eye whether the higher scores in 1995 are directly related to the higher TVRs in this year (2.1 times as many as in 1994), or whether there is an increase in the base for awareness (the level it falls to when you have been off air for some time).

Nor can you get a good estimate of the half life, or rather the fade parameter, from this figure by considering the decline in the scores during the unadvertised periods: the average ratio of the scores in successive periods during 9401 to 9404 and 9413 to 9503 is 0.936, corresponding to a half life of 11 weeks, but the ratio varies between 0.70 and 1.18 and the noise in the system makes the average rather unreliable. Also, it is possibly affected here by a trend.

First you must calculate adstocks for a range of half lives, using the method explained in the last example. Then you add these for weeks 1 to 4, 5 to 8 and so on. The results are also in Table 7.

When the numbers are moved into a multivariate package, you can look at the correlations between all the variables; and you can carry out stepwise regression; you can look at other regressions.

Some values from the correlation table follow:

	Trend	Ads4	Ads6	Ads8
Awareness	0.67	0.94	0.96	0.95
Trend		0.52	0.58	0.61
Ads4			0.98	0.94
Ads6				0.99

The explanations given by adstocks will be stronger than by the trend : 0.94 to 0.96 is larger than 0.67. It will not be easy to distinguish between the adstocks for such similar half lives which are highly correlated: coefficients of 0.94 to 0.99. Of those shown, Ads6 (adstock with a six-week half life) gives the best fit. In fact a stepwise procedure goes straight to trend and Ads6 as the explanation.

The R-squareds for all the possible explanations are:

Trend alone	0.450		
Ads4 alone	0.877	Trend plus Ads4	0.924
Ads5 alone	0.914	Ads5	0.943
Ads6 alone	0.924	Ads6	0.944
Ads7 alone	0.919	Ads7	0.934
Ads8 alone	0.905	Ads8	0.918

Trend alone certainly explains something: from a simple regression, you calculate that the increase every four weeks is 0.23 with $t = 4.4$. Trend also adds to the explanation at each half life, so it is probably real, even though the improvement is small for the preferred half lives. For the six-week half life, for example, 0.944 is larger than 0.924.

The best fits are with both trend and adstock with five or six-week half lives. At six weeks, the coefficient for trend falls to 0.06, $t = 2.9$, while t for Ads6 is 14.2. The fit for Ads5 is almost the same. Here it is not easy to say how large the trend effect is, but +0.06 per four weeks is a better estimate than the +0.23 coefficient with trend on its own.

The preferred fit is with adstock with a six-week half life and a trend term. The equation is:

$$\text{awareness} = 5.21 + 0.04 \times \text{adstock} + 0.06 \times t$$

The practical results of adstock modelling, and these have just been shown, are:

- an advertising effect has been demonstrated, not always an easy task;
- the rate of decay has been indicated;
- the size of the effect has been estimated, by the size of the coefficient; this number is used to estimate the sales effectiveness of the copy when sales are the objective variable, and is used extensively below.

8.4 Explaining the Results of Modelling

There are three main ways of graphing those findings which you do decide to show. Plots explain to managers what is going on better than equations and significance tests. These are now demonstrated, based on the previous example, but come into their own in more complex cases, when you are modelling sales.

The equation agreed says that awareness is estimated by

$$\text{constant} + C_A.\text{adstock} + C_T.\text{trend}$$

In words, the model is a constant base (plus a trend), to which the score falls back eventually, while after advertising bursts there are temporary increases or blips. Such a model is often fitted and it is deduced that the advertising effect consists of these blips.

You recognise this as one of the ways advertising has effects, as described in Section 5.8 – it can happen to sales when the effect is a reminder, and moves a brand to the top of the repertoire, but later on the need for variety or some other cause pushes another brand ahead.

This interpretation is incomplete, and it may undervalue the advertising contribution. The key question is, how did the base get there? You may not have enough data to answer this question. But it would be wrong to assume that previous advertising played no part in it, or that it is permanent and without advertising support it would not decline.

Later in this chapter I am more specific about possible movement in the base. For now, I simply record that it may not be constant, that it can be made to step up by suitable marketing activity and that advertising may play some part in the trend now being fitted.

In the example just given, it is believable that the advertising caused the awareness. Relationships are not always so easily sorted out. Every statistics course warns that correlation does not prove causation. This statement cannot be repeated too often. The line joining cause and effect may run in the reverse direction to the one we assume, or there may be some third factor which affects both of the variables we are studying.

Example: Sales cause the advertising
Annual data, on the size of the advertising budget and on sales volume, seemed to support the statement that so much spend produced so much sales. In fact, sales varied for a different reason: when product improvements were made, sales went up. Since it was known in these years that increased sales were expected, and because the advertising budget was determined by forecast volume times a fixed rate per case, the advertising budget was also higher than usual.

The worrying part of this example is that there may indeed be an advertising effect, but it has been made impossible to measure because analysis cannot distinguish between the relation the advertiser put there (sales cause advertising), and a second relation (advertising causes sales). Luckily, in such cases the apparent sizes of the effects measured can be so untypical that they are unbelievable, so at least there is a warning that something else is going on.

8.4.1 Explaining the Results of Modelling: Time Plots

If you plot the actual awareness against time, and on the same plot show the fitted estimate, you see quickly whether the equation represents the main actual movements – if so, it is a 'good fit' and will be trusted (to keep the two distinct, use another colour, or symbols instead of a line). This can be a powerful way of demonstrating the reality of adstock, that is, the growth and then the gradual decay of effects after a burst.

Another useful plot is of the residuals (actual – estimate) against time, though you may be able to draw the same conclusion from the first plot. The conclusion you would like to draw is that the estimate is in error for purely random reasons: 'noise' in the system and in the measurement. You may however see something more systematic, in which case you have to look for an explanation. Was there one execution in the campaign which seemed to do particularly well, for example?

Example: Time plots
The results from the fit explained above are shown in Figures 23 and 24.
The observed values of the awareness score are clearly matched closely by those calculated. Since you know that the R-squared was high (0.94), this is no surprise. However, most managers find the plot more convincing than the statistic.
You also have the chance to look for any systematic deviations from the actual observations, which may be a clue to the factors having an influence. In

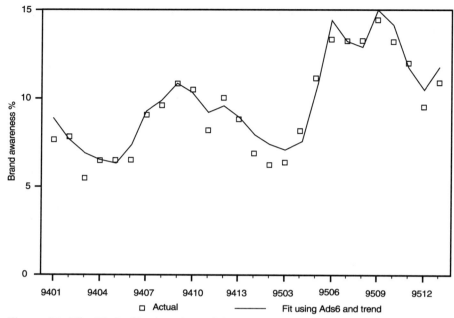

Figure 23 The Fit is Close to Actual Awareness

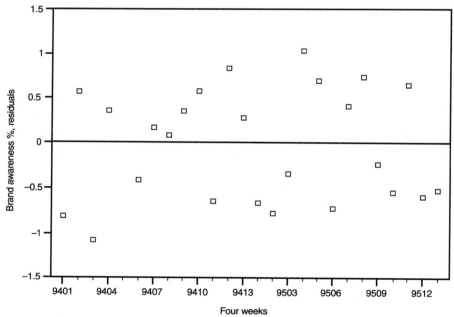

**Figure 24 The Residuals from the Fit show
        No Systematic Pattern**

this case there appear to be none – which is shown also by the plot of the residuals. Here, if there were any outliers, they would be investigated.

8.4.2 Explaining the Results of Modelling: Each Effect Separately

In this example, there are two reasons why the estimate varies over time and you should make a plot showing them separately. That is, you make a new plot with one line showing C_A times adstock and another showing the trend line, which is C_T times trend. The advantage of this is that the *sizes* of the effects become clear: you see how large the blips are when you advertise compared with the size of the trend (and of the constant). You cannot see this from the coefficients alone, only when these multiply typical values of the variable. You cannot see it clearly from the plot of the combined estimate because the two effects are simultaneous.

Example: Plot of effects
Figure 25 shows the two explainers' effects separately. A naïve view of the equation sees that the coefficient for trend (0.06) is larger than for adstock (0.04), and it might be thought that trend has a larger influence. But the trend variable is in the range 1 to 26, while the adstock range is 12 to 205, so the adstock effect is much larger.

In Section 6.7 the effects of different activities on sales – price, promotions and distribution – were discussed, and Figure 13 was derived in the same way as Figure 25. The work is described in Section 8.6.4, and again in 8.10.

When marketing activities are reported in this way as having separate effects, you are over-simplifying. You are reporting the association of sales with one activity *in the presence of the other activities*. The effects cannot really be added like building blocks in this way, with the implication that if you take one away, the rest will not change. A brand is holistic, the activities have synergy. It is possible, with enough data and experiments, to find out how much one activity affects another, but this is rarely done. In direct mail and direct-response press advertising it is very desirable. If all your right-hand pages were in colour, and left-hand pages in monochrome, it is obvious, I hope, that we cannot say whether it was position or colour which gave higher response. The danger of error is no less when we are talking about a price effect with or without the presence of advertising.

When you plan ahead you should not write a scenario very different from history and expect each factor to behave in the same way as before, so do not take this deconstruction too literally. It is reasonably precise under constant conditions. You can use it as a guidance system for relatively small changes.

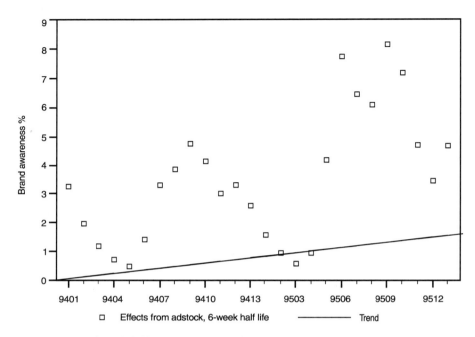

Figure 25 Adstock Effects are Larger than Trend

8.4.3 Explaining the Results of Modelling: A Scatter Plot

If you are explaining how a trend is fitted, it helps to show a scatter plot of the data against time, with the regression line shown.

If you have fitted adstock as well as a trend, make an XY or scatter plot of the observed values on the Y-axis against the adstock at each observation, with the period number as the data label. You may see very clearly how awareness is high when adstock is high and low when it is low. This is often a very convincing way to show an effect and its size. If there is a trend, then this will show, within a band of adstock values, by awareness being high for the earlier, or for the later periods, depending on the direction of the trend.

Example: Scatter plot

Figure 26 plots the actual awareness against the adstock in each period, and shows the period number at each plotted position. First, the association is obvious, and like the plot of actual and fit, is suitable for convincing a manager.

Second, the effect of trend is relatively small in this case, but can just be glimpsed by noting the highs at 9504, 9505, 9511 and so on – all in 1995 – opposed to the relatively low positions at 9403 and 9401. In some cases this inspection gives clearer results.

170

Figures 10 and 11 were further examples of scatter plots. The fact that Figure 10 showed a tighter relationship between prices of 102 and 114 than did Figure 11 for distribution between 91 and 98 tells us that the price effect is stronger than distribution.

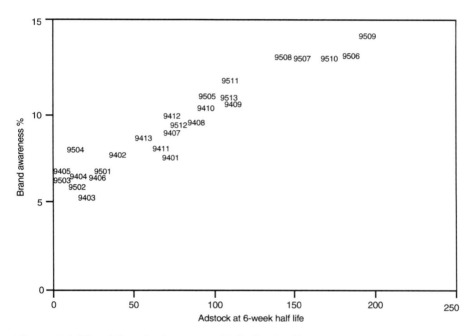

Figure 26 The Adstock–Awareness Relation is Clear
and the Trend Effect Just Visible

8.5 Forecasting for the Sector

Three sensible questions about the sector are: What is its seasonality pattern? What will its size be, for example next year? What will its average price be?

Forecasting is a specialised branch of statistics and the more complex methods will not be described here. Now that I have described the approach to modelling, a similar simple approach which is often adequate is recommended. In this case adstock does not enter. It would do so, if you had one of those cases in which total advertising noticeably accelerates the growth of the sector.

Start as usual by examining the plots over time for volume and for price. Both are treated in the same way. It is likely that you will decide the plots can reasonably be fitted by a linear or quadratic term plus a seasonal pattern. So you estimate these two together. Sometimes there are sharp spikes caused by price promotions of large brands, which can be smoothed away by a moving average (such as 1:2:3:2:1). But if there is a regular pattern in these you may not want to remove them (Christmas promotions for drinks, for example).

It is also possible that sector sales are influenced by some economic or demographic variable which can itself be reliably forecast: births, for example, or the number of cars on the road. In these cases another explanatory variable enters your equation.

Next, get the averages for each week of the year (or four weeks etc) and plot these. If you have, say three and a half years, there will be three observations for some weeks and four for the rest. The different dates for Easter, Christmas and school holidays may have to be allowed for. When this is done, a moving average will again smooth out the data and give a fair view of seasonality over the year (if the trend is strong then some growth over the year will appear in the seasonality numbers but this is not a problem). For four-week or monthly data it may be best to leave the averages as they are.

Then return to the raw volume data and calculate the deseasonalised equivalents, which are finally fitted by a linear or quadratic equation. The forecast is the extension of this, with the seasonal adjustments.

Price is separately forecast but by exactly the same process. Seasonality itself is often less of a problem, but instead there may be steps as the price leader makes a change, followed quickly by other brands. Interest rate changes often have a similar effect for financial products.

Example of forecasting for the sector
Data in Table 8 show the volume and value for the category, and the price (from value divided by volume), for 1992 to 1995 in four-week periods.

Plotting the volume you see regular peaks around April and November, with lows in January, June and December. It is important to estimate the size of this seasonality. It is not clear from the plot whether there is overall decline though 1995 is lower than preceding years.

A regression against period number indicates that you need not allow for an overall trend, so you estimate seasonality directly from the raw data. This shows a systematic pattern for the periods, with period 12 as much as 25% above the annual average in volume sales, periods 1, 6 and 13 at between 11 to 14% below.

Price is more complex, rising slightly to mid-1994 and falling to the end of 1995. There are clear price promotion battles, for example near the end of 1992, but more regularity recently, as overall lower prices take over.

In order to forecast, you not only do some sums, you also talk to people in touch with retailers and used to studying what the brands have been doing and to guessing competitors' plans.

The calculations you do are to fit price over the whole period with two terms: period number and this number squared. Projecting this to 1996 you get an average price of £4.99 per kilogram, compared with the £5.03 in 1993–95. You also fit the price since mid-1994. Projecting this, the 1996 average is £4.96, and for 1997 it is £4.92.

The experts' view is that the recently lower average price is due mainly to the rise of low-priced brands. This is expected to continue.

Finally, a scatter plot of category volume against price shows no relationship, and you would not expect one at the small range of £4.95 to £5.10.

Our forecast is therefore for no volume trend from 1995, but continued seasonality, and a price which continues the small decline from mid-1994.

The forecast for volume was plotted in Figure 1; for price, in Figure 2.

8.6 More about Modelling

8.6.1 More about Modelling: Price Elasticity, Advertising Elasticity

Suppose that the equation for sales share is linear:

$$\text{sales share} = \text{base} + C_A.\text{adstock} + C_P.\text{price}$$

where 'base' is some constant (this assumption is important – *see Sections 8.7.1 and 8.10* about this). C_P is negative. This equation is often used in marketing, since it is easy to explain, though econometricians generally use the multiplicative or logarithmic version (more on this later). Clearly the linear form is an approximation unlikely to hold at large changes; a price change of 20%, for example, will probably not have 20 times the effect of a one per cent change.

Adstock is in units of ratings per week, so typically has values like 10 (for ratings of about 500 a year), or 40 (for 2,000 a year), but it may fall to zero. Relative price is normally calculated relative to the category average = 100. Thus, 20% or 40% above the average is represented by 120 or 140.

I am now going to discuss the two coefficients, first C_P and then C_A.

It is convenient to have a number which tells us by how much sales or sales share will change if price changes by one per cent. This was introduced in Chapter 4, where the breakeven price and advertising elasticities were defined and calculated from the brand's budget. I define the measured, or marketplace, elasticity to price; *price elasticity* for short. This is *the percentage change in sales share when price increases by one per cent*. You can derive it from C_P, but you need more information first.

You can also estimate it roughly from only two points on the price–volume plot in the last chapter, often useful when you have drawn a line by eye and want a quick and rough estimate of elasticity.

Example: Elasticity from two points
Suppose sales share was 12% at a relative price of 120, but 11% when price rose to 125. The percentage change in price was 100 x 5 / 120, or 4.17. The percentage fall in sales was 100 x 1 / 12, or 8.33. Thus for every one per cent price rise, the percentage change in sales was –8.33 / 4.17 or –2.

Suppose that P is average price (and that adstock is at its average); so at these values the expression above gives S for the (average) sales share. Now increase price by one per cent, so that the new price is 1.01P. The increase in sales share is clearly 0.01P times C_P. What is this as a percentage increase? It is 100 times (0.01P x C_P) / S. This can be written C_P x P / S.

In words, you get the elasticity for any activity (this applies to adstock as well as to price) by multiplying its coefficient by the average value for the activity, and dividing the result by the average value of sales share (or whatever the objective variable is).

Example: Calculation of elasticities
The equation for sales share as a percentage is:

$$34.8 + 0.04 \text{ x adstock} - 0.2 \text{ x price}$$

and the averages are: sales share 12%, adstock 30 TVRs/week, relative price 120.
The advertising elasticity is 0.04 x 30 / 12 or 0.1.
The price elasticity is –0.2 x 120 / 12 or –2.

Advertising elasticity has another interpretation, though this is to be used with care. Suppose advertising stopped. What share of sales would we lose? The answer suggested by the model is not realistic because advertising has other effects than immediate short-term sales. However, we get an insight.

Apparently the answer is C_A times (average adstock). As a percentage of current sales this is 100 times C_A times (average adstock) / S, which is the same as 100 times the advertising elasticity. You can derive this also in words. If the percentage change in sales resulting from a one per cent change in adstock is E_A, then the effect of 100% change in adstock is 100 times E_A. In the example above, you can say, 'Ten per cent of sales are the short-term result of advertising,' provided you do not assume the remaining 90% is independent of advertising.

8.6.2 More about Modelling: The Size of Advertising and Price Effects

There are two comments to make about the entirely realistic example above. First, the advertising *elasticity* is a small number compared with the price elasticity. Do not assume, or let your manager think, that advertising is therefore relatively ineffective – still less that it must therefore be uneconomic (this depends on the brand budget, as shown in Chapter 9). Point out that the 'one per cent change' in adstock, or the media spend, is only a small part of the brand's turnover (even if the advertising-to-sales ratio is as high as 10%, it is only one-thousandth). But a one per cent change in price affects *all* the turnover.

Second, the advertising *coefficient* is a small number compared with the price coefficient. Again, do not let your manager assume that advertising effects are therefore negligible compared with price effects: you have to take into account typical values in the factors themselves.

These are warnings to be taken seriously. It is so easy to misinterpret the size of the elasticities and coefficients found in modelling. Even professionals can fall – an American professor has published a paper claiming that these numbers explain why marketing expenditure has swung away from advertising and towards price promotion. There are actually other explanations for this fact, such as the perceived difficulty of measuring advertising's effects, compared with the visibility of price effects (which says nothing about their profitability) – and the power of retailers, who see promotions as a weapon in their own war in the High Street against competing retailers and so insist on manufacturers arming them in this way.

Example: Calculating typical effects
The way the equation above works for different values of adstock looks reasonable: when adstock is zero, no sales are added by advertising, when adstock is 10, then 0.4 is added to sales share, when it is 40, 1.6 points are added.

But for a price of 125 (at zero adstock), you have to subtract 25 (that is, -0.2 times 125) from the base of 34.8 to get the sales share of 9.8 or a fall of 1.0 from the average (that is, $34.8 - 0.2 \times 120$). At a price of 130, the fall is 2.0.

So actually, for normal levels of variation, the sizes of effect in this case are similar in size.

A more realistic example of discussing typical effects is given after weekly data over two years have been modelled.

It is advisable to demonstrate to the manager what sort of effect has actually occurred. This is done by the calculations in the examples above, or more thoroughly by plotting each effect separately, as was recommended in Section 8.4.2, for awareness fitted by adstock and by a trend term. If you plot C_P times adstock against time you can show exactly what its effects on sales are estimated to be.

You cannot do quite the same for price. Do not plot C_P times price, which is a large number – compared with the average sales share of 12 – and call this the 'price effect'. It is much too large. Instead, proceed as follows.

Determine the minimum price during the period analysed, say C_{min}. Rewrite the equation as follows:

$$(\text{base} + C_P \text{ x } C_{min}) + C_A \text{ x adstock} + C_P \text{ x } (\text{price} - C_{min})$$

This shows you can represent the situation as:

- a more reasonable-looking constant value $(\text{base} + C_P \text{ x } C_{min})$, when adstock is zero and price is at a minimum;
- an adstock effect on sales share, which you can plot;
- a price effect, $C_P \text{ x } (\text{price} - C_{min})$ which you also plot; it is negative and largest at the highest price, zero at the minimum price.

Example: Rewriting the equation
In the last example in Section 8.6.1 where elasticities were calculated, the equation was

$$34.8 + 0.04 \text{ x adstock} - 0.2 \text{ x price}.$$

Suppose relative price never fell below 110. You can rewrite the equation:

$$12.8 + 0.04 \text{ x adstock} - 0.2 \text{ x } (\text{price} - 110)$$
$$\text{where 12.8 is } 34.8 - 0.2 \text{ x } 110.$$

8.6.3 More about Modelling: Multiplicative or Logarithmic Model

There is another version of the adstock and price model, which has the multiplicative form:

$$\text{sales share} = B \text{ x adstock effect x price effect,}$$

Here the 'adstock effect' is $(1 + \text{adstock})$ to the power E_A and the 'price effect' is price to the power E_P, 'price' now being price relative to the category average $= 1$, that is, as a ratio not as an index with average 100. Thus:

$$\text{sales share} = B \text{ x } (1 + \text{adstock})^{E_A} \text{ x } (\text{price})^{E_P}$$

This equation, when it shows the reaction to changing price, produces what is known as the 'demand curve' and is widely used.
When you take logarithms:

$$\log\{\text{sales share}\} = \text{base} + E_A \log\{1 + \text{adstock}\} + E_P \log\{\text{price}\}$$

The reason for adding 1 to adstocks is that you could not write log{adstock} since you cannot take the logarithm of zero. But log{1 + adstock} does not have this problem, and when adstock *is* zero the expression has the value zero which means, as it should, that adstock then has no effect. Similarly, when price is equal to the category average, price then has no effect.

If the log model holds, you can plot the *log* of the objective variable against the *log* of one of the explaining variables and get (approximately) a straight line again. You either take logs before plotting on the computer, or you use log-log paper if doing the job by hand. This makes it easy to estimate the slope (now the elasticity), by eye or by a simple regression.

Though the expression with logs *looks* very different from the multiplicative model, the results are of course identical. 'The log model' and 'the multiplicative model' are in practice synonyms. Either of them generally fits data better than the linear model. Why should you ever use the linear model, then? First, the linear and log equations give very similar results when changes are small, as shown in Figure 27 and in the example below. Second, the linear model is much more easily explained to managers – 'added' sales by advertising or a price drop is a natural idea. Third, many people find taking logs, or raising one number to the power of another, difficult concepts, and these procedures are not available on most hand-held calculators.

The analyst needs to be familiar with both models – linear and multiplicative or logarithmic. In general, use the log model, but when results need to be explained as simply as possible, and the linear equation gives similar results, present the linear equation. Some people find that natural logs (to the base e) are easier, when you are used to them, than to the base 10. Program writing is clearer with exp{ } than with 10^. The differentiation of formulae, though almost never needed, is simpler.

Which you use is a matter of choice.

Example: Equivalent linear and logarithmic models
Return to the linear model:

$$\text{sales share} = 34.8 + 0.04 \times \text{adstock} - 0.2 \times \text{price}$$

where 'price' is indexed on the category average = 100, in order to be able to talk conveniently in percentages. You have established elasticities of 0.1 and –2. Write the equivalent multiplicative model:

$$\text{sales share} = B \times (1 + \text{adstock})^{0.1} \times (\text{price})^{-2}$$

where *price* is now indexed on the category average = 1.

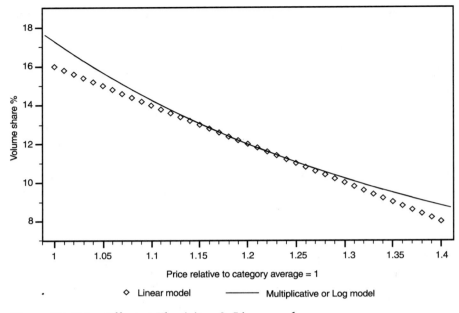

**Figure 27 Price Effect at Elasticity –2: Linear and
Multiplicative Models are Similar for Small Changes**

Calculate B by substituting the known average values:

$$B = 12 / (31^{0.1} \times 1.2^{-2}) = 12.26$$

The logarithmic version is:

$$\log\{\text{sales share}\} = \log\{12.26\} + 0.1 \log\{1+ \text{adstock}\} - 2 \log\{\text{price}\}$$

In Figure 27, the effect of changing *price* is shown for the two sorts of model. Both go through the sales share average of 12% when adstock and price are average. Both have the same slope and elasticity there.

The linear model keeps this slope at other prices; the multiplicative or logarithmic model keeps the same elasticity.

The practical difference between the models is small if you reduce *price* from 1.2 to 1.1: sales share is then 14.0% for the linear model, 14.3% for the other. If you were to increase price to 1.3 then the differences in sales share are much the same: 10.0% and 10.2%. But at a price of 1.4, 20 percentage points above the current level, the difference starts to become serious. Sales share is predicted to be 8.0% for the linear model, 8.8% for the log model. At extreme values the difference is very large, but the models would then break down anyway.

The log model results in an *interaction* between the two effects. Some synergy is built in. A change in adstock has a larger effect when price is low and sales are high – and vice versa.

The linear model can be modified to allow for differing amounts of interaction, by adding the variable (adstock x price) multiplied by some coefficient. This coefficient can be estimated during the fitting of the model.

Even when the linear model has been used, the effect of changes in two variables may be shown by multiplication of the effects. It is of course an assumption that their joint result will be as this calculation predicts.

Example: Two effects together
One effect is a fall of 10%; so is another. Together the result is a fall of 19%, not 20%, since 0.9 (the multiplier for a fall of 10%) times 0.9 is 0.81.

Example: Volume effect from two changes
Let your ad and price elasticities be 0.12 and –2.8. You plan to change your TVRs by a drop of 25% and the relative price of the brand by an increase of 2.1%. The sales estimate is at present 24,167 tonnes. How does this change?

The linear sum is that the sales change, as a per cent, will be about

$$0.12 \text{ x } -25 - 2.8 \text{ x } 2.1 = -3.0 - 5.9 = -8.9\%$$

Combining the separate effects by multiplication, the change is

$$(1 - 0.12 \text{ x } 25 / 100) \text{ x } (1 - 2.8 \text{ x } 2.1 / 100) - 1$$

which is:

$$(0.970 \text{ x } 0.941) - 1 = -0.087$$

Applying these to the present volume, the estimates are that the loss will be 2,150 or 2,100 tonnes – not a meaningful difference.

The multiplicative model is that sales in tonnes will be:

$$24,167 \text{ x } 0.75^{0.12} \text{ x } 1.021^{-2.8} = 24,167 \text{ x } 0.966 \text{ x } 0.943 = 22,015$$

which is a loss of 2,150. When you work with ratios of the TVRs, or their equivalent adstocks, in this way, you need not add the 1 which is necessary when using individual adstock numbers which could be very small or zero.

The log model is that log{sales} in tonnes will be:

$$\log\{24,167\} + 0.12 \log\{0.75\} - 2.8 \log\{1.021\}$$

Whether logs are taken to the base e or 10, the prediction is that sales will be 22,030 or a loss of 2,140 tonnes. The difference from the sum above is only because the numbers above were rounded.

In this example, all methods gave results which are in practice identical. The numbers were chosen to make the point that there is no rule that the multiplicative model always gives larger results (as Figure 27 for a single variable suggests). It depends on the sign of the elasticity.

From the way the log equation is written above, you see it has the same form as the linear equation. Thus you fit it by ordinary least squares in much the same the same way as the linear model, except that logarithms are taken before starting the regression, and the coefficients found are themselves the elasticities, so you do not have to go through calculations like C_p times (P / S) to calculate elasticities.

I demonstrate that the coefficients *are* the elasticities by writing the relation, for fixed adstock, as:

$$\text{sales share} = \text{constant x price to the power } E_p$$

which is differentiated with regard to price to give:

$$\text{change in sales share} = \text{constant x } E_p \text{ x price to the power } E_p$$

hence the proportional change in sales share is:

$$\text{constant x } E_p \text{ x price to the power } E_p / (\text{constant x price to the power } E_p)$$

which is just E_p. For this reason the curve is also called the curve of constant elasticity: at every point on it the elasticity is the same (this is not true for the linear relation).

8.6.4 More about Modelling: Adstock Modelling for Sales

The following example draws together the calculation of a practical model with the resulting elasticities and the demonstration of the size of the effects.

In Section 5.8 it was argued that long-term effects are not identical to short-term ones, but can arise from separate mechanisms. In analysis you keep an open mind about this: you allow for both to appear, but are quite ready to accept that you may get neither, or only one. There are two techniques. One is explained in Section 8.10; one is introduced here, and is simply using adstock with a long half life as one of the explainers. 'Long' means in practice times like 26, 39 or 52 weeks. You can define 'short' as up to 10-weeks half life, and long as over this, but normally there is a clear distinction between the two half lives, even if not as dramatic as this example's two and 39 weeks. In any case, there is usually little to choose between the fits at, say, 20, 26 and 39 weeks.

For simplicity, this example has been constructed without a term for competitors' advertising. It is obvious that if their advertising increases their sales share, it decreases ours. In practice it should always be allowed for. You may look at some major and direct competitors individually, creating separate adstocks for them. Or if the brand is large, it may be enough to take the competitors' total. Quite often you do *not* find a clear effect, probably because their presence is fairly uniform (it contributes to the 'constant competition' of Section 8.10 which causes a general tendency for your share to decline unless you do something about it), or because they steal more from each other and you are able to resist them.

Example of adstock modelling for sales
Turn now to the weekly data for your brand for 1994–95. This is given in Table 9. You have 104 observations, but not enough time to expect a firm view of long-term advertising effects; you will nevertheless look for them. The data show observations for volume share, relative price, distribution and promotions. Adstocks were created for a full range of half lives, but to save space only those for a two-week and 39-week half life are included here.

Inspection of the data gave the warning that price has a clear effect – see Figure 10. The job now is to quantify this and to study the effects of the other factors.

You also inspect the correlation array for the volume share and explanatory variables. In part, this is:

	RelPr	Dis	Promo	Ads2
Vol%	–0.84	0.57	0.77	0.52
RelPr		0.42	–0.51	–0.21
Dis			0.67	–0.07
Promo				0.16

The first line shows strong associations between volume share and all the explainers. Among these, promotion and distribution are clearly linked (0.67), which is going to give us a problem in disentangling their effects. You have also tended to get better distribution during price promotions (–0.42, where the negative sign means higher distribution at lower prices). Such correlations in this work; they show both synergy (one activity works better in the presence of the other), and plans which employ both together (often because the synergy is assumed).

These data were constructed in order to give a clear result and the reader may check that the findings are clear. The value of R-squared for the regression is unusually high, 0.96, and so are all the t-values, except for Ads39, and even that has a satisfactory 2.6. Figure 12 shows the fit.

The effects of the three non-advertising factors are shown in Figure 13. Above the line you see the rise due to promotions of up to two share points, during which distribution also rose. Below the line, the benefit of low price periods, and the damage caused by competitors' price promotions, show in the fluctuations of nearly five share points.

The fit uses separate terms for the short-term effect of advertising (two-weeks half life) and for the long term (39 weeks). In this case both are significant. In other cases, one only may matter. Figure 14 shows the sizes of both effects: the short term has a large, rapid result, often of one or two share points, and up to three in the largest burst. At the same time there is a fluctuating long-term contribution.

The two effects are distinct, although related – the correlation coefficient is 0.33, less than, for example, for distribution with price or promotions. This is because two weeks and 39 weeks are very different. The method could not be used, for example, with both a 26 and 39-week half life, for which the correlation coefficient is 0.9. In a stepwise procedure with several half lives, after the first adstock has entered you may next get another with a negative coefficient. This is not a meaningful explanation and the second adstock should not be used.

More systematically, you can review the effects by looking at the average values and ranges of each variable and multiplying by the relevant coefficient. You can then say:

- Relative price varies in a range between about 103 and 114: its effect is up to 11 x 0.39 or four share points in a maximum week.
- Promotions, as measured here, total six units spread over eight weeks twice a year. Each eight-week period contributes (6 / 8) x 1.6 or 1.2 share points per week over eight weeks.
- Distribution varies between 91 and 97: its effect is up to 6 x 0.21 or about 1.3 share points in a maximum week. Of course if distribution were ever to fall seriously, the result could be much more than that. You are talking about its current range.
- Advertising's direct effects can be looked at as the total of short and long-term effects, resulting from 100 rating points. These give rise to 100 units of adstock of each type. Thus 100 x (0.036 + 0.040) or 7.6 share points (if it were concentrated in one week).

To turn these into tonnes, use the average 1995 category volume of 2,575 tonnes per week to multiply share points.

The regression coefficients are:

Relative price	–0.393	(elasticity –3.0)
Ads2	0.0357	(elasticity 0.055)
Promotions	1.605	
Distribution	0.213	(elasticity 1.40)
Ads39	0.0404	(elasticity 0.066)

The price elasticity is high but not unduly so. The distribution elasticity is not expected to be above one, so this coefficient is rather large. The short-term advertising elasticity is low, which is not unusual, and you do see a rather poorly defined long-term effect – the regression can hardly distinguish between a 26 and a 39-week half life.

This was the analysis reported in Sections 6.6 and 6.7, Figures 9 to 14.

Note that this analysis is repeated later (in Section 8.10), with longer periods (four weeks) but over a longer time (four years). The method is much the same, and the results are similar, but the long-term effect of advertising is modelled there in a different way. The reasons for showing two different regressions are as follows, as well as simply showing the two techniques.

First, you do get such changes of time periods in practice. Some data (such as tracking studies, or sales data), are not available weekly, or not over the longer time you require. You prefer weekly data, but may not have enough of it.

Second, it is more convincing, and preferable, to look for long-term effects over many months or even years. It is not strictly necessary, since it is the period-by-period decay which you are actually estimating, not the overall effect as such. Note that the length of the period can have a result on the findings and this is discussed in Section 8.11.

Having now completed a successful fit, it is appropriate to point out that things do not always run so smoothly.

Example: Insufficient data

This is a true request. 'Would you please analyse these data and tell me what the advertising effect is: what size, what half life, what shape of response function?' The data was a table of six bi-monthly sales shares, rounded off to the nearest whole number, averaging a 4% share, with TVRs for the same periods.

There are only six values, and the request is for three parameters: the half life, the height and the steepness of the response function. You cannot expect so much information from so little.

You cannot tell, with one year's information, what is trend and what is seasonality.

You have not been given a previous rate of advertising, with which to create adstocks.

Bi-months are too coarse a period length for this sort of question.

Rounding off numbers near four means that you cannot distinguish between, for example, 3.5 and 4.4 – the second is over 25% more than the first.

You have no information about any other factors: price, competitors' activities, and so on.

8.7 Consumer Brand Equity

8.7.1 Consumer Brand Equity: Definition

Distribution has an effect on sales, just as price has. This relationship was studied in Chapter 7. You can look at the simultaneous effects of price and distribution with the equation:

$$\ln\{\text{sales share}\} = \text{base} + E_P \ln\{\text{price}\} + E_D \ln\{\text{distribution}\}$$

There are three ways you can define 'base'. Most people treat it as a constant. Second, you can model the possibility that the base changes in response to long-term effects of advertising and other factors, which comes later. This is followed up in Section 8.10. Third is what I now consider: observations allow you to study how the base does change.

This is seen by rewriting the model:

$$\text{base} = \ln\{\text{sales share}\} - E_P \ln\{\text{price}\} - E_D \ln\{\text{distribution}\}$$

This means defining the base as the brand's volume share less the short-term effects of price and distribution. If you further define the elasticities used as those common to all the brands in the category, you have developed a method of quantifying the underlying 'value' to consumers, or Consumer Brand Equity, of each brand, as promised in Chapter 2.

You are creating a level playing field on which each brand is seen without the volume advantage given just by being at a low price, or having exceptional distribution. This is a way of comparing one brand with another, or one brand today with the brand yesterday, uncontaminated by the temporary effects of price and distribution. It is an estimate of how much the brands would sell if they were all on the same shelf and at the same price.

As I have defined it, Consumer Brand Equity is emphatically not a constant – though it usually changes more slowly than volume share itself, which is so driven by current relative price, hence by all the promotions and price deals in the category. The 'base' as defined in this way is often the place where the larger part of advertising effects are felt. This definition of equity is affected by advertising, and of course by other marketing factors – except price and distribution.

Now consider what happens when there is a steady rise in equity, perhaps because of a successful brand-building campaign. Suppose you increase price at the same time – or your relative price rises because a competitor cuts his price. This price increase causes a certain loss in sales, but now the harm done seems to be less, because the 'base' has risen at the same time, due to the 'steady rise'. The measured price elasticity is now smaller.

The benefit of a 'reduction in price elasticity' is often mentioned – the 'added value' of Section 2.7 appears in this way. It is more than a useful phrase: 'adding value so as to sustain a premium price' sets a different agenda for creatives and different expectations in management. In extreme cases, you may even see a positive price elasticity: the volume has risen when the price went up. An example is given in the next section. This very desirable outcome indicates a large rise in equity. Similarly, if price decreases at this time, you apparently observe a very large (negative) price elasticity. The slope for price increases is flat, but for price decreases is steep.

Thus the usual calculation of price elasticity, set out in Section 8.6.1, which depends on the assumption of a constant base, falls apart. It is worth calculating the price elasticities for increases and for decreases separately as a check, or once during the time of share growth, once for decline.

Another aspect of these facts is that when advertising adds value (ie increases equity), it is up to us to decide how to take this added value. Sometimes you do so as a volume increase. At other times you take it as a price rise. The profit results and the strategic fallout of how you take the value are different.

8.7.2 Consumer Brand Equity: Working

To turn this into a practical tool, suppose your brand:

- has present sales volume share V
- is at the relative price P (the average for the category is 100)
- has distribution (or equivalent measure) D, while the average for the category is D_A
- and suppose that E_P and E_D are average price and distribution elasticities in the sector.

Then I have defined Consumer Brand Equity as:

$$Q = V / [\exp\{E_P \ln\{P / 100\}\} \times \exp\{E_D \ln\{D / D_A\}\}]$$

This is the second equation in the section above, but expressed directly in terms of volume share, *less* the effects of current price and distribution (if these elasticities applied). It was reached by expressing each side of the equation as a power of e.

It looks a complex expression, but once written it is just another column on a spreadsheet, derived from current volume, price and distribution. When relative price is 100, and distribution equals the average for the category, Q = V. If price rises above 100, and V is constant, Q increases – to sell the same volume at a higher price means higher equity. If distribution rises above the average, Q falls – selling the same amount although you have more distribution means lower equity.

This is a quantity which you may calculate across all the brands for their average positions (for volume share, price and distribution) over, say, a year. You may also calculate it for a second year, and so you may look at changes from one year to another. Table 10 is an example of calculating equities for annual averages. The brands may be put in order of their changes in equity. Further, you may calculate it for a single brand for each period (for a number of individual weeks, for example), and see how it changes while, say, adstock varies.

Consumer Brand Equity contributes to your view about how the brand is doing. Part of the brand's sales movement is due purely to price changes (ours or competitors), and part to distribution gains and losses. What remains is due to other factors: perceived quality, trends, promotions which add value rather than cut-price, and so on.

These three reasons for a change in a brand's sales share are multiplied together to give the actual change. The formulae for the effects are:

- due to a relative price change, when P changes to p, then the effect is $\exp\{E_P \ln\{p / P\}\}$;
- a similar expression for distribution: $\exp\{E_D \ln\{d / D\}\}$;
- and the third is the change in the ratio of the equities.

Table 11 shows this in practice.

Because the ratios are often not far from one, the numbers can sometimes be presented as percentages which are added or subtracted, even though they were not originally handled in this way.

Example: The effects of changes on Consumer Brand Equity
You increased your relative price by 3% but lost 1% of your distribution. The elasticities were –2 and +0.9. Your sales share increased 2%. Then the real calculation is that the proportional change in equity is:

$$1.02 / [\exp\{-2 \times \ln\{1.03\}\} \times \exp\{0.99\}\}]$$
$$= 1.02 / [0.943 \times 0.991] = 1.091$$

The linear interpretation, rounded off, is that our relative price change was expected to lose us 6%, our distribution loss was expected to lose us 1%, but you improved equity (by other activities) by 9% hence your share gain was 2% since $+9-6-1=2$.

Note that this is an example of a price increase and a sales increase simultaneously. To interpret +3% in price and +2% in sales is a problem if you assume – as is so common – a stable base.

Example: Hiding the price elasticity
Modifying the example above, suppose relative price is again increased with an elasticity of –2, so you expect from this a loss of 6% in share. Suppose this time distribution did not change. If the base or equity were steady, this 6% is what would show. But if equity declined at the same time by, say, 2% then a loss of 8% in share is seen; if equity increased by 2% then a loss of only 4% shows.

The superficial result of the price changes in this example conceals two simultaneous effects. If the change is interpreted as a price effect alone, an incorrect estimate will be made for its elasticity. This error is often made. A common situation is a price decrease accompanied by advertising which raises equity – the apparent elasticity is very high. Another is a price increase accompanied by advertising which again raises equity – the apparent elasticity is small.

A table of the effects on each brand of its price, distribution and equity changes is a powerful way of describing the category. It quickly becomes clear what are the main drivers in the category from the sizes of these effects.

In some categories (eg spirits on the Continent), volume changes depend very much on distribution changes. In others (eg some groceries in the UK), price changes matter most. In yet others, it is changing equities which most determine changing sales.

It can now be argued that there are three groups of drivers for profit. *Pricing* strategies are the first. You have to get your list or normal price at the optimum position, and you should discount from it the least that is sensible. The 'optimum position' depends on your perceived quality, which is discussed below, and balances volume against profit, with an eye on your strategy against competitors. Discounting may be necessary to satisfy retailers, to attract occasional users whom you hope you can convert, to add excitement and create goodwill.

Distribution strategy has a simple aim – to get the attention of the consumer as often and as conveniently as possible. However, this has to be bought, so it is balanced against a cost.

There remains *Consumer Brand Equity*. This has been defined as a number, but there is a qualitative interpretation. Equity is about the values at the heart of the brand. It includes perceived product quality but there is a lot more. Brand essence, defined in Chapter 1, is part of it. It is what marketing is about, in every aspect except the specialised jobs of pricing and distribution. It has been suggested as the scorecard number with which marketing activities should be evaluated. Management control of advertising, in particular, could be exercised in this way. It would still be necessary to allow for other reasons why it rises and falls (a competitor withdraws from the category, you have a technical breakthrough), but the idea is attractive. I have experience of it *helping* to evaluate advertising, but not of it being the sole criterion.

8.7.3 Consumer Brand Equity: Calculating Category Average Elasticities

Elasticities for individual brands from time series were discussed above on the assumption of a fixed base. This is inappropriate for the situation now considered, where equities are changing. You can approximate to this by allowing a trend over time to represent rising, stationary or falling equities. So you fit to all the brands this expression for ln{sales share}:

$$\text{base} + E_P \ln\{\text{price}\} + E_D \ln\{\text{distribution}\} + \text{coefficient} \times \text{trend}$$

Here the sign and size of 'coefficient' is a rough indication of the overall movement in equity you are going to find for each brand. Then the average values of E, or at least for those with reasonable t-values, indicate average elasticities.

Another way is similar to the plots described above, of the *per cent changes* in sales volume share for each brand against *per cent changes* in relative price and in distribution. A multivariate regression, through the origin, of the changes in sales, against changes in both price and distribution, indicates the elasticities directly from the coefficients.

The plots should be inspected first since outliers explained by neither factor are very likely to be due to equity changes. These should be excluded from the regression.

A third way is to use other data, especially for the main brands of interest, which indicate elasticities, if these are available. Care must be taken that these are not naïve calculations assuming a fixed base. Measurements made in store at different prices are likely to be most useful.

8.7.4 Consumer Brand Equity: Plots for Constant Equity

Once an average price elasticity has been agreed, there is an addition to the price–volume plot which is sometimes useful. This shows 'contour' lines on the plot, which a brand would follow, if all it were doing was to respond to price changes. On the other hand, if it climbs across the contours (towards the top-right), it is gaining in equity. This might be, for example, because of improved distribution. To check this, a similar plot can of course be done for distribution–volume.

The lines follow this expression for sales volume share:

$$\text{equity} \times \exp\{E_p \times \ln\{p / 100\}\}$$

You have to choose a sensible range of equities (after inspection of the actual equities calculated), and plot a line for each equity over the range of prices in your plot.

As noted in Section 8.6.3, you can take logs before making this plot, and the 'contours' become straight lines. Further, if you plot on the X-axis not just $\ln(p)$ but $(-1 / E_p)$ times $\ln(p)$, and also ensure that the sizes of the scales of the X and Y-axes are equal, then the 'contours' are straight lines at 45°. This makes it easy to see whether one brand's equity is higher (more to the top-right) than another.

8.7.5 Consumer Brand Equity: Direct Plots

In Chapter 6, I suggested making a scatter plot for the brands, with the X-axis being volume shares in year two, and the Y-axis being the per cent changes in volume share from year one. It is revealing to make a similar plot here with the X-axis the Consumer Brand Equities in year two, and the Y-axis the per cent changes in equity from year one. This tells us not only which brands have high equities or low, but also how they are moving. Top-right is again a desirable position. This was Figure 17.

You can also compare the equity changes for brands with movements in those factors which might affect equity. For example, when changes in equity are plotted against changes in share of voice, you often see a remarkable association between these two (see the comments on share of voice in Section 7.5.3). Note that equity plotted directly against share of voice (not *changes* in these terms) may *not* show such an association. This is telling us that equity itself depends on more than the decision to advertise (product quality, brand history and consumer satisfaction are much more likely sources), but that share of voice has an influence and that the other factors are rather stable.

This is another example of the importance of distinguishing between the average *position,* and *changes* round that position. It is also an example of the advertising being run by competitors in a category having comparable sales effectiveness, despite the often observed large differences of effectiveness of campaigns in pre-testing development. This is probably because the specific criteria used in pre-testing (communicating sales points, for example), are not the way the campaign actually works; just being there, for example, may be a major factor.

Example: Changes in share of voice and in Consumer Brand Equity
Figure 18 is the plot just suggested. It shows two brands (A and B) in the top-right quadrant. They increased their share of voice, and perhaps as a result now have higher equity. A did proportionately better than B in this way. Brand C spent less on advertising and its equity has fallen. Own label did not advertise specifically in this category, but its equity has risen, perhaps because of a growing reputation for value.

8.7.6 Consumer Brand Equity: Continuous Calculation

The formula for Consumer Brand Equity does not use advertising or promotions as input. It is therefore reasonable to examine the effects of these activities on the equity, using the data period by period. You then see what benefit these activities produce in the underlying base of sales of the brand. You have removed the effects of price and of distribution when you do this.

So instead of looking in summary across all the brands, as you did above, you now look at a single brand across the periods. The equity can be regressed and plotted against adstocks and other variables.

Example of calculating equity continuously
For your brand, using four-week data for 1994 and 1995, regression of Consumer Brand Equity against Ads2 and promotion shows clearly significant effects. Scatter plots against these variables also show them. The longer term adstock effect is not so clear.

The result of the regression is shown in Figure 19. The dates show the actual movement of equity, with peaks at 9408 and 9508. The line shows the fit with Ads2 and promotion, and tells us clearly why these peaks occur: they are when you advertise and promote most heavily. The lows, for example at 9502, are when you are losing equity because of competitor's activities. Changes in your Consumer Brand Equity are responsible for movements of four or more share points.

8.8 Response Functions

The normal, or linear, adstock model states that the effect of, or response to, increased advertising pressure increases indefinitely in a straight line. This assumption is reasonable only for moderate amounts of exposure. If the pressure, or opportunities to see, get large, then diminishing returns must set in. You need to model this situation too. The logarithmic model does this in part, but not satisfactorily. Another and more explicit way is to use adstock in a function which says what the different responses are to varying amounts of adstock.

8.8.1 Response Functions: The Shape

The units for adstock are normally ratings per week. In this application the most appropriate units are OTS per week; remember that ratings / 100 measure the average number of opportunities to see.

A convenient way to represent response to n opportunities to see is another geometric function h x $(1 - r^n)$, where h is a scale parameter, the maximum height reached by the function, or the effectiveness of the activity, and r is a parameter between 0 and 1. This *steepness* parameter determines whether you have a very convex function, or a gently sloping one.

At n = 0 the function is always 0; at very large n it is close to 1. At n = 1, or at the first opportunity to see, the function has the value $1 - r$; for small r, this is a large proportion of the maximum value 1 and the function is steep. For large r the function is more flat; it approaches a straight line as r

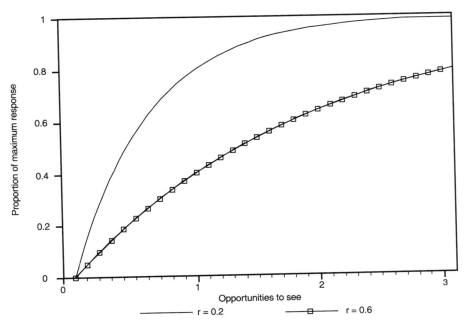

Figure 28 Two Response Functions
At r = 0.2, the function is steeper: at r = 0.6 it is flatter

increases. Small r has been suggested for most cases, large r for small budgets and new products. Note that a rate of one OTS a week is given to very few brands: this is 5,200 TVRs a year and requires a substantial budget.

Figure 28 shows the steeper function, for r = 0.2, going through 0.8 at one OTS; at 2 it is 0.96 and at 3 it is 0.99. For r = 0.6, it has reached only 0.78 at three OTS, so additional advertising exposures would still give some return, though less than for earlier exposures.

The 'steepness' of the function depends which part of it is being discussed. The weight of advertising and the length of time being considered both matter. For rates of advertising equivalent to fractions of an OTS per week, even the two very different-looking curves in Figure 28 are quite close to linear. The definition of 'response' is also relevant.

For completeness, I mention that some theorists have suggested that response is s-shaped. That is, response is very small at small n, then grows more sharply, only to become convex so there are still diminishing returns at high values of n. A method to model this is suggested below. The shape may apply in special circumstances – a new and complicated advertisement for a low interest product, for example. It is in practice hard to distinguish between a convex function, with large r, and an s-shape which is also close to linear.

This shape is associated with the idea of 'effective frequency'. This applies to a schedule analysis (which shows how often people see a commercial – not at all, once, twice, and so on). The concept is that you should disregard effects on the lightly exposed, and count all those who saw two commercials (or whatever frequency you decide is 'effective'), as equally affected. Thus 'effective frequency' corresponds to a step function, and this is the extreme form of an s-shape. Put like this, such a theory is hardly realistic, but it has proved a useful way of setting targets for TV buyers.

8.8.2 Response Functions: Adstock + Response

With the more acceptable geometric response function you can define an 'adstock + response model' where the response at any adstock is proportional to $1 - r^{(\text{adstock} / 100)}$. You do not know r in advance, just as you do not know the half life to use in the adstock you are going to fit. You use the same method – you try out different values of r and use the one which fits best. Thus, you first find the best half life for the linear adstock model, then for this adstock (and ideally for one with a smaller, one with a longer half life), you make columns or variables for various r. The columns hold values which are nearly proportional to adstock when these are small, but you see diminishing returns as adstocks increase. Remember, for most people, for most campaigns, OTS per week are usually under one. In a multivariate regression, you find out which r gives the best explanation. The coefficient found for this term in the regression corresponds to the effectiveness parameter h.

Note that other transformations of the adstock variable are possible. The method introduced in Section 8.3, the linear adstock model, is the simplest. Then diminishing returns were discussed above. It is also possible to model with a threshold: the effect is nil unless adstock exceeds the threshold D; beyond that diminishing returns apply with (adstock – D) as the variable.

Example of fitting adstock + response
The weekly data for 1994–95 is now known to be well-fitted by the brand's relative price, its distribution and promotions, a short-term adstock with two-week half life, and a long-term adstock with a 39-week half life. As has been explained, the example was in fact constructed to give this fit. However, what happens when you try a geometric response function instead of this linear response to short-term advertising?

The answer is reassuring: in this particular case you are advised that the linear response is best. In real life, of course, you expect, and I have often found, some diminishing returns. Values of r can be as low as 0.2 for weekly data, but are usually nearer one.

The method described above was used on the file of weekly data: creating columns of $1 - r^{(\text{adstock}/100)}$ for the current adstock during each week, for various values of r. The goodness of fit, which still included price, distribution, promotion and long-term adstock, for several r is shown below.

r	Per cent of response at one OTS	R^2
0.1	90	0.941
0.3	70	0.961
0.5	50	0.969
0.7	30	0.973
0.9	10	0.975

So in this case you are led to the correct decision – that response goes on increasing roughly in proportion to the number of times your advertising is seen.

8.8.3 Response Functions: Fitting Response Directly

On occasions you need to fit the geometric response function directly. That is, you have data about response (which is called v here, since it is often a volume sales measure), at different amounts of pressure or numbers of opportunities to see (which is called n). In general, the function says that, when n = 0, v has some base value B. There must be some asymptote or maximum conceivable value; for example, if response were the percentage of the target who are aware, this could not rise above 100. Suppose in general the maximum is B + H. Then you have to estimate the three parameters in:

$$v = B + H(1 - r^n)$$

which you can write:

$$\log\{B + H - v\} = \log\{H\} + n.\log\{r\}$$

A quick approximate solution can be got in the following way. For any asymptote B + H you can create a column for $\log\{B + H - v\}$. Make a scatter plot for these values against the corresponding $\log\{r\}$, and regress them against $\log\{r\}$. Choose B + H which gives the best linear fit, or looks straightest on the plot. The coefficients give us estimates for r and H. You then get B via the known B + H.

8.9 Budget Allocation over Time

Now a special use for the adstock + response model is described. This is to help the media planner with the decision about allocating a budget over the weeks of the campaign. TV language is used here and the method is called BAT.

Each timing decision depends critically on two factors – as well as on the rate of decay of the effects which half life in adstock represents, and on the diminishing returns which the response function caters for.

8.9.1 BAT: The Value in Different Weeks of Having an Effect

There are always reasons why having an effect in one week will be different from others. The two most common are these. You may be running some other marketing activity which the advertising is to support – a consumer promotion, the announcement of a product improvement and so on. In these cases you insist on timing the advertising appropriately. The second reason is when more purchase decisions are being made in your category at certain times, so it is more worthwhile to exert pressure then. In other words, category seasonality matters: toys, for example, are advertised before Christmas. In these cases, if there are twice as many sales in this week, we want twice as much pressure, or a similar requirement.

8.9.2 BAT: Media Costs Over the Year

There are some cases when the cost of placing advertising is the same whenever it appears. It is however more usual – and certainly the case in television in Europe – that you pay more at the two cost peaks of spring and autumn. When you allocate a budget you would rather buy at the cheaper times, all other things being equal.

The allocation problem arises precisely because other things are not equal and you have to balance opposing requirements. You would like to be on at a cheap time; you would like to be on when category sales are high; you do not want too much advertising at once or diminishing returns set in; you do not want to be on again just after a previous burst because you still have the benefit of that advertising.

Fortunately the adstock + response model can cope with this situation and can guide us to an efficient allocation.

Example of 'values' and 'costs'
In Table 12 is the seasonality of the category in 1995, as calculated earlier, indexed to average 100. You know there is a general climb from around 90 in January to about 115 in July. Apart from another peak in November there is then decline, with the two weeks at the end of the year at about 50. You take category seasonality as the worth to us of someone in your target seeing a TV commercial at that time, because he is more likely to make a buying decision then.

From your knowledge of TV costs you can produce another index, from the cost each month (of four or five weeks) of buying 100 housewife ratings. This climbs sharply from about 75 in January to 110 in May, declines to under 90 in August, climbs to its annual peak of nearly 120 in October, then falls again.

The question is, what happens when you put together the two indices to make the value/cost index? All three items are in Table 11, and the value/cost index is plotted in Figure 20.

January (because of its very low costs), and August (because of low costs and excellent category volume), are clearly preferred times.

8.9.3 BAT: Evaluating an Allocation

A TVR allocation is a set of numbers – the proportions in which TVRs are bought over the weeks of the campaign. Given a TVR allocation, the costs of television and a budget, you can say how many TVRs will be bought each week. From this schedule, you can calculate adstocks. Using the response function, you can calculate response. This should be weighted by the value you have given each week. The sum of these weighted responses is the effectiveness of the allocation.

To execute this model is harder than this outline sounds. You have to collect the relevant data and decisions. You should have previously fitted a model to give the half life for adstocks and the steepness for response – or if you have not fitted one you need to make estimates (you can check the sensitivity of your decisions to these estimates: it often turns out, for example, that steepness or r is not a critical parameter for normal weights of advertising). Then you need to write the model in a form which media planners can use.

BAT is written as an aid to judgment and does not itself allocate the budget; it assesses a given allocation and shows how to improve it. This is because optimisation requires further decisions (What is the least number of TVRs you would buy in a week? How much do you allocate to a promotion or announcement, compared with the rest of the year?), which are more easily made when you see the numbers involved, and the changes in effectiveness at various allocations.

The process just described may be contrasted with traditional TV planning. The allocation of money to different months is often less thought about than is ideal. It may even be based solely on the sales pattern, as in the case history of Chapter 6. The other extreme is that it may be based only on cheap time, to make the money stretch further and produce low TV costs. Next there are the questions of how much is enough? Or, how many exposures are needed? In other words, the effective frequency debate. A conventional solution is to fix on a magic number, usually one, two, or three, within some period of time like a week, or the purchase interval. BAT uses both 'values', such as the category sales pattern, and 'costs'. It side-steps 'effective frequency' by giving all frequencies *some* value, but acknowledging that there are diminishing returns. BAT then considers all parts of the problem at once, and uses the allocation of TVRs as input, a single number for effectiveness as output.

8.9.4 BAT: Improving the Schedule

The 'improvement' suggested by BAT comes from a brute force technique. Starting from the existing schedule, you add a small sum to the budget and spend it in week one. This adds to the TVRs then and improves the effectiveness. You record the improvement, deduct the amount from week one and instead spend it in week two – and repeat this process until you have estimated the effect of changing the expenditure in each of the 52 weeks of the year. The results tell us in which weeks it is best to spend more, and for those weeks where you already have expenditure, where it is best to reduce it.

By following this advice (and meanwhile obeying other constraints, like supporting promotions, and not buying less than some minimum number of ratings in any week), you improve the schedule. By several repetitions of this process you soon get to a schedule which is for all practical purposes the one to be recommended.

Example: Evaluating a schedule and improving it
The model is set up with the TV values and costs already described, a response parameter and a half life for advertising effects. You first use two weeks for the half life since this was found in the fit to the weekly data for 1994–95.

BAT is first run to calculate the weighted responses to a standard schedule. This consists of TVRs each week which are in proportion to the value/cost index that week. The sum of the weighted responses to this schedule are taken as an effectiveness of 100.

Then you input the actual 1995 schedule, shown on Table 11. This had no TVRs for the first 12 weeks (sales were comparatively low then and this had led to the decision not to advertise). There were then peaks around June (when sales were high, and before the holidays), and about September (at the shoulder of high sales).

The actual schedule was based on the sales history and largely ignored costs. The value/cost index suggests this could have been a mistake.

Indeed, when you calculate the effectiveness index of the actual schedule you find only 83.9. You know you got 1,575 TVRs at an average cost of £235,000 per 100. The standard schedule got 1,624 TVRs at a cost of £228,000 per 100. Hence on conventional media grounds the standard schedule would have been better, and when you take sales effects into account it is 19% better (100 as a percentage above 83.9).

BAT also indicates how to improve the actual schedule. With this short half life you cannot do much better than the standard schedule. You cut out the last two weeks, strengthen the first quarter and so on, but basically a rather continuous schedule with small modifications is suggested. Its effectiveness is 19.4% above the actual schedule.

In cash terms, on the budget of £3,700k, this represents an added £720k. It is rare that such a large improvement is available, but this shows what is possible with a thorough analysis.

So much for short-term effects; the model you have fitted tells us there are also advertising effects with a long half life (39 weeks). What would you do to maximise the return from scheduling in this way?

Going through the same process you find the actual schedule had an effectiveness index of 95. The recommended schedule shown in Table 11 is for the long-term effects and concentrates much more on the early part of the year. This makes sense in the total TVRs you would have bought (1,755) and their average cost (down now to £211k per 100). It means also that the adstock from these TVRs is working during the climb to the value peak; the effectiveness is up to 104.6, suggesting a cash benefit of £375k.

The two schedules are different – the first, for short-term effects, which is nearly continuous, and the second, for the long term, which concentrates on January to March and July. Which of these two schedules should you have bought – and which route will you follow for 1996?

The answer depends on how much you value an immediate return, and how much you believe you are investing in Consumer Brand Equity and the longer term.

The application in this example is made in Section 9.10.4, where priority is given to the long term, since you see that the short term is satisfactorily improved anyway.

8.10 Long-Term Adstock Effects and General Modelling

Adstock has been used to explain short-term blips in what is otherwise a stable variable, or one which trends steadily. The cases initially considered had a constant base, or a constant plus a simple trend, and with only one or two other terms besides advertising. Half lives were short – less than ten weeks. All this is often not adequate, either because there are additional explainers, or because advertising effects last longer.

Additional explainers may be required and they are just added to the regression process. Competitors' activities is the one most obviously missing from the examples here. To have many explainers makes the interactions between the so-called 'independent' variables more likely, and also harder to make judgments about. A correlation matrix among these variables is a sensible aid when you are deciding between possible explanations. But all the principles described above in the case of two explainers still apply.

I have added to the initial model three other ideas. First, that adstock with a long half life (20 weeks or more) may explain long-term movements in the base. In the set of adstocks entered in the multivariate regressions you try out, include half lives like 20, 26, 39 and 52 weeks. You find out whether one of these is a significant explainer. You may simultaneously look for short-term effects: it is quite possible for advertising to have both these two different sorts of effect – or either one or the other. Some people say, 'you cannot have a long-term effect without a short-term one'. They may not be distinguishing properly between two sorts of effect. They may also be observing that even when you have a long-term effect, you get more of it at the beginning, as the adstock model predicts. The long-term effect is not a 'time bomb', undetected at first but which suddenly explodes.

The second change considered is to let the data decide how the base moves: Consumer Brand Equity. You have no preconceptions, but you find out after the event how your activities affect equity.

Third, I have allowed for diminishing returns in the short-term advertising effects.

This might seem to be an already extensive armoury, but in this section another method is added. The reason for the variety is that any one of these models may be appropriate for a particular situation. There is no one way in which advertising has effects: you have to study the data and then describe it appropriately.

They are in any case broadly similar models: there is always the possibility of a short-term effect, which may be sensibly in linear proportion to adstock, or some response function may be detectable. The other variations are all in the way the base behaves – that part of a brand's sales movements which changes more gradually. You may study this movement, from sales less the short-term influences such as price fluctuations. You may fit it with a long-term adstock.

Or, you may fit it with the 'floating base' which follows. It is unlikely that the base is genuinely constant, though it may look that way, with the support the brand actually received. That is much the most frequently-fitted model, but it usually cannot be used when the modelling helps us fix a budget. This is because ignoring the support which kept the base nearly steady, or helped to grow it, or slow down its decline, results in *undervaluing* advertising. A budget based on this false assumption may be totally inadequate.

In the case which follows – and in many I have met – the floating base model is the most satisfactory. It represents the roughly stable base without assuming it is constant or that advertising has no long-term effect. It may be the norm that the explanation for stability is a balance between erosion and maintenance which this model provides. A full discussion of the complex issues now raised is not attempted, but a practical guide to action is outlined.

So the final way in this book of accounting for the effects of advertising is as follows. It replaces the constant base with a more complex term which can be thought of as a floating base: in some circumstances this base sinks, in others it floats up again. The base is in dynamic balance between two forces.

The first force is the rather constant competition a brand faces. Of course there are special aspects of competition you model separately: the general level of prices, competitors' promotions and their changing advertising weight – these can be allowed for explicitly. But their continual presence as an alternative to your brand must erode your share. You can represent this by a constant fall, say c, each period.

There is the possibility of this being countered by a second force: uplift from your brand's current advertising pressure, or adstock with a long half life. In each period you may add e times $Lads_t$ where e is some coefficient and $Lads_t$ is the value of a long-term adstock at time t.

Counting from the beginning of your data (t = 1), the cumulative effect of these two mechanisms is that the base is changed to base + c.t + e.$Lads_t$ where c is negative and the sum is from 1 to t. These will cancel out and the base will stay roughly constant if $-c.t = e.Lads_t$, or if $-c$ / e equals the average adstock or TVR rate. A collection of real examples has in fact been successfully modelled in this way, with the average constant fall amounting to −16% each year, sometimes in equilibrium with a contribution from advertising, sometimes resulting in decline and sometimes in growth in the base.

All this suggests that it is worth trying to fit a model which, in addition to short-term advertising effects and other factors, includes as explanatory variables a trend term and cumulative adstocks for half lives like 26, 39, 52 and more weeks. For a floating base, you are looking for a fit with a negative trend and a positive contribution from cumulative adstock.

Example of long-term modelling
Four-weekly data is used in this example, for Brand B, 1992 to 1995. The objective is to explain sales volume share, and the variables available to do this are its price relative to the sector, its distribution and promotions, and its advertising.

Because the data is constructed with a relatively small error term and little correlation between the variables, you get a clear result from a forward stepwise regression. The value of R-squared (0.96) is high and the t-values are satisfactory for this reason. The fit is good, as Figure 15 confirms.

The regression suggests that price, a short half life adstock (two weeks) and promotions are the important explainers, in that order. The effects of the short-term factors could be seen in a plot similar to Figure 13, and an extra figure is not given here. A cumulative adstock (with 39-weeks half life), and a trend term add to this explanation, but are less strong. Distribution is not prominent, but also contributes.

The base, which is the balance between cumulative long-term adstock and a negative trend, does not vary much, as Figure 16 shows. However, there is a trace of overall decline from 1992 until the increased advertising in 1995 kicks in.

The regression coefficients are:

Relative price	−0.38	(elasticity −2.8)
Ads2	0.0090	(elasticity 0.049)
Promotions	2.00	
Distribution	0.092	(elasticity 0.58)
Trend	−0.217	
CAds39	0.0029	

This is again a high but not unusual price elasticity. The short-term advertising elasticity is low, but there is also a long-term effect. Distribution elasticity now looks low.

The promotions coefficient is the same as with the two-year regression. You have three promotions a year, so the overall result is 3 x 2.00 or six share points for four weeks. Category volume in 1995 is 10,300 tonnes per four weeks. Therefore promotions contribute directly 0.06 x 10,300 or 620 tonnes. The distribution effect is confounded with this and cannot be estimated reliably on its own.

The price effect can be stated as the reaction to a one per cent cut, or the reduction of relative price by 1.07. The coefficient is similar to last time at –0.38 and the share improvement is 1.07 x 0.38 or 0.41. Over four weeks this is 42 tonnes, but remember you lose revenue to get this.

I return later to the advertising effect, but the simplest approximation is by using the sum of the short and long-term elasticities in Section 8.6.4, which is 0.12, so a one per cent addition to the average 1994–95 spend on TV, or £24,000 in four weeks, gives 0.12% of 10,300 or 10 tonnes.

Example: Long-term effects
In this model you have estimated a decay (c) of –0.217 share points every four weeks, or 2.8 share points every year. This is 19% of average sales in 1992–93 (14.6 share points); it is near the norm reported above, which is 16% decay a year.

How can such a result be compatible with the obvious stability of the brand?

The reason is that the stability is dynamic. It is a balance between this erosion and support by the long-term advertising effect: a coefficient (e) of 0.0029 times Ads39. The result is no change if –c / e or 0.216 / 0.0029 = 74 is the four-weekly TVR rate. This is an annual rate of 965 TVRs.

In fact the annual rates have varied round this, which is why you see overall stability, but can detect a slight fall in 1993–94 and recovery in 1995. The following table spells this out, though it reports an effect which is actually spread out beyond the calendar year.

	TVR	Calculated change in share points
1992	1012	+0.1
1993	824	–0.4
1994	747	–0.6
1995	1574	+1.8

For example, for an average four weeks in 1995, the drop of –0.216 is countered by adstock generated by 1574 / 13 = 121 TVRs, and multiplied by 0.0029. This is 0.351. Then 0.351 – 0.216 = 0.135 is the increase in base every four weeks. Over 13 periods this is 1.8 share points.

It is only through a forecast using the full model that you can see what the effect of changing advertising weight will actually be. This is provided in Continuous Budgeting in Section 9.10.

There are two practical conclusions from the model. One is to help set a budget which will ensure stability: this is the cost of 965 TVRs a year. Average scheduling is assumed. Another is a justification for advertising at all – if you stopped doing so, in a couple of years you could find your brand declining at the rate of 19% a year, which is surely unacceptable, unless you found some technique which did the job of maintaining equity as well as advertising.

This was the analysis briefly reported in Section 6.8.

8.11 Note on the Results of Grouping Data

We have now looked at one example of modelling two years' weekly data, and another of four years' four-weekly data. The two years were included in the four years. Are the results the same, and which is preferred?

Such a situation is often met. We prefer one set of data for one reason (weekly numbers give a more detailed view), and another set for a different reason (there is a longer run of four-weekly data and so greater reliability and a more convincing estimate of long-term effects).

The differences in findings in the examples here are partly due to the different years covered, but the grouping has a larger effect and this is a general problem which has to be faced. It has long been known, and was pointed out above, that there is an 'interval bias' when the effects of advertising are modelled: the longer the interval, the more likely you will choose a longer half life for the fit. The shorter the interval, the more extreme and the faster will the results appear. In addition, as already pointed out, you lose definition when you use a longer interval and the results of this are not well understood except that it introduces uncertainty.

The recommendation already made is to collect ratings and media data generally at the shortest reasonable interval, a week. If possible, use this length throughout. If not, after weekly adstocks are created, group these to the interval in the sales or tracking data, where only longer intervals may be available.

Example: Compare results for different intervals
Looking back at the two sales models – Section 8.6.4 and immediately above – you find unusually almost the same price and short-term advertising elasticities; if they had differed, the weekly one would have been more 'real'.

The effects of promotion and distribution were estimated differently in the two sets, undoubtedly because the promotions were brief and associated with distribution. This association caused the unrealistic distribution elasticity in the weekly result. The size of the promotion effect is reasonably well determined, but that for distribution is not – since distribution itself has varied little, this is not surprising.

The biggest difference is when the long-term effect of advertising is estimated. For forward planning, the four-year data, with the floating base, gives the result to use. But no elasticity from this calculation is available, as in this model the 'one per cent increase' in advertising has effects over later months when the downward effect of the trend term will also be felt. It is not a one-off increase, as the traditional calculation assumes. You have to go to the Continuous Budgeting Model in Section 9.10 to see the accurate effect of changes.

For the elasticity approach, the model with Ads39 (elasticity of 0.066) and Ads2 (elasticity 0.055) is preferred. You can legitimately add these to give an overall elasticity of 0.12.

8.12 Experiments

8.12.1 Experiments: Introduction

Although theorists often suggest area tests as a way to evaluate TV advertising alternatives (especially copy and weight), and although the UK structure of ITV and other TV transmissions allows such tests to be designed, they are uncommon. In other countries, with controllable TV transmissions via cable to a panel – like IRI's service in the US – they are more frequent but still unusual. The reasons are the costs involved, uncertainty about getting a clear result and even unwillingness to admit that the current plan may be less than ideal. Equally, some tests are run for poor reasons – to postpone or merely to justify a decision.

In other ways of communicating, such as database marketing or direct mail and other direct response media such as print, tests are common or even normal. Certainly, testing should always be considered as a way of extending your knowledge and improving your communications. So this section outlines the principles involved in designing and evaluating a test.

In TV tests, TV regions are most often employed in a test design and this is the language used here. But transmitter areas are possibilities, cities may be used for posters, split runs for direct mail and some print media, a randomly-chosen set of addresses in your database. For all these designs I say here that there is a *test area*.

What you may do next looks simple: you make the change in the test area and see whether sales go up and by how much. Many people have done just that and then been disappointed. Either sales continue to vary much as before, or conditions obviously change – for example a competitor drops a coupon in the test area, whether as a deliberate spoiler or not. For one reason or another, most tests analysed in this way are unreadable.

8.12.2 Experiments: How to Design Them

Ensure that only *one variable* is tested: do not make two changes at once unless that is the strategy you want to evaluate. New copy, an upweight in adspend, a sampling promotion – these are examples of test variables.

Agree on the *criterion measure*, the number you will use to evaluate the test, usually volume sales share of the category (removing most seasonal and category trend effects), so this is the criterion used below. Brand awareness and penetration are other examples.

Agree on the *success measure* – the change which makes it commercially worthwhile to execute the change. For example a 50% upweight may require 10% more sales to make it profitable. In some cases any improvement would be worthwhile, as with a creative shift which incurs little extra cost. This is not a calculation of statistical significance, but a business judgment.

Review the possible *test areas*: look for those large enough to have reasonably stable sales share (this is covered in detail below), but not too expensive to test in. If you use several areas you will eventually combine them in analysis. In the US it is common to pick as many as three test areas in case some catastrophic reason later makes us drop one – or even two. This advice may or may not be relevant to your design.

Review the possible *control areas*, perhaps the rest of the country. Often care is taken to try and match test and control, demographically and in category behaviour, but this is hard and, as we shall see, not always necessary.

Collect back data, during a *base period*, about the criterion measure in both test and control areas.

Also collect data about *factors which you think may affect sales share*. This means numbers like relative price, competitors' advertising, and so on.

For each possible pair of test and control areas, using the back data, calculate for each period the *ratio of your sales shares in the different test areas and control*. Call this the *test ratio*. It removes national effects like a competitors' list price change. Plot it over time. Ideally, the ratio averages one, meaning you have the same sales share in test as in control. Also ideally, the ratio varies very little, meaning that the two are influenced in the same way by the same factors.

In practice, the test area will be slightly biased. It shows a sales share consistently slightly higher (or lower) than control. This is not fatal provided the bias is not large. A large bias makes extrapolation of the test to the control area difficult to believe. What matters more is the variability of the ratio. Calculate its coefficient of variation (CoV). The test-and-control pair to choose is the one with an acceptable bias and the lowest CoV.

If all the CoVs are high, can you explain movement in the ratio by a regression against the ratios of the different possible factors? For example, relative price in test, divided by relative price in control, may be an explainer. If you can explain most of the movement in the ratio in this way then you may still get a readable test, provided you continue to use this explainer in the way described below.

If you do use some of the explaining factors, a plot of the residual from the regression shows us how variable the ratio is, once you have allowed for the explainers. The effective CoV is now calculated from the amount of variation unexplained by the regression. The lower the variation, the more readable the test. This means you will reach a conclusion more quickly, or a smaller difference will be determined as significant.

When you apply the whole of this process you can raise the efficiency of a test remarkably. You have agreed in advance what to measure and what success is. You have allowed for the effects of seasonality, of category-wide changes and area differences – all factors which can ruin tests. You have picked the test and control areas which give the best chance of reading and extrapolating from the test. If other factors affect results, like competitor's pricing, you have allowed for them.

8.12.3 Experiments: Analysis

You can now calculate how long the test is likely to last, in order to give us a usable result. If this is unrealistic, drop the test. In order to explain the calculation, I must first describe how the test will be evaluated.

During the test, as each period's data arrives, you add to the file of test ratios and of those variables which you have found to be useful, explainers of the test ratio in the analysis of the base period. You carry out a regression in which the log of the test ratio is the dependent variable, the logs of the explainers are the independent variables plus a dummy variable.

The dummy variable is zero during the base period, and taken to be one during the test period (other shapes of response than a step-up can be used). Its coefficient, say i, tells us by how much log sales increased during the test period. The ratio of sales in the test period, compared with the base period, allowing for the other effects in the equation, is estimated by $\exp\{i\}$; or, the proportional increase is $\exp\{i\} - 1$. Comparing this with the success measure, you see whether the test has been successful. It is likely you will not rely only on the numbers analysed here, but some qualitative data will be collected to throw light on how the test variable is working.

The plot of ratios over time should show a step up when the test starts, and the average ratio during the test should exceed the ratio during the base period, by the success measure at least. That is, if no factors were used as explainers. If explainers were used, it is the residual from the regression you should plot.

You can now answer the question, before the test, of how long you expect it to last. Suppose you have observed enough periods before the test to assume that the coefficient of variation is exactly determined (if the number of periods is small, so you have to allow for the CoV being only an estimate, the sum is more complicated, using an F-statistic). Pick the appropriate t-value for a one or two-sided test, and for the significance level required. Multiply this by the CoV and then divide by the success measure (the percentage change in sales share decided as commercially viable). Square the result. This is the number of periods which you expect the test to last in order to reach statistical significance.

This is because, if the number of periods required is n, then the coefficient of variation of the observed average ratio is CoV / √n. This is multiplied by the t value to give the percentage sales change which will just be significant.

In practice, and if you are doing a lot of testing, it is worth writing a program which outputs the number of periods for which the test is expected to last. The input will be the calculated SoV before the test, the number of periods used in this calculation, whether the test is one or two-sided, and the percentage sales change anticipated. The table output shows a number of different CoVs and sales changes. This is more useful than a single figure. The reasons are because you may have to choose between several test-and-control alternatives; the manager may decide on a different success measure after he has seen the table – one he is more likely to find significant within a reasonable time.

Once the test has been agreed and starts to run, you return to the analysis you do each period, until you are satisfied that the results are positive – or until it is clear that the results are not going to reach the success level.

8.13 Single-Source Data

8.13.1 Single Source: What is it?

Up to this point, the data used to measure sales (panel, audit or point of sale), have been collected separately from the numbers about advertising exposure (BARB panel, National Readership Survey, and so on). For many years we have hoped to get better information about the effects of advertising from shoppers who tell us about both their purchases and their media exposure. Such data is called Single Source.

This sort of information does exist, though it is exceptional. Diaries were used in the 1960s and 1980s for this purpose, but data collection has become more mechanised. Set meters and people meters for the TV numbers are now common, and purchases can be recorded at point of purchase electronically, or by a 'wand' in the home, which is used on the bar codes. Details and comments on the subject are in the Appendix.

Single Source offers a special way to detect the effect of advertising exposures on brand purchase – you know what advertising each shopper saw, and you know what she bought. Apparently you have only to compare one with the other. The comparison is in fact quite difficult to make.

This section describes a way of studying TV advertising effects on the choice of grocery brands, using Single Source. This subject is more controversial, and less understood, than the study of separate sources. It is clear how the findings from normal data should be aggregated when movements over time are studied: category totals, brand shares, average prices, actual ratings, and so on, either for the whole sample or for specific segments. In the earlier sections of this chapter you were able to compare factors like price and ratings with sales, only because they happened on the same timescale. The pressure from advertising was high; people then bought more; other factors could not explain all the increase – this is a summary of most of the arguments so far.

Similar summaries exist for Single Source, as is shown below, but these do not utilise its special characteristic – that individual advertising exposures and purchase decisions can be studied for the same people. How connections between the two should be analysed is not obvious. In the rest of this book I have ignored the detailed analysis of individuals in a panel. I am forced to it here because there is no other way to take advantage of this special feature of the data.

8.13.2 Single Source: Description and Influences on Purchase

When you review the information available to describe how the brand is doing, you will realise that Single Source, just like the other sources described in Chapter 7, contains a lot more than information about viewing your campaign and your brand share. Note also that if you have separate information, you should use it too – product changes or launches, changes in copy, general movements in the way the category is made up, economic conditions, and so on.

Consider what the raw data consists of for an individual shopper. When she makes a purchase in the category, you know the brand chosen. You also know the size of the pack, the price paid and whether some promotion was recorded. For each day before this occasion, you know if she was 'exposed' to TV advertising, for any brand in the category, and how long the exposure was. You also know the demographics of the shopper and of her household.

Think of a single purchase occasion. What might influence the decision to buy your brand? Out of the many ways the data might be used, the following is recommended.

The most important factor which influences the shopper's decision to choose your brand, on any one occasion, is her total purchasing history. For what proportion of *all* buying decisions did she decide on it? Call this the shopper's *brand preference* – it is not the *volume* share studied with normal data, but is derived from the *number* of times she chose or rejected the brand. Is she fairly loyal to the brand, giving it a high proportion of her category requirements? Or loyal to others? Or promiscuous? You also know her weight of purchase in the category, ie whether she is a light or a heavy buyer.

Next is usually the *relative price* of your brand at the time of purchase, compared with the category average. You can sum for each week total volume bought and total price paid (most price promotions and special offers run for a week at least). This is only an average number, and will not apply exactly to individual cases (not in the relevant store, and not for the particular pack size), but experience shows that brand choice is indeed related to this number.

Then should come the *promotional detail*, whether a coupon was available and used, whether there was a two-for-one offer, and so on. Unfortunately, in this data, you know about a promotion only when it was actually taken up, not when it was just on offer, and you will find it hard to determine its influence if you know only about the successes. Promoted and non-promoted decisions can be studied separately. In any case, much of the promotional effect is captured in relative price.

You would like to know about *distribution*, facings and other store activity, but this is not recorded in Single Source. You may have figures from a separate source. Other relevant influences – advertising in other media, for example – may also be separately recorded.

Finally, you know about the shopper's *TV exposure* in detail. You can count her total exposure to all category advertising (in seconds, usually transformed to 30-second equivalents); this tells you her weight of viewing, ie whether she is a light or a heavy viewer. You can create adstocks from her previous exposures to your campaign, for any half life – and you can do the same for competitors in total, or individually. You can if you wish also count the number of exposures she had to your campaign in, say, the seven days before the day of purchase. This is another, and not particularly efficient, way of estimating recent ad exposure, or its current pressure.

As well as the shopper's overall weight of purchase and weight of viewing, you know her household's demographics – whether there are children, the household size, and so on. These general descriptions are often linked to other summary figures: weight of purchase, weight of viewing, and brand preference. Large households buy more, young working people watch less TV, and so on. As pointed out before, in data as it falls there are many associations, few of which are causal. Hence, some tests are suspect. Demographic factors (household size, presence of children, household income, and so on) are often genuine causes.

Before you decide what to do with this database, note that it can be large – the number of category purchases in many analyses can be between 5,000 and 100,000 or more, and the number of variables listed above to describe the circumstances about each purchase occasion can total 30. You may reduce the number of occasions by looking only at households of particular interest, for example excluding those who never bought the brand, who cannot tell us much in this way about the positive effects of advertising (they can still tell us whether advertising exposure is linked to ever buying the brand, but not about the detail within buyers).

Normal data (sales, ratings) are initially made up of even larger data sets, but analysts dealing with brands do not often get into such detail; they are used to dealing with convenient summaries. Perhaps Single Source will have similar agreed summaries one day, but at present the necessary consensus does not exist.

You approach such data in exactly the same way as any other. First, recall what the advertising is *meant* to do – spell out your mental model. Second, use the data to *describe* the situation of the brand and its competitors. Only after that, attempt to quantify or model the effects of the marketing factors. As usual, we expect short-term advertising effects to be smaller than long term, certainly smaller than price and promotions, and in this case considerably smaller than the shopper's habits or loyalty.

Some of the ways the data tell us about the brand's situation are now shown by an example.

Example: Ketchup in BehaviorScan
This American example is chosen because the category is simple and the conclusions are straightforward. The raw data was collected from 636 households over 84 weeks in 1979–81 and consisted of 5,598 purchase occasions. Every nine weeks, on average, shoppers made a decision on which brand to buy.

There were two advertised brands, Heinz and Hunts:

	Brand share %	Relative price	Ratings, per week
Heinz	37	125	55
Hunts	28	96	11
Rest	35	78	–

For this example, suppose the Heinz advertising strategy was twofold: most important was to reassure more loyal users, those who bought Heinz more than any other brand, that they should continue to do so even at its high price (a long-term objective). Second, to persuade irregular buyers, those who normally bought other brands, to try Heinz again (a short-term objective), despite its price and because of its quality.

Even for the brand leader, shoppers did not split simply into buyers and non-buyers. Occasions can be split by the shoppers' brand preferences (this is equivalent to splitting shoppers and weighting by frequency of purchase) into shoppers who never bought Heinz (546 occasions), and then the remainder (5,052), by the share they gave Heinz:

	Never buy	Low share	Medium share	High share
No. of occasions	546	1,684	1,684	1,684
Brand share %	0	10	32	89

For the remaining analyses of occasions, look only at the 90% of occasions for shoppers who ever bought Heinz.

An important table tells us whether the shoppers' weight of viewing is linked with the share of purchases they give Heinz:

Viewing	Light	Medium	Heavy
Brand share %	48	43	40

Light viewers are the group most likely to buy Heinz. Demographics reveal that these tend to be small households; it is logical that the high price of this rare purchase will not put them off as easily as those with very full trolleys in the supermarket who therefore count their pennies. A number measures this: the purchase/viewing index. The index divides 40 in the table above by 48, and multiplies the result by 100. The larger the result is, then the more heavy viewing is associated with choosing the brand; this is called a positive index. If the result is 100, there is no association. In this case the index is 83, indicating a noticeable negative bias.

The calculation just shown is a way of summarising the association of two variables, as were Figures 10 and 11 in Section 6.6 (scatter diagrams of volume share against price and distribution at the time). Indeed I could show here a plot like those, and I could have used an index there rather than show the detail in the figures. The reason for preferring the plot then was that the few exceptional points are easy to see and might repay investigation. Here the numbers are large and it is the general association which is of more interest.

Example (continued)

A similar summary is to look at the brand shares for each of three groups of occasions divided by relative price at the time:

Relative price	Low	Medium	High
Brand share %	50	43	38

The association of low price with high share is obvious and expected.

The last part of the general description given here looks more carefully at the loyalty of Heinz buyers and contrasts it with Hunts. It also asks a marketing question: Are coupons used most by more loyal users, or by irregular buyers? In other words, do coupons support the long or the short-term objectives?

The share of category requirements of each shopper which Heinz meets is now divided into 12 groups: none, all, and 10 inbetween (more than none but less than 0.1, 0.1 and more but less than 0.2, and so on). The occasions are now sorted into these groups and Figure 29 is drawn. This gives the results for Hunts as well.

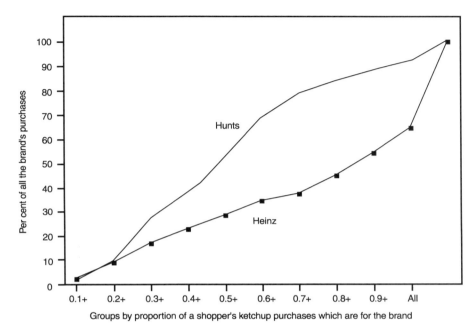

Figure 29 **Individual Loyalties and the Shares of
a Brand's Purchases**

This shows the percentage of all the brand's purchases for which each group is responsible, cumulating the results for loyalties less than 0.1, less than 0.2, and so on. A brand which gets a high share of its sales from loyal shoppers (here Heinz) is a strong brand (it is not a coincidence that Heinz has a higher Consumer Brand Equity). It gets a lower share from the irregular buyers, therefore starts low on the left-hand side, stays to the right of weaker brands, and climbs steeply on the right.

From shoppers who gave Heinz less than half their purchase decisions, the brand got only 28% of its turnover. For Hunts, such shoppers are responsible for over half its turnover. Conversely, from shoppers who gave Heinz more than half their purchase decisions, the brand got nearly three-quarters of its turnover. Hunts got less than half.

Now look at the way Heinz coupons were used. First, there were not very many. Only 9% of sales were with a coupon, but 28% of Hunts sales were with a coupon. From shoppers who gave Heinz less than half their purchase decisions, 13% were made with a coupon; from the rest, only 6%.

This meant over half of all coupons were used by loyal buyers, many of whom would have bought Heinz anyway. From one point of view, with over half its coupons Heinz was giving money away. But consider the company's aims – to maintain a high average price and to keep its loyal customers. The cost of this small present may well have been worthwhile.

Just under half of all coupons were used by irregular buyers, but the 13% of their purchases made this way meant that Heinz was getting them to try the brand again occasionally.

This is a good mix of coupon results, contributing to both the long and short term.

8.13.3 Single Source: Weekly Summary

Another summary is by weeks, which results in a file which looks very like the brand file of Section 7.4.4. You have the brand share (of occasions), TV ratings (for the brand and for competitors), relative price and the proportion of purchases made each week with promotions; you could add distribution and other measures if you had these from another source. Advertisement and purchase information for individuals is no longer used: you are back with time series and aggregated data, and you know already how useful those are.

Example: Weekly summary
In the Heinz case, the weekly summary is itself best described by adstock modelling of the sales share, using also relative price and a trend term. This confirms that, as usual, price has a clear though small effect (t was -11.9); there is also a strong, positive trend (t was 4.5) amounting to an increase of 18% each year of the average share (another sign of a strong brand).

Adstock was tried with various half lives; the best fit was with 26 weeks. For Heinz advertising t was 2.4; competitors' advertising effects were negligible. Thus aggregate data suggests that advertising decay rate was of medium length at least, which is not unusual for an infrequently purchased category, a well-known brand and well-established claim (the thickness and flavour of the ketchup). Most of the effect seems to be to reinforce loyalty and to justify price. The advertising effect coefficient and elasticity are now known and can be used as in earlier parts of this chapter.

8.13.4 Single Source: Regression in the Occasions File

Now I return to the occasions file, and ask how the individual brand choices are influenced by advertising and what sizes the effects may be. Although the data could certainly be used to look at long-term effects in ways additional to the weekly summary, this has not yet been done. It is traditional to ask only what the short-term effects are, since the data seems uniquely suited to display this.

Example: Multivariate work in the occasions file
Much the clearest explainer for whether Heinz was bought or not (a variable
which is 1 or 0 represents this) is the shopper's brand preference. Habits are
strong. A regression with this alone explains 49% of the variation (R-squared).
This may not seem large, and much of the variation looks random, ie for reasons
not captured by our explainers. Using the other variables therefore does not improve this much, but the t values for some of the explainers are satisfactory.

Of the short-term half lives tried (between 2 and 14 days), the longest gave
the best fit. The regression chosen showed effects from trend (positive, as in the
weekly summary, and with a similar coefficient), price (once more small but
clear), Heinz adstock (positive) and competitors' (negative). The short-term advertising effect was estimated to be 4% of current sales (this is the coefficient,
times average adstock, as a percentage of Heinz's sales share).

This regression gives information additional to the aggregate, weekly summary. The two agree on trend and price effects. The disaggregate data emphasise
the importance of loyalty to the brand and point to a short-term advertising effect, while the weekly summary indicated a slower rate of decay.

Such regressions can go on to use the adstock + response model of Section
8.8.2, so investigating diminishing returns at the individual level. In this case, a
linear effect was (just) clearer than gently diminishing returns. Since the brand's
2,900 rating points a year (a heavy weight by UK standards) brought its average
adstock up to only 0.55 OTS per week, Heinz is still at a part of the response
curve which is not so far from linear.

8.13.5 Single Source: When the Explainers are Associated

Using data about individuals emphasises the need to allow for confounding
between the variables, the fact that they may be associated. In the aggregated data which is analysed by regression, correlation between variables
did not bias the estimates you made for the size of the effects. The same is
not true for the sort of indices calculated above.

Example: Effects of confounding
The positive effect of advertising found above is not visible if you look at an
over-simple table, where the occasions are divided into groups by the pressure at
the time from Ads14 (the adstock which gives the best overall fit). It is clearly
the shoppers with low exposure to the campaign which have a slightly higher
brand share, as expected from the category viewing analysis above.

Ads14	Low	Medium	High
Brand share %	45.7	42.3	42.2

From the table above you can make an index (as described earlier) of 92,
which is 100 x 42.2/45.7. The fact that it is less than 100 means that more advertising seems to mean less sales.

You may find it surprising that an advertising effect which was positive in
the regressions above is now not merely invisible, but appears to be negative.

That interpretation would be over-hasty. Category viewing is a very strong influence on whether the shopper has a low or high Ads14 on any occasion; brand preference is the major influence on whether the brand is bought. The two are associated, and this is a major reason why the index above is below 100. You have to look within the multivariate detail to understand this.

This point can be further demonstrated by repeating the calculation of the index within two equal-sized groups of occasions: those for shoppers with a low brand preference (averaging 14%), and those with a high preference (73%). The result is an index of 125 for the shoppers with a low share, 99 for those with a high share. For the more loyal buyers, a short-term ad effect is not visible; it is those who do not usually buy Heinz that recent ad exposure seems to persuade more.

Again, there is a surprise here. How can an index of 125 and of 99 seem to have an 'average' of 92? The answer is so important it is worth spelling it out with the actual numbers. First, how many occasions were there?

Brand preference	Low	High	Total
Ads14 high	894	787	1,681
Ads 14 low	762	923	1,685

This table shows the purchase/viewing bias: 787 and 762 are lower than 894 and 923.

Next, on how many of these occasions was Heinz bought?

Brand preference	Low	High	Total
Ads14 high	142	567	709
Ads 14 low	97	673	770

From these two tables, you may calculate the brand shares and so the index for the apparent effect of Ads14. Note that this is only an indication, as further interactions with price and competitors' advertising have not been taken into account.

Brand preference	Low	High	Total
Ads14 high	16%	72%	42%
Ads 14 low	13%	73%	46%
Index	125	99	92

Another reason for the initially surprising index of 92 lies in the timing of a price increase and of heavier advertising. The weekly summary showed that part way through these weeks there was a step-up in average price. Probably to lessen the bad volume effects of this rise, advertising was increased before and during the increase. Some sales were nevertheless lost at this time. The outcome was that for the heaviest adstock occasions the sales share was lower than average.

The net of the Heinz case history is that both short and medium-term advertising effects have been measured. More has been learned about the kind of households in which the short-term effect is produced. Coupon effects are also clearer. The interactions of brand preference, household size, price and viewing weight would never have been seen without Single-Source data.

An aside is that any attempt to analyse an advertising effect by directly linking recent ad exposure with more decisions to buy would have been misleading, since it would have suggested a negative association. A purchase/viewing bias is the main reason in this case.

9 Combining Marketplace Analysis and Brand Budget

Since it has often been said that advertising cannot be evaluated by its behavioural and financial effects, this chapter starts with examples which show that it can. These lead to a structure for dealing with your own case, a series of questions which determine whether you are easily able to show you have accounted for your investment, or whether you are in a more complex situation. The manager should be encouraged by the simplicity of many of these solutions to the accountability question.

If the analyst has constructed a successful model, as described in the last chapter, then the manager and analyst can do more. They can consider possible scenarios for the year or more ahead, and improve their recommendations about, for example, the size and timing of the advertising investment.

Accountability to senior management and finance is achieved by the combination of a satisfactory explanation of the past, and convincing arguments about future plans.

9.1. Case Histories

It has so often been said that communications *cannot* be made accountable that it is appropriate to start this chapter with some examples of success. After encouraging optimism with these case histories, I go through the possibilities methodically.

The examples are the same as those used in Chapter 7 when campaign evaluation was introduced. The reference numbers are again to the volume number of *Advertising Works* followed by the paper number (given in the contents list of each volume and at the head of each paper). In some of the papers real profit figures were kept confidential so the sums given there are sometimes incomplete. Of course you will not have to be guarded, as these authors were, in describing actual marginal profit levels and other figures.

9.1.1 Case Histories: Volume Increase

These cases are for straightforward calculations of sales increases. Other aspects are mentioned below, but how the extra volume was calculated, and the comparisons with costs, are simple.

Abelour (8/16) is a malt whisky from Speyside whose 1989 press campaign was a mix of direct and theme advertising. It offered a hogshead (360 bottles) at £1,350, to be delivered in 1999. At the time of writing, the sale of 175 hogsheads was reported, 64 by coupon. These sales were at a higher profit than if the whisky had been used in blends. Counting only the 64, and the difference in profit, the advertising paid off. There were other hogshead sales, new distribution for bottles was achieved in supermarkets, and there were applications of the idea in other countries – all of which added to profit.

In Scotland, milk advertising by the *National Dairy Council* (8/19) was aimed at 10 to 15-year-olds from April to March, 1994. Knowing their rate of consumption before the campaign, and assuming this would have continued, added sales were calculated and multiplied by profit per bottle. The advertising paid for itself three times over.

By running television advertising in 1990 and 1991 for *Whipsnade Wild Animal Park* (7/14), incremental revenue from visitors was generated. Running costs were hardly affected so this is added to profit. The increase exceeded the advertising cost. Also, sponsorship deals were thought to be easier to negotiate.

Boddingtons Bitter sales (8/6) were measured in core accounts before and after their advertising. An increase was believed to have taken place in other outlets, and to have lasted after the campaign stopped, but these were not used in the calculation of payback.

Marstons (8/7) is another brewer who estimated consumption before and after advertising. The increase in profit was calculated at three and a half times the advertising cost. In addition, visits to Marston's pubs increased. Whitbread were forced to sell a large proportion of its Marston's holding in 1993 and placed this with institutional investors. The *Financial Times* commented that recent advertising had been an important factor in this placement.

9.1.2 Case Histories: What if? How much to?

By making assumptions about the share of market or the price which a brand would have had without advertising, it is possible to estimate its benefit.

PG Tips (6/1) was relaunched in 1955. Then and for most of 1956 it was the number four brand and average in price. What would have happened if it had stayed in that position or risen only to number two? Or if it had stayed in this price bracket? These situations were compared with its actual volume share and price premium, and the difference turned into a cash estimate.

Lanson Champagne (6/4) was switched to a new distributor and a new agency was appointed in 1985. Its actual performance up to 1989 can be compared with what would have happened if it had performed in line with the total champagne category – or if it had been in line with its most direct *Grande Marque* competitors.

Another way of making the same point is to work in reverse. Rather than calculate extra profit and show that it exceeded the cost, it is possible to calculate how much the difference in behaviour must have been to be profitable, and then to make the case that the actual effects were larger.

The *Health Education Authority* ran HIV/Aids advertising between 1988 and 1993 (8/3) which cost £15.4 million. From the cost of treating an individual with Aids it was possible to calculate that the investment paid back if it prevented 51 cases of HIV infection a year. The numbers presented, it was claimed, indicated that 'it is likely the commitment has been more than justified'.

9.1.3 Case Histories: Lifetime Value

In some categories it is inappropriate to count only the profit made during the campaign or soon afterwards. Converting someone to the brand can be shown to produce revenue, on average, for many years. The examples now given estimate this benefit.

Perhaps tampons are an extreme category in this respect, since loyalty is established very early and is fiercely held to. *Lil-lets* (6/14) advertised their Mini variant in 1988–89 in the teenaged press with a bias towards 10 to 14-year-olds. Their normal profit calculations were based on over 30 years of use of the brand but in this case payback was planned over three to six years. An advertising spend in one year of £453,000 was calculated to bring in incremental profit in millions of pounds.

Alliance & Leicester (6/17) lent a first-time buyer in 1989 on average £33,000 on which they made a gross profit in the first year of £440–£990, depending on commission earnings on the endowment policy and insurance. On average these loans last five years, and in each of the rest of these the profit is between £490–£540. The majority are replaced immediately with a second loan, and most of these are with the same lender. A range of estimates was generated, based on only the first five years, on various assumptions and between £4 million and £28 million, with a best estimate of £16 million. Since the advertising cost was £3 million, the return was clearly positive.

Scottish Amicable (7/18) believe that its annual policies have a typical life of 20 to 25 years. Using pessimistic figures, the total profit from business attributed to their 1990–91 campaign was 100 times the cost.

Amnesty (6/13) estimate that recruits brought in by advertising have a greater probability of renewing membership than other members as they are likely to have a deeper commitment. But even if they follow the pattern of the average member they are more likely than not to renew at the end of the first year, and, even after six years, renewal probability is about 40%. It is therefore possible to extend the average income per member of £12.87 over a number of years. Taking six years only, an advertising investment of £82,000 returned £115,000. This compares favourably with total income from an alternative investment with the best commercially available interest rate: £91,000.

British Telecommunication's Call Waiting service (7/13) data suggest a retention level of over 90% a year. Even at the conservative figure of 75%, advertising for Call Waiting in 1991 covered its costs in just over a year.

The *Health Education Board for Scotland* (8/18) advertised on television a booklet 'You Can Stop Smoking', and a telephone helpline. They estimated that 6% of adult smokers used the helpline and (based on a panel run for a year) that there was a 1.4% reduction in adult smokers. This compares with an annual average of 0.8%. The real benefit is the 'life-years gained by quitters ... the value of which to them, their families and friends is inestimable'. A cost was however calculated from costs to the National Health Service, and losses of working days, from smoking-related illnesses. These are conservatively put at £238 per smoker. There were 8,400 additional quitters, so the saving from a campaign costing £654,000 is put at £1.35 million.

9.1.4 Case Histories: Price Premium

When a product is deliberately positioned to consumers at a premium price, a 'triangular relationship' can be set up between the brand, the consumer and the retailer. The consumer accepts that the price is high, believing that the quality and reliability are to match and knowing that to purchase the brand is to make a statement about himself and his ability to pay. The latter is especially true for publically purchased and consumed products: cars, clothes, drink, and so on. The benefit of branding to the purchaser is often much more emotional than physical, but none the less real for that. At the same time, the retailer can make an above average profit so is encouraged to stock and display, and will himself pay the manufacturer an above-average price. The justification for communications is likely to come from the price premium, provided volume does not suffer.

Stella Artois (7/7) faced the problem of getting distribution in the free on-trade, since this meant putting another lager font on the bar. The argument about extra profit to the publican was key. The extra retail price paid for the advertising which told both consumer and retailer that the brand was expensive. Between 1983 and 1989 total outlets doubled, with free-trade volume growth at 140%. The premium in the wholesale price was between 4 and 6% above competition, averaging £7.50 a barrel. When this is multiplied by turnover, the result was about twice the media cost.

The first *CICA* trainers for children (8/9) from *Clarks Shoes* were made and advertised in 1991. They were not significantly different from their existing own label products, except in price. Value was indeed added, and volume rose above the pre-campaign level. The additional revenue justified the advertising. This ignores other benefits: the volume would probably have fallen without advertising, like other trainers, so the comparison with the pre-level is cautious; prices of competitors fell and it is unlikely that this drop could have been resisted; longer-term revenue from the new brand is ignored; CICA brands for adults and for infants were later launched.

9.1.5 Case Histories: Statistical Analyses

These do not have to be complex. In fact the examples start with very simple cases where the calculations are straightforward.

Doorstep deliveries of milk were in decline in 1990 at 0.43% of total milk sales per month. The *National Dairy Council* (7/1) were able to calculate what sales would have been without the advertising they ran in May to December 1991, and hence the sales added by their campaign. The profit from these sales was 12p per bottle, not allowing for other sales made by the milkman or the higher volume bought when milk is delivered. In comparison with the cost of the advertising, 'our wildest dreams were exceeded'.

For *Volkswagen Golf* (7/5), what sales would have been in 1988–90 could be calculated on the assumption that it experienced the decline normally experienced by other models. From the known profit per car, let alone possible extra replacement sales after this purchase, the benefit was shown to be three times the advertising cost.

Optrex (7/8) evaluated their increased advertising in 1983–91 in conventional ways (overall volume share increase, an upweight test in the HTV region), but they also modelled the effects of price and stock changes. They concluded that advertising had reduced the price sensitivity of Optrex, thus allowing them to take price increases. Good stock levels at pharmacists generally result in higher sales, as counter staff select from what is on the back shelves. Advertising also reduced sensitivity to this factor, so that Optrex's reduced share of stocks did them less harm. The financial effects of these factors could be calculated. Other benefits, not used in the calculation of payback, were in excluding potential rival brands and in improving their own new product development potential.

K Shoes (7/15) produced a model for the volume sales of women's washable leather trainers. This depended on seasonality and on the cover of the advertising and gave an excellent fit to weekly sales through their shops. Running the model without the advertising term gave a lower sales figure. The difference is attributed to advertising: 56,730 extra pairs (allowing for sales through independent retail stores). The advertising cost was equivalent to £4.72 per pair, and since the marginal contribution per pair was larger than this, the campaign was profitable.

Alliance & Leicester (7/19) modelled net receipts for 71 months between 1986 and 1991. The explainers included an adstock term (TV ratings allowing for decay over time), as well as financial indices and an allowance for promotions. The extra net receipts due to the short-term effects of TV advertising can be estimated at £656 million. There were press advertising effects which were difficult to separate out from the natural effect of launches. Reduced sensitivity to interest rate changes, and longer-term income from new savers were also not allowed for.

Survey data were used to estimate of the increased 'acceptability' of the society. There were twice as many people prepared to do business with the Alliance and Leicester after the 1987–91 campaign, which translated into an increased share of total building society customers. The larger savings balance due to this growth could be calculated. The increased gross profit from lending was £93 million and the advertising cost was £22 million.

Roses (8/4) have seasonal sales peaks which coincide with advertising peaks. It looks hard to disentangle cause and effect here. A model was written which unusually took only the Christmas data, but did so over ten years and individually in nine regions. From this data, an elasticity was estimated, both for price and for advertising. The advertising effect could then be calculated, at 36,709 extra tonnes. Using the cost of advertising, the minimum profit for breakeven per tonne sold could be worked out. The real contribution was considerably more.

Canned *Boddingtons* (8/6) sales growth from 1991 to 1994 was largely due to distribution growth. This can be allowed for by looking at its rate of sale, where it had distribution. This in turn was modelled, using as explainers its own advertising, competitors' advertising, price and seasonality. Thus the additional rate of sale due to its own advertising could be estimated. Additional volume is then obtained on multiplying by distribution. During the campaign evaluated, the added sales were estimated at 62,818 barrels. However, because delay in the effects of advertising had been estimated by adstock modelling, it was possible to calculate what additional sales were created by this advertising after it had appeared, and this grew the estimate to 94,341 barrels. Meanwhile, growth in the total canned bitter sector was only modest.

The campaign benefited both the bitter (described above) and the canned products. The cost was £7.3 million. The minimum profit per barrel needed to pay back was exceeded. Two additional benefits are not counted in: being able to charge above average despite being a weaker beer than the competition, and the distribution growth achieved by canned Boddingtons.

9.1.6 Case Histories: Conclusions

Reviewing all these examples, you will see three common themes.

First, they are all comparisons of money paid out with money taken in. They talk the language which the manager and the finance director understand. They are not about awareness, improvements in survey scores, brand penetration, and so on. These are not needed here, useful though they are in explaining *how* the campaign worked, in making it more effective next time and in adding conviction that it really was the campaign which had these effects.

Second, only a single benefit is costed in each case, most often volume sales which would not have been achieved without the campaign. Other advantages are described, but are not part of the accountability. Remember that these are case histories of outstanding success. In real life you cannot always be as cavalier with other benefits: you may have to cost these too in order to make a successful case.

Similarly, estimates are often conservative in the case histories. A range may be given: 'We could have brought in £X to £Y, but even at £X we made a profit.' You cannot always afford to work with the lowest possible figures.

Third, these cases naturally all look backwards. Analysis usually contributes most when it helps forward planning.

There are five main ways to show accountability:

(a) There is an *obvious improvement in sales volume* during the campaign, and costing that volume at the marginal profit rate shows you brought in more than you spent.

(b) You may need a *more roundabout way of showing what 'improvement' means*: it may mean an argument about what sales 'would have been'.

(c) The improvement may *not be only during the campaign*. Perhaps you have been able to calculate what its effect was, or would have been, after the campaign stopped. Or, the individuals affected may reliably be expected to provide a profit stream for years to come.

(d) It may *not be volume, or not volume alone*, which benefited. You may argue that the price you were able to charge was higher than it would have been. The examples in Section 9.1.4 showed price deliberately set high: it was part of the brand essence. This is not the same as adjustments upward in price, which may put the brand above average but are not meant to make it seem expensive. See Section 9.7.1 on this point.

(e) Statistical analysis, or *modelling*, may allow us to estimate the size of an effect.

These are possible ways you can check when it comes to your own communications.

9.2 The Easy Case

When you look back at the marketplace results of a campaign, you hope to find that advertising is identified as the source of a rapid volume increase, which pays for the cost of the campaign.

The ways you may have measured such an increase were described in the last two chapters. Direct response is one clean way to see a return, but it can be apparent with sales through retailers too. An experiment is a method hard to argue with, but a blip on the sales plot may be equally clear.

It is of course not enough to look only at the additional revenue or income generated. You have to allow in nearly every case for extra costs involved in making and distributing the additional volume. This is the whole point of the variable costs discussed in Chapter 4. Fixed costs are going to be ignored: you are operating at the margin.

You know the marginal rate of revenue from extra sales. You multiply the extra volume by this revenue rate and get the extra contribution (after the costs of production, distribution, and so on). If the cost of the campaign is less than this, you have made money.

Example: A simple evaluation
In Section 7.6, you estimated in Example 1 that advertising was responsible for an extra 2,000 units per week. After four weeks you have generated 8,000 units at a marginal revenue of £100 each. The cost of the campaign was £600,000. This is less than the total marginal revenue of £800,000 so the advertising was profitable.

There are no serious problems in these cases. There could be some uncertainty about the size of the extra volume, or debate about the overall cost of the campaign – staff time involved, production costs, and so on, as well as media spend.

It can also be easy to extend a historical finding to the decision about the next campaign. It may be a reasonable judgment that a similar result can be expected, that costs will not have changed much, and so further investment is justified.

9.3 Other Simple Benefits

There may be other advantages which you can attribute to the campaign, and which were also felt almost immediately. These are to do with your own staff and sales representatives, and other sales tools you employ, plus the reactions of retailers.

Most of these cannot be easily costed: improved morale, the use of an advertising theme in a promotion, the more effective performance of this promotion, greater co-operation of retailers. A few may have obvious value: more favourable trade terms for example.

Others may be given some vague future value: higher distribution, better penetration of category purchasers, or purchasers getting familiar with new uses of the product. These may be detectable in sales terms as a rising trend.

If the direct and immediate return was shown to be a profit, you will probably not spend much time thinking about these other results. What happens when you do *not* seem to get back the advertising investment? It may then be that some of these benefits make the difference between judging you are in loss, or in profit. This can happen even with direct response. The immediate return may not be all that should be taken into account: you could also be storing up goodwill of some kind.

If the margin between profit and loss is small, it may be reasonable to do a very rough costing of the benefits to show that, overall, the advertising contributed enough to take us into profit. Or, to ask the *'how much to?'* question described below. You may find that a modest assumption is enough to show that pay-back is more than likely, without having to work it out exactly.

> *Example: A small profit gap*
> Suppose that in the previous example, the advertising cost was instead £850,000. There is a gap of £50,000 between this and the marginal revenue of £800,000.
>
> The manager may well say, 'We opened a new retail account as a result of this campaign. That makes the exercise worthwhile.' Or, 'We've only got to shift 500 more units in the next week or two to break even. I'm sure the advertising has put us in a position to do that.'

9.4 The Normal Case

But if the gap between investment and short-term return is large – and it often is – then the real work starts. There can be a further problem when you cannot easily assume that the future will be very like the past, so you have also to do serious forecasting in order to take responsible decisions.

These are the situations now tackled. The easy case is no longer assumed.

Some reminders must first be issued. You have to remember the business objectives, discussed in Chapter 2, where 'worthwhile' was defined. It is often the case that immediate profit improvement is not the only, or even most important, criterion. Volume and sometimes other criteria may also have been specified – for example to establish a new brand in the marketplace, to get adequate distribution, or to raise awareness on which you can capitalise later in some way. The question which management is asking is not just, 'Did we make a profit from the advertising?', it may be, 'Was the combination of volume with profit or loss satisfactory – taking also other outcomes into account?'

You have to review the other factors affecting your sales – and your ideas about exactly how advertising affects your brand in the marketplace. The reasons are not only that factors like price, distribution and competitors' promotions have to be allowed for in estimating what advertising really achieved. Your other marketing activities should be evaluated because they may be alternative investments to advertising. It is no use saying advertising does not pay off, if it nevertheless achieves management objectives more economically than other means, and the cost is considered worthwhile. 'Being accountable' means doing the job at the price agreed. An advertised new product launch, for example, may not have made money at the end of its first year. Advertising money could still have been well-spent. You have however to decide whether another activity – sampling, for example – would have been a better or worse investment.

9.5 What if ? How much to?

Just as there were simple descriptive estimates of the size of an effect at the end of Chapter 7, there are equally simple questions which appear to make the accountability decision quite easy – and on occasions will do so.

An example of this approach is: 'What would our situation be if we could charge only the same price as Brand X?' You extend your volume sales at this price and see how much worse off you would be. The argument depends on the belief that, without advertising, this is all you could charge. There had better be some evidence of the way advertising supports your price, and of the volume you would sell at a different price, for this method to be convincing.

Another form of the same argument is '*how much to?*' An example was given above, and another follows. This calculates what difference in price would justify the adspend, and compares this with prices in the category.

Example: Own label price
For your brand, the price at retail level in 1995 was £5.38 per kilo, while own label charged £4.33. Your actual revenue, after retailer margin, was £94,976k. Suppose you could charge only the price own label does. The revenue would fall by £18,700k. This compares with your advertising cost, including production, of £4,455k. 'Clearly' the revenue difference justifies the spend.

Or, starting the argument at the other end, your media spend including production, divided by volume sales of 24,167 tonnes, was £184 per tonne or 18p per kilo. In theory, with no advertising, you 'could' reduce your price to retailers of £3.93 per kilo by 4.6%. If they passed on all this reduction to consumers, the cost at retail level could fall by this proportion and you should gain in volume. Even if sales stayed level you would break even.

These arguments are hypothetical. They have only to be spelled out for their weaknesses to become clear. You would never drop your price to the level of own label and, if you did, your volume would hardly be the same in the convulsions which would follow, since retailers would certainly retaliate. For example, they could simply maintain the consumer price and pocket the difference. Until such sums have been tested in retailer negotiation and in extended field tests, they are not worth much. The effect of advertising cuts is explored later through the modelling results and this is the approach recommended.

You may also ask how much volume would have to change to justify the advertising.

Example: The volume equivalent of advertising
Your adspend in 1995, including production, was £4,455k. At the gross margin of £1,790 per tonne, this is equivalent to 4,455,000 / 1,790 = 2,489 tonnes or 9.7% of your volume.

Do you believe that advertising 'produced' more or less than 9.7% of your volume? To put this amount into context, your volume increase in 1995 was 7%. It is credible to say that such a proportion could be put down to advertising.

Again, this is not a rigorous argument, but it helps you to grasp what is involved. It is just another way of allowing common sense to get a grip on the situation. It also raises the thought, 'if we cut advertising, we'd probably lose *some* sales; could it be as much as this?' In this case the answer looks debatable; there are times when the balance tips more clearly one way.

Another application is to the rate of change of volume. 'We have grown at X% a year. How much would the rate of growth have to be without advertising to make the same profit?' Or, 'Sales are steady. How much decline would justify being without advertising?'

So far, all the argument has been about the advertising decision. Other activities can be evaluated in a similar way. Since price is one of the major decisions, the way this combines with the budget is now discussed.

227

Look again at the marketplace data in Figure 10, about the relation between price (relative to competitors) and volume share. In this case other influences have been less important than price, and the points on this plot can be taken broadly to represent price effects, plus the inevitable variation due to 'other factors', which was dissected in Chapter 8. How do these points look, from the point of view of profit? How much should the price be, to keep us at the current rate of profit?

On a plot which shows price and volume, each point determines a profit rate (if nothing changes but these two variables). A contour line can be drawn, showing the positions which all return the same profit. Above this line, profit is higher; below, it is lower. This is not a *prediction* of the relation between relative price and volume share – that sort of line was drawn in Figure 27. This is a *calculation* of the volume share needed, for any relative price, to give the stated profit. If several lines are drawn, movement on the plot may be seen to cross contour lines and so change profit.

Price changes, and projected sales and profit movements from these changes, can now be judged visually. When the method is used to examine the effect of promotions on this plot, the results can be striking. A typical finding is that the sales share did rise, but not enough: the promoted period fell down the profit contours.

Example: Profit contours on the price–sales plot
The budget for 1995 in Section 4.2 may be written in a different form. Put X for relative price, currently at 107.3. Put Y for sales share, currently at 14.44%. The current revenue rate is £3,930 per tonne sold to retailers, but at X we suppose the revenue rate is $(X / 107.3) \times 3,930$. The sales share is derived from marketplace data, where the category size is estimated to be 133,900 tonnes; at the factory gate sales are 1.25 times as high (due to under-reporting by the consumer data source), so the real category size is 25% higher, at 167,400 tonnes. This allows your volume sales in the budget to be written as $(Y / 100) \times 167,400$.

It is now possible to write the budget, in £k, as:

$$\text{revenue} - \text{variable cost} - \text{other costs} = \text{profit}$$

where the three terms on the left are respectively

$$\text{revenue} = (Y / 100) \times 167,400 \times (X / 107.3) \times 3,930$$

$$\text{variable cost} = (Y / 100) \times 167,400 \times 2,140$$

$$\text{other costs} = 26,025 + 3,930 + 1,575 = 31,530$$

You may check that when the current values of X and Y are used, profit is correctly calculated as £11,700k.

Now write P for profit and, using the identities above, rearrange the budget equation as

$$Y = (31{,}530 + P) / (61.31X - 3{,}582)$$

This curve may be plotted for any value of P. An example is given in Figure 10 for a profit of £12 million, close to the current level. Other contours may be drawn for other P; for steps of £1 million, they turn out to be about one-third of a market share point apart.

Look at Figure 10 to see how your actual points fall (the calculated line using the measured price elasticity, and explained in Section 8.6.3, runs through the centre of these points and indicates the same result). For relative prices below 106, the points move sharply above the contour. For relative prices above 109, they move below it. In periods 9406, 9508 and 9509 the profit rate was well above £12 million; for 9404, 9412 and 9511 it was well below.

This is only another way of saying that marketplace elasticity is above break-even, and if other things were equal the price should be reduced, but seeing the contour and the actual points on the same plot brings the point home.

9.6 Effects Beyond the Campaign Period

You may use the *how much to?* approach to work out what the lifetime value of a new customer has to be, in order to make up the difference between immediate revenue and total advertising cost. You count not only what the customer spent in the campaign period, but what experience shows a new customer spends on average in total. This argument is particularly relevant in business-to-business, and to buyers of financial products, white goods and cars.

This is only one of the ways you need to think about the time after the campaign ends. To credit advertising in a copy or weight test with additional sales only during the test is to underestimate its effects. In a summary of 44 BehaviorScan tests, it was found that an average increase in year one of 22% was followed by a second year of sales which were still 14% above average, even though there was no unusual advertising then. Sales were also 7% higher in year three. The mechanism was probably that the floating base or 'natural' share of the brand had been raised in year one, and this took time to fall back to the national level. The result was that the return from the campaign was twice that which would have been traditionally allowed.

The description of adstock in Chapter 8 makes it clear that you expect effects after the period of the campaign. The amount depends on the half life of the advertising and on the length of the campaign. With a short half life and a campaign lasting a few months, there will be only a small proportion of the effect seen after this time. But with a half life of 26 weeks, and a brief burst of two or three weeks, a quarter of the overall effect follows more than a year later.

9.7 Indirect Effects

Some of the indirect benefits of advertising may be quantifiable, while for others it would be difficult to do so. Even so, they should not be omitted from discussion. This is especially the case when other calculations do not justify the adspend and you are searching round for all likely benefits.

9.7.1 Indirect Effects: Price

The price you charge for your brand has so far not entered the calculation of benefit, except that the higher the price the larger the marginal return.

It may be that the price has changed during the campaign, in which case you have a more complex argument to follow. It could be said, for example, that advertising 'has allowed us to charge a higher price'. Or, that you 'have a low price elasticity' and so suffered little loss in volume when competitors cut price.

Being able to charge a higher price, and affecting volume little or not at all, is often called an 'indirect' benefit, that is, advertising is not acting directly on volume. This is thought to be different from selling more volume at the same price. The distinction is actually not real.

You have to return to earlier discussions (particularly Section 8.7.2) about the volume you expect to sell at different prices and when the brand has increased Consumer Brand Equity. This *may* show in raised volume. Or, you *may* sell about the same volume, because you have simultaneously raised the price.

These two eventualities can be identical benefits. Advertising adds in both cases to equity. The question is only whether you also change the price. You *either* take the higher equity in more volume, *or* in higher price. Note that the two need not have the same profit outcomes or strategic value.

Example: Equity, price and advertising
For your brand, you already know that Consumer Brand Equity rose from 16.6 to 17.3 between 1994 and 1995; that is, by 4.1%. You think this is a possible change you might make again, and you apply it to the 1995 budget in Section 4.2. Should you take the benefit in volume, or use it as an opportunity to raise price and keep volume steady?

You could expect the same proportional increase in volume. This would have increased tonnage sales from 24,167 tonnes by 990 tonnes. Since the gross margin is £1,790 per tonne, this benefits the bottom line by £1.8 million.

On the other hand, volume would have remained steady if you had increased price by 1.35%. You calculate this from the price elasticity of –3 and the volume change in proportion to $1 / 1.041 = 0.961$. That is, the effects of equity improvement and of the price increase would have cancelled each other out. What price p, in proportion to the old price, causes the new volume to be, in proportion to the old volume, 0.961? You solve:

$$\exp\{-3\ln\{p\}\} = 0.961$$

or,
$$\ln\{p\} = \ln\{0.961 / -3\}$$

which gives the new price to be 1.3% above the previous one. More simply, for a 4% drop, with price elasticity –3, you need a price rise of $4 / 3\%$.

Because price elasticity is quite high, this is not a large rise, nevertheless you would have to be cautious about retailers' acceptance of the price increase, and about competitive reaction. The increase applies to all the turnover, so your revenue (after retailer commission) goes up by 0.013 times £95 million or £1.2 million.

In this particular case you would choose to grow volume. It is both safer and more profitable.

9.7.2 Indirect Effects: Internal

Advertising may help inside the firm, especially when it shows customer service, demonstrating for example to telephone, counter or forecourt staff how they should relate with customers. Even for staff who do not deal with the public, there are benefits from increasing pride in the product. Recruiting may be assisted. The solitary representative on the road, far from the office, knows he is not alone. Unless you can quantify such improved staff performance, such benefits are impossible to cost and must be the subject of judgment.

9.7.3 Indirect Effects: Trade

By 'trade' is meant all those who contribute to or handle the product but are not employed by the firm.

Retailers are the most conspicuous example: 'as seen on television' has not completely faded away as an argument for distribution and display. Retailers want products which they believe will be bought by consumers. Suppliers and other middlemen are also affected. If improved distribution has already led to higher sales, or promotions have worked harder than before, you must consider whether some of the gains are due to advertising.

Some of your other activities may use your campaigns, directly or indirectly. Packaging may be more relevantly designed and accepted if the creative content is shared, or the product already more valued because of the advertising. The same applies to promotions and sponsorship.

9.7.4 Indirect Effects: Corporate

The firm may get other advantages than directly from the performance of the product. In the world of acquisitions, mergers, analysts, shareholders and share prices, a reputation can be helped if not built by advertising.

In this book it is generally assumed that the unit on which management concentrates is the brand. But advertising may have also an umbrella function, under which are gathered other sub-brands. Further, it is not only in the financial arena that a company has a value. Increasingly we are following the Japanese concept of the source of products (the company) adding its own value to them, as well as drawing its own worth from them.

Thus, benefits may not be felt only by the brand whose budget is discussed here, but may extend to other brands. These situations can become very complex: launches and range extensions may be more successful because of the company or brand umbrella.

9.7.5 Summary on Indirect and Later Effects

The general approach, when you review the past effects of advertising investment, is now clear. It starts by estimating a volume effect of advertising, over a period similar to the campaign. If this is confused by price changes, then you have to allow for them; for example, by calculating a Consumer Brand Equity and allotting part of the volume change (or stability) to price and part to advertising. You then compare the direct benefit via volume with the cost of the campaign. More work is needed if the cost is greater than the benefit, that is, the direct effect on its own does not meet the brand objectives.

So you list, and attempt to cost, indirect benefits and those later than the campaign period. These have been outlined in Sections 9.6 and 9.7. It may be that one or two of these can be given a cash value and that this closes the gap, in which case the advertising cost is justified.

It may be that the gap still exists, even on an optimistic reckoning. Then the advertising cost has not been paid back. You must ask whether, for strategic reasons, the cost was worth paying. If so, then the advertising investment was worthwhile. Even if it was, could other methods have been more economic?

In each of these three cases, you have achieved accountability in a rigorous and transparent way.

Or it may be that the benefits cannot be costed with sufficient accuracy and that management has to give its opinion. For example, suppose you have been locked in battle with another major advertised brand, both advertising fairly continuously. The category is stable and advertising appears not to gain sales, but it could be dynamic stability. Or suppose you have advertised only at the same time as you have promoted and cannot disentangle with any precision the effects of the two activities.

In such cases – and they are few though important – the formal conclusion of analysis may be non-proven. This fourth case is at least tackled with the facts, and the size of the uncertainty, clearly laid out. You have made your best attempt and there is nothing unusual in forming a judgment.

This sequence of judgments is now laid out as a decision tree:

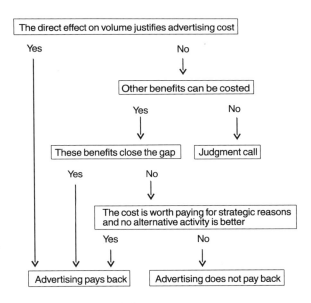

Figure 30 Advertising Accountability

9.8 Benchmarking

The *action* which should be taken by management, after the accountability question has been given a reasonable answer, is beyond the scope of this book because it raises strategy decisions for the company, not tactical decisions for the brand. All that the analyst can do is to provide input for corporate planning.

There is, however, one further step which the analyst can take, which is to benchmark your performance as well as to evaluate it.

Management want to know whether the job has been done well, in comparison with best practice, as well as to make it accountable. That is, you compare your estimate of your advertising's effects with the best guess you can make for your competitors. It makes a difference whether you have failed – but so has everyone else – or whether your work is below standard and that is why you failed. Management is much more likely to call for a fresh try in the second case. There is evidence that the job can be done, it is just that you have not done it very well. And even if you have made money, management will still wonder whether you could have made more.

Example: A comparison of equity changes
For the top three brands in your category, you know the changes in Consumer Brand Equity between 1994 and 1995 – and the media spend for each brand. The details are in Section 8.7.5.

You are not surprised that Brand C, with a recent share of voice of only 3%, has a sharply falling equity. You cannot be complacent that your 24% share of voice grew your equity only 4%, while Brand A, with a share of voice one and a half times yours, grew equity more than one and a half times as fast – and from a higher base.

Management might well call for a review of why Brand A is doing better than us.

9.9 Modelling

There are increasing degrees of complication when you come to combining financial data with modelling. You may be dealing with the current situation, or you may have to forecast because you are looking a year or more ahead. You may use only price and advertising elasticities, summary financial numbers and a simple linear system; you may use these elasticities with a multiplicative model. Note that in this section time is not taken into account (for the effects of advertising to be felt).

The choices are as follows:

(a) Deal with the current year, and look only for guidance on the *direction* to move – more advertising or less, price up or down. This can be done with the linear or with the log model.
(b) Forecast for next year, and agree on a feasible budget, which is what will happen if you buy the same ratings and keep at the same relative price.
(c) Test single alternatives round the feasible budget for next year – the first one to try is the one suggested by the current marketing plan.
(d) More systematically, map out a set of alternatives and evaluate them all.

(e) Finally, and I cover this in Section 9.10, you may include *all* the variables you found to be important when you modelled. You then add financial data, in all its complexity, to the full equation you fitted. And you allow for the effects to feed in gradually over however long it takes.

9.9.1 Modelling: Linear Model – Current Year

You start by evaluating the likely effects of changing your current advertising and pricing policies, by the simplest calculations. They are directionally very important.

You use the model defined in Section 8.6.1 to write down the effects on sales of changing your advertising spend and your relative price; I prove here the results quoted in Chapter 4. The underlying formula is:

$$v = V \left[1 + E_P (p / P - 1) + E_A (a/A - 1)\right]$$

– where v is the sales volume you move to when you change, V is current volume
– where p and P, a and A are similar figures for the price to retailers and for advertising spend
– and where E_P and E_A are the price and advertising elasticities.

You use the budget data for the brand in the form:

$$r = v (p - c) - a - F$$

– where r is the profit you move to
– where c is the marginal cost of one more unit, so (p – c) is gross margin per unit and
– where F is fixed costs.

By differentiation you can write the rate of change in volume sales when you alter p and when you alter a:

$$E_P V / P \text{ and } E_A V / A$$

Similarly, substituting for v in the equation above, for the rate of change in profit:

$$(p - c) E_P V / P + V \text{ and } (p - c) E_A V / A - 1$$

235

From the last expressions you can write the condition that changing price (by a small amount from your current position), makes no difference to profit. This is when

$$(P - c) \, E_P \, V / P = -V \text{ or } E_P = -P / (P - c)$$

In words, this is price per unit divided by gross margin per unit. This value for E_P is called the 'breakeven price elasticity'; note that it is easily determined from a couple of items in the brand budget. It is obviously an important figure, especially when compared with the measured price elasticity in the marketplace. For, if measured price elasticity is larger than breakeven, or $E_P - P / (P - c)$ then you can increase the price you charge and profit will go up.

However, volume will decrease, and you have to balance the overall effects of these two results. You know also by how much profit will go up, or volume go down, at least for small changes.

Exactly the same calculations for adspend give us the breakeven advertising elasticity: $A / [V (P - c)]$.

So an increase in adspend is profitable, locally and short term, if $E_A > A / [V (P - c)]$, or the measured advertising elasticity is greater than adspend divided by [sales volume times gross margin].

Example: Which direction should you go?
In Chapter 4 you used the equations just proved to calculate the breakeven elasticities: price –2.2, advertising 0.09.

In Section 8.6.4, the marketplace price elasticity was –3.0; the long-term model of Section 8.10 suggested –2.8.

Thus your measured elasticity is larger (a bigger number) than breakeven: cutting price should be profitable. There may be other implications and this is not a recommendation.

The advertising elasticity measured in Section 8.6.4 is 0.12 (short plus long term). This too is greater than breakeven. Increasing adspend should be profitable in the long run, cutting adspend loses us money. But in the short term alone, your elasticity is below breakeven. Increasing adspend reduces profit for a short time. In a crisis – and making planned profit at year-end is often treated as a crisis – you improve cash flow by cutting advertising, though you pay for it later on. All too often this is next year and someone else's worry.

These comparisons, of actual or marketplace elasticities with the breakeven elasticities from the budget, can get confusing. A table of the alternatives may help.

Price Elasticity

	Marketplace < breakeven	Marketplace > breakeven
Raise price	Profit up, volume down	Profit down, volume down
Drop price	Profit down, volume up	Profit up, volume up

Advertising Elasticity

	Marketplace < breakeven	Marketplace > breakeven
Raise adspend	Profit down, volume up	Profit up, volume up
Drop adspend	Profit up, volume down	Profit down, volume down

If the marketplace elasticities are close to breakeven, the profit effects of changes are likely to be small. For volume effects:

Raise price or drop adspend: volume down,
Drop price or raise adspend: volume up.

9.9.2 Modelling: Log Model – Current Year

Now I move on to the log model, which is likely to give more realistic forecasts for larger changes and allows for some interaction. So I return to the relation between sales, price and advertising spend in Section 8.6.3, and write this:

$$\log\{v\} = \log\{V\} + E_P \log\{p / P\} + E_A \log\{a / A\}$$

The relation between profit and volume remains close to linear, as in Section 9.9.1, at least when the changes are of moderate size. You can use the two sorts of equation together, so that for any price and adspend you can predict not only volume but profit.

Example: Cutting price, spending more
Suppose that, after inspecting the example above, you agree on a one per cent price cut over the year, and to spend another £250k on TV. Thus p / P is 0.99 and a / A is (for television, the medium you have evaluated) 3,950 / 3,700 or 1.068.
  Using the elasticities given in the last example,

$$\log\{v / V\} = -3.9 \text{ x } \log\{0.99\} + 0.12 \text{ x } \log\{1.068\}$$

which gives v / V , or the change in volume as a ratio, as 1.048, the larger part of the increase coming from the price change.

Instead of selling 24,167 tonnes at £3,930 per tonne, you sell 25,327 tonnes at £3,891. Your revenue increases £3,571k. However the extra volume, 1,160 tonnes, results in higher variable costs of £2,482k, so from this aspect you are £1,089k better off. After paying for the extra ratings, your improvement is £839k.

9.9.3 Modelling: Next Year – a Feasible Budget

You normally assume that the *same* elasticities will apply for the year to come as in the year you measured them. There is evidence that elasticities are quite stable – provided the category does not change dramatically, that you do not introduce completely different advertising and so on. But the financial numbers you saw in these formulae will change, and normally can be predicted, so it is worthwhile to do so.

The numbers are:

(a) The *cost of buying advertising*, since it is the number of ad exposures which has an effect on purchasers, not your spend. The adspend change does not translate automatically into a ratings change, or whatever corresponds to ratings in the media you are using. You need a *media price change forecast* by which to modify the spend forecast and to get the per cent increase in advertising pressure.

(b) From the forecast brand budget, check the per cent change expected on this year in average *price*. The budget is costed at the price to retailers, so it is necessary to go through the steps between this and the consumer price. Are there new retailer terms or other reasons to expect that the price to the consumer will not change in proportion? Next, what is your forecast of competitors' prices? This will give the number by which you expect your relative price to change next year.

(c) The *variable cost* of making one more unit.

(d) *Fixed cost* changes affect the actual profit calculation, but are irrelevant for comparing one scenario with another.

(e) Finally, you need the *category volume forecast* for next year, as it is share which the equation above predicts.

You now use all this information to write a feasible budget, that is, one you are pretty sure you can achieve. You assume that if you keep up the same advertising pressure, and do not change your relative price position, you will reach the same sales share. Of course, in some circumstances you cannot assume stability, but then you write in the relevant assumption. For example, that your historical decline in share will continue, if this is your situation. Or, as in the case below, that there are long-term benefits still to come.

You have not yet decided that this scenario is where you want to be, but it gives us a relatively secure foothold in the uncertain future, from which you can explore alternatives.

Example: Writing a feasible scenario
Suppose you are in 1995, and you are to calculate the feasible situation in 1996. First the checklist just given is completed.

TV costs are expected to rise 10%. Excluding production, the spend on time in 1995 was £3.7 million. To buy the same TVRs will cost £4,070k. £230k was spent on space in magazines. The print schedule is not discussed here, but suppose it will increase to £320k.

Price in the category is expected to fall on average by 0.8%. Your variable costs are expected to be a little down at £2,130 per tonne. Fixed costs will be up to £26,400k.

Category volume is not expected to change.

The feasible budget is shown below. What this does is to change your selling price from £3,930 per tonne to £3,900, in line with the category, so your relative price is unaltered. The other changes from 1995 are made. Volume share is not expected to change, as your relative position in the category is the same. In this case actual volume is therefore unaltered.

Note that in some cases the 'feasible' budget, or 'same as last year, allowing for inflation' is quite realistic. In this particular case it is not a serious forecast since it ignores the trend in sales which will be supported by the long-term effects of 1995 advertising. This more sophisticated method is used in Section 9.10, but the simpler method is completed first.

	£000
Revenue from 24,167 tonnes at £3,900 per tonne	94,250
Variable cost at £2,130 per tonne	– 51,470
Gross margin at £1,770 per tonne	42,780
Fixed cost	26,400
Adspend (TV 4,070; print 320)	4,390
Profit	11,990
	42,780

9.9.4 Modelling: Check a Proposal

This section describes the evaluation of a scenario proposed for next year. This is done by considering it as a change from the feasible budget produced above. Note how you have taken *two* steps, rather than apply the changes directly to the current year. You have gone from this year's (actual) budget to a feasible equivalent next year. Then you modify the price and advertising spend of that feasible budget in order to estimate the volume and profit which will result from the proposed plan.

Arriving at the brand's forecast budget is a negotiation. Sometimes the brand team is forced to agree what they know could be unrealistic targets for sales and for the bottom line. This can happen because management is tempted to lay down required volume and profit targets, with restrictions on marketing activities, and then to assume that the package is feasible. It is thought to be good practice to stretch brand management in this way, in order to encourage them to find ways out of the corner they have been painted into. There is much to be said for this approach, but it is not one I take here – because in this work there is no liberty to make changes other than in the budget, while in reality there are innovations in copy and new marketing and media techniques which can be explored by the team.

Note that for all its apparent realism, a forecast such as that below is still incomplete. Other cost changes are ignored. It is assumed that the effects of advertising are instantaneous, again with the result that carryover from the current year is ignored, and all the effects of next year's spend are assumed to benefit the contribution in that year. But as a rough guide, this approach can be very helpful.

You input the changes in price and advertising pressure implied by management's requirements, and then find the change expected in sales share. Multiply this by the category forecast to get the brand volume forecast. Using the forecast brand costs, turn the volume forecast into a profit forecast.

Compare the resulting figures for volume and profit with those the team has agreed. If the two are similar, well and good. It is more likely there is disagreement. You should follow through the team's argument and compare it with yours. It may be that they rely on benefits from other parts of the marketing plan, in which case you now have a ballpark figure for the contribution expected from these activities.

Example: Next year's plan evaluated – using only elasticities
This follows through the case history from Section 9.9.3. In Sections 8.6.4 and 8.10, the estimates were derived of –2.8 for price elasticity and 0.12 for advertising elasticity (this is the sum of the short term 0.055 and long term 0.066, as the best approximation for the total return).

Suppose that management has asked for volume to increase from 24,167 tonnes in 1995 to 25,000, and profit from £13,500k to £14,500k. Price is to rise from £3,930 to £3,980 per tonne, and TV spend has been cut from £3,700k to £3,060k.

What do you expect if you raise the selling price and reduce adspend, as asked? You apply the elasticities to the percentage changes in price and adspend from the feasible budget (not from last year). In this case the rough linear method is chosen, from the alternatives set out in Section 8.6.3. The example in that section showed that other methods would give similar results.

– For price, the difference from the feasible budget is +2.1% and the effect will be –5.9% (–2.1 x 2.8);
– for TV spend the difference is –25% and the effect –3.0% (–0.12 x 25);
– the total effect is –8.9% so the forecast volume is 22,020 tonnes.

Working this volume through the budget you have to allow also for a higher gross margin rate and a lower spend on advertising. These improvements are not enough to compensate for lower volume: profit is down.

	£000
Revenue from 22,020 tonnes at £3,980 per tonne	87,640
Variable cost at £2,130 per tonne	– 46,900
Gross margin at £1,850 per tonne	40,740
Fixed cost	26,400
Adspend (TV 3,060; print 320)	3,380
Profit	10,960
	40,740

Clearly the budget requested is very unlikely to be met with the activities which management are suggesting. Volume is nearly 3,000 tonnes below their request. Profit is £3,500k down.

9.9.5   Modelling: Plotting a Course

Again you have to start from a feasible budget for the year to come, and then find the effect of various alterations to it. Each calculation is done by the method described above.

First, decide on the maximum changes to price and advertising which are likely. Then set out a table which covers all combinations. For example, if you have two higher and two lower prices there are five possible prices. With five possible adspends there are 24 combinations, plus the feasible budget itself.

For each cell of this table, work out the volume you expect to sell. It is easier to read the table if the *difference* from the feasible or central budget is shown. Then in a second table show the difference in profit. Remember again that the findings are approximate, but you will get an indication of where to go, if any direction takes you nearer management's goals.

The interpretation of these tables depends on the brand objectives and in what way the plan being evaluated falls short of them. From the business plan for the brand you will know what the acceptable possibilities are. For example, perhaps volume is to be maintained and profit must not be below a given amount. These restrictions will correspond to some entries on your tables being unacceptable, and such areas can be marked no-go. What is left is an estimate of the combinations of price and adspend strategies which are consistent with the business plan – provided such combinations exist.

You can also be helped by two formulae, stated here and detailed in the references.

(a) Volume remains constant when you increase both price and adspend, provided the proportionate changes in these are themselves in proportion to the advertising elasticity divided by minus the price elasticity.

Example: Holding volume steady
For an advertising elasticity of 0.12 and price elasticity of –2.8, the ratio is 0.12 / 2.8 or 0.043. So a price increase of 2.1% requires an advertising increase of 2.1 / 0.043 or 49% in order for volume to be steady.

(b) You also increase profit provided that the advertising elasticity divided by minus the price elasticity is greater than the advertising-to-sales ratio.

Example: Will you raise profit this way?
Continuing the example above, if advertising is 3.5% of turnover, this condition is met since 0.043 is greater than 0.035.

The converse question can be handled in the same way: can I cut adspend and replace it with a price cut? Of course there are longer term and strategic considerations in such decisions. Below I give them more careful consideration.

Example: Tables of alternatives
The example in Section 9.8.4 gave the objectives and an evaluation of management's plan for 1996. This delivered neither the volume nor the profit required.

Management wanted to raise the price more than you expect the category to do, and to take from the advertising spend. Are there alternatives to the feasible 1996 budget which meet their objectives? Compared with this, you want to raise volume by 830 tonnes, and profit by £2,500. These are the increases you look for in the table below.

You decide to look at alternatives with price £50 and £100 per tonne each side of the suggested £3,900 (price fall in line with the category), and with TV spend £500k and £1,000k each side of the £4,070 needed to buy the same TVRs as in 1995.

Change from feasible plan in sales volume, tonnes

		TV spend, £000			
	3,070	3,570	4,070	4,570	5,070
Price, £ per tonne					
4,000	−2,500	−2,100	−1,700	−1,400	−1,100
3,950	−1,700	−1,200	−900	−500	−200
3,900	−800	−400	−	+300	+700
3,850	+60	+500	+900	+1,300	+1,600
3,800	+1,000	+1,500	+1,900	+2,200	+2,600

Change from feasible plan in profit, £000

		TV spend, £000			
	3,070	3,570	4,070	4,570	5,070
Price, £ per tonne					
4,000	−1,130	−870	−690	−590	−540
3,950	−790	−520	−340	−	−180
3,900	−460	−190	−	+110	+170
3,850	−140	+140	+330	+450	+510
3,800	+160	+450	640	+770	+830

The position which management has taken is in the top left of this table: TV spend very close to £3,070k and price just below £4,000.

From inspection of the table, you see it should not be very difficult to get the additional volume required. A price reduction to £3,850 would do, if combined with a TV budget around £4 million. No price reduction is needed if the TV spend is over £5 million.

The profit requirement is much harder: a price cut (since you are above breakeven elasticity), and adspend increase are indicated. But nowhere on the table exceeds +£1 million. To reduce price below £3,800 per tonne might invite competitive response, and the evidence for spending over £5 million on advertising may not be convincing.

The conclusions are:

- the request to cut the TV spend should be resisted, and you have a strong case
- price reduction is a strategic question although analysis suggests it
- you might manage to reach the volume requirement, but the profit request is going further than price and TV spend manipulation can reasonably suggest.

To end this section, note again that it has assumed advertising effects from previous years were nil. This is too restrictive; the evidence is anyway against it. The next section deals with more reasonable assumptions about long-term advertising effects.

9.10 Continuous Budgeting

9.10.1 Continuous Budgeting: The Full Marketplace Model

Our purpose is now to give the best possible help to decisions about marketing activities, particularly the weight and timing of advertising. You start with a model of the type described in Section 8.10. It is essential in what follows that there is a reasonable representation of the majority of advertising's effects, which usually means in the long term. You are going to estimate the overall results of changing the advertising spend, and to follow this through over several years. More detail is given in Table 13.

You would be misled by a model which assumes that advertising has only short-term, and probably uneconomic, effects. The purpose is no longer to *fit* the model, so that you understand better the results of your activities, as far as the data allow. It is to *use* your best estimate of what the marketplace situation really is. You cannot, however, go too far outside current experience.

If you believe the advertising has significant effects on distribution, which will not be quickly lost and so have long-term benefits, this is the time to say so. In the case where advertising spend has been so steady that it is just background, and the size of the effect cannot be estimated by regression, it *was* reasonable to say just that. *Now* you may have to give your best guess. For example, you know from Section 8.10 that stability can be the result of a constant fall in share each period c countered by an adstock term which on average is e (the coefficient) times the average rate of TVRs. Thus, for any value of c you can calculate the value of e which produces stability. You may estimate c from the fate of other brands, or from an overall average: for highly competitive categories you have a guess of –16% each year. A base produced this way may look indistinguishable from a constant – while you advertise at the historic rate. If you make large changes in adspend, it will behave rather differently.

Earlier, I was using the elasticities derived from the marketplace model, plus summaries from the brand's budget, to evaluate possible changes in advertising spend and price. Those sums are useful directionally. They have their limitations and are too crude for the purpose now. They assume that effects are instantaneous and so do not adequately describe what happens over the months after the decisions.

The time dimension is critical in marketing. For accountants, the volumes and profits required have to be delivered when stated. But some expenditures incurred now may not pay off for months or years to come.

Hence the name 'Continuous' Budgeting. The job is to construct a marketplace + financial model which is based on the accounting unit of time, say months. But this series can be grouped into longer periods as you wish – quarters or years. You can look further ahead, and in more detail, than the current period. This is the only way to handle the classical dilemma, which is that advertising has to be paid for now, but usually produces results beyond the immediate accounting horizon.

The model may cover the current year and two or three years ahead. To go further usually means that this level of detail is not required. One year ahead may not be enough to show the long-term benefits you expect.

Now you see the reason for emphasising above that there must be a realistic long-term advertising element in the model, and you must be convinced that you are representing most of advertising's benefits. Otherwise you put up a proposal which under-represents your case.

Realism is a matter of judgment. It may sound as though you have to attempt an impossible task – to build a full business model representing all aspects of the organisation. We are not being so ambitious. Making a Continuous Budgeting Model convincing and usable is hard work enough – though the trouble is well worth taking. It also gives a structure for the forecasting work which Marketing has to undertake in any case.

You want to be precise enough to capture the broad picture, and more detailed than the over-coarse view often taken. As in modelling the marketplace, you do not expect complete accuracy, you want a workable view which leads to better decisions.

9.10.2 Continuous Budgeting: The Data Required

Suppose you have assembled the following information and forecasts:

(a) A marketplace model which predicts the sales share of your brand, depending on such variables as your relative price, routine promotions, distribution, any special activities of which you have experience (added value packs, two for one offers, joint promotions), a trend term, your advertising and competitors' advertising, and so on.

(b) A forecast of the relevant environment facing your brand: the size of category, average price, media and promotion costs, competitors' activities, and so on.

(c) A forecast of your own costs and other budget constraints, fixed and variable; the delays with which you receive income and pay your bills, and so on; and whether there are any volume thresholds at which costs change (if you have to bring in a new line, for example).

In the examples already given, modelling has been adequately covered and so has forecasting for the category. You could use the model to evaluate scenarios for their effects on brand share. What if you reduce price, for example? What does the model say will be the gain in volume?

But you are going to do more than forecast in this way, though you certainly will predict volume. The company already has forecasts of its own costs and knows its ways of operating. It is important that stage (c) is realistic. A model may be disbelieved if it does not reflect, say, that the December advertising burst is not paid for until January and so the costs appear in the *next* year's accounts. It matters that the accountants work in months and the research data is four-weekly: you have to build in the conversion between the two timetables (based on the numbers of weeks or days in the two systems). Future contribution is evaluated in different ways in different companies – by comparison with some opportunity cost, using discounted cash flow, or whatever.

The reason for emphasising this is that Continuous Budgeting is the best way known to get the marketing people and the accountants to talk the same language. The budgeting model you are building must be worked on by both departments and agreed by both departments. There is no place for disagreement or vagueness when the job is translation and co-operation.

Example: The material for Continuous Budgeting
The marketplace model of Section 8.10 tells you that your sales share depends on the following, and gives you the coefficients to use in forecasting sales share:

- a base made up of decay and a long-term advertising term
- relative price
- promotions
- distribution
- a short-term advertising term.

You need your schedule of TVRs to make adstocks. Ratings will come from knowing your TV spend each month (to be input each run, depending on the scenario you are to evaluate), and a forecast of TV costs.

You get relative price from knowing the price you decide to negotiate with retailers, your judgment about the price passed on to purchasers, and a forecast of the category's price.

Your distribution has to be forecast. So does the price of future promotions, and your press spend – if you are going on with the same activities.

Once you have estimated your sales share, you have to apply this to the forecast of category volume to get retail sales volume – and then translate this to ex-factory volume.

Internally, there are timings to be investigated – ex-factory sales becoming retail sales, bills to retailers and bills from media being paid, factory and overhead costs falling due.

The sizes of the fixed and variable costs have to be forecast.

9.10.3 Continuous Budgeting: Constructing the Model

The model is described here as a spreadsheet, with months as the time periods, but may of course be in other forms.

The first part consists of input, where a particular scenario is specified. This includes the price at which you sell to retailers, the spend on various media and promotions.

Then, these inputs are translated into marketplace conditions: relative price is such and such, so many TVRs, the execution of a promotion. The ratings are converted to adstocks, more than one set if there are both short and long-term effects, with the half lives previously determined. You take into account the various costs and time frameworks specified. The object is to create all the variables needed for your marketplace model.

Third, the model predicts your volume share, which is turned into the volume made and sold to retailers, and into your revenue less discounts, again period by period.

Then you go through the financial steps needed to calculate profit. The various costs are subtracted from revenue: for media and promotions, then the fixed and variable elements of the budget.

Thus you are able to evaluate the outcome of marketing decisions – not just by their market share and volume results, but by revenue and profit. The final stage is to display and print out the results, in summary and in detail, as tables and plots.

Example: A Continuous Budgeting Model
A specific model is now described. It was based on actual sales in 1992 to 1995. It shows history for 1994 and 1995; it predicts 1996 and 1997. It continues the example started above.

The category volume and price forecast are as in Section 8.5. The price at which you plan to sell to retailers is forecast, and the way this translates into a price relative to competitors at retail level is specified – hence the price effect on volume share can be calculated.

The costs forecast for TV time allow us to turn TV spend each month into TVRs every four weeks and hence the two adstocks you need. The advertising effects, short and long term, can be calculated.

Promotions, spend on press advertising, distribution – these are also forecast. So are fixed and variable costs.

The model predicts sales share at retail level and volume sales ex-factory, and calculates revenue and profit through to December 1997 (in practice I usually look three years ahead).

You can look at the details of each step, but usually you will concentrate on:

– the four-weekly retail sales volume share prediction
– and the monthly volume and profit figures.

Two key figures sum up any plan:

- the volume sales, usually next year's are looked at first, - the profit total for 1996 and 1997 (the latter discounted in this case by 15%).

9.10.4 Continuous Budgeting: Using the Model

The main use of the model is to arrive at a plan which both meets management objectives and is feasible, that is, the achievement is compatible with how the marketplace works and with your forecasts of future conditions. If this is not possible, then the model is used to propose feasible alternatives which are discussed with management so that new, more reasonable objectives are arrived at.

I concentrate here on the use of Continuous Budgeting to evaluate marketing activities. Runs do not ordinarily alter inputs like category data, half lives for advertising effects, the advertising coefficients, terms of business, media costs and your own cost structure. Nevertheless, you may sometimes choose to do more than change marketing decisions. For the model can also comment on changes in the environment. What will happen if the category declines faster than expected, if your ad effects last longer, if new copy moves sales more than previously, if media costs become higher or if your product is more expensive to make? These are important questions to which numerical answers can now be estimated.

In running the model, all you usually do is to alter the adspend and/or the price and/or the promotions plan for the year (or more) ahead. This is the scenario you are to evaluate. By experimenting with different scenarios you learn in which directions, and by how much, you alter profit, and from what new volume. You are in effect moving on the same table of alternatives as for the example in 9.8.3. The differences are that the calculations of effects are more precise, they allow for time and so you may see the effects over any set of periods ahead which you decide to look at. You can, for example, comment on how you affect the year for which the expenditure is incurred, and how much you impact following years.

Some examples are now given. These show what happens when you use the model to check out a plan which is not achievable, and how you arrive at a compromise with management. The avenues also explored are different pricing decisions and different amounts and schedules for TV advertising, in addition to some other applications.

Example: Checking a given plan
In Section 9.9.4, management gave the price and TV spend it wanted followed in 1996. You have already found difficulties in meeting the volume and profit requirements which management also laid down.

The input for 1996 and 1997 implements the price increase in March, the earliest feasible month, and takes a TV lay-down rather similar to 1995, but with the new expenditure total specified.

The model is used to explore changes in price and advertising. For 24 months in 1996 and 1997, you have to enter the price per tonne at which you agree to sell to retailers, and the money you spend on TV advertising (as well as all the other inputs explained in the example above).

The input summary is the first two columns below; the output the last two columns:

	Price to retailers £ per tonne	Adspend £000	Volume tonnes	Profit £000
1994	3,870	1,814	22,234	8,966
1995	3,930	3,930	24,167	11,725
1996	3,980	3,315	24,487	13,907
1997	3,990	3,509	24,843	14,893

Compare this output with the result of the simpler work in Section 9.9.4. The major differences are due to the addition of long-term benefits from the heavier investment in 1995, part of which pays off in 1996. There are also effects from differences in the timing, and other small items not taken into account in the earlier example.

Example: Changing the TV schedule
In Section 8.49 it was explained how the 1995 schedule was analysed by BAT in order to discover whether it could be improved.

The same method is applied to the 1996 plan which, as stated above, was roughly similar in lay down. Using the short half life it was found that you could move some money to January from February and the summer, and to September from October and November. This raises the effectiveness on short-term grounds by 9%, and generates more TVRs (from 1,200 to 1,300) which will do us good long term.

When these ideas are applied in 1996 and 1997, no extra cost is involved, but the last two lines above become:

	Price to retailers £ per tonne	Adspend £000	Volume tonnes	Profit £000
1996	3,980	3,315	24,656	14,219
1997	3,990	3,509	25,603	16,311

This takes us nearer the management objective, and this becomes the initial scenario which you now try to improve.

For volume, you are looking for a further 350 tonnes. For profit, £300k.

Example: Cutting the year-end burst
In October and November 1996 you planned to spend £349k on TV, but suppose management refuse to authorise this burst, claiming that the money is required for other purposes.

Because you lose some volume immediately, you calculate that the actual saving is not £349k but only £58k in 1996. Over the two years 1996–97, far from a saving, you actually lose £381k off the bottom line. In addition, you lose 583 tonnes sales over these two years.

Example: Exploring improvements
It is now much easier to explore scenarios: you just enter the desired TV spend lay down, or the selling price, and run the model. In this way you can see what happens if you cut advertising (disastrous in this case), raise the price above £4,000 per tonne (equally misguided), or look at the more realistic alternatives below.

They are evaluated by two key figures: volume in 1996, and the profit total for 1996 and 1997 (the latter being discounted by 15%, the rate agreed in this case). In practice, management will look at the 1996 profit more carefully, and perhaps also at the quarterly profit forecasts. To simplify the example, the two-year figure is given as having the greater real significance. You examine the differences from the new base scenario.

As well as changing price and TV spend, the two last lines in this table are about changes commented on below.

	Volume 1996	Profit, £000 1996 & 1997
Base scenario	24,656	28,083
Differences from base		
TV spend halved	−1,200	−4,500
TV up 25% 1996	+590	+1,770
TV up 25% 1996 &1997	+590	+2,240
Price £3,930 1996	+880	+350
Price held as '95 in '96 &1997	+880	+720
Ads2 effect 10% up	+150	+500
Margins up £10 per tonne	–	+460

The preferred route here is through adspend. Price cuts have an uncertain effect in the marketplace and although they deliver volume (if there is no retaliation), do less for profit than might have been expected.

The line with TV up 25% in 1996 was the recommended plan in Section 6.14. This is quite a step up from management's initial proposal, though it is not so much up from the successful experience of 1995. The case history was written as the conversion of a management initially sceptical about the return from its advertising investment. At the end the marketer is sufficiently persuaded by the believable modelling results that the increased investment will pay off. This can be the result of a convincing analysis; indeed it is the theme of the book that this analysis should lead to better decisions, whether they are to increase spend, as in this case, or to decrease it, or to decide that copy must be changed. Very occasionally, the outcome is to agree a test. While in theory desirable, this takes time.

Example: Other changes
The last two lines in the table of alternatives examined above show how the underlying model can also be changed. You easily evaluate two other ways of raising profit.

First, suppose you are considering new copy, perhaps getting ready to test it as you did in Section 8.12, and want to know how much you will benefit from improved effectiveness.

The hypothesis is that the direct sales effect of your short-term adstock is raised 10%. The cost is that of a new film – but perhaps you were going to incur this anyway. The finding is that volume would rise by 150 tonnes – hardly detectable in a short test, by the way, as this is only 0.5%. The benefit in the same year is £360k, over two years £500k. This gives us a feel for what is worth spending, and what is worth testing, in addition to gut feel about the chances of getting this improvement in effectiveness.

The margin improvement finding is a very different story, and makes it clear why management pursues this objective so keenly. The table shows no cost involved, but these will perhaps appear in another part of the accounts, for example in that year's fixed cost if you are discussing new machinery. A very small change, of £10 in £1,850 per tonne, goes straight on the bottom line here, giving £250k in 1996.

The improvement is close to what you are looking for in profit. It should be taken with great caution, and strategic issues may again be raised. Does the advantage come with any reduction in product quality? If so, this is a slippery slope. If, however, this figure encourages a search for a gain in production efficiency which does not impact the consumer's experience with the product, it is worth taking.

This completes the examples of Continuous Budgeting being used. They take us straight into the heart of management discussions about the future. Are the forecasts believable? Is the model sufficiently reliable – do the findings feel right? What are the other consequences, which the model does not attempt to cover?

In the particular case described, the advantages of using the model are to show management that its first directives about marketing activities for the year to come are unlikely to have the desired consequences, but that you can reach these by a combination of a moderate increase on last year's TV spend, plus smarter scheduling. There is also a major lesson about taking into account later effects of advertising, both when forecasting for next year and when justifying this year's budget.

10 The Process

This describes the steps to go through as you make your advertising campaign accountable. It is a checklist for the managers responsible for the brand, for its finances and for its communications.

To apply the ideas in this book you need a practical process. If you follow this one methodically, it is easy to administer and control. The work is broken into seven steps and fourteen separate headings. As each point is made, I refer back to relevant parts of the book. The analogy used in the headings is building a house.

10.1 Clearing the Ground, Laying the Foundations

Too often, the early parts of the job are skipped – but this is fatal. Choices are made at the beginning which seriously influence the outcome.

The main decision is of course to make an optimistic and realistic attempt to be accountable (*see especially Sections 1.2 and 1.6*).

Category

What brand are you working on? What are its main competitors and what is the definition of the category?

The definition of competitors and category may be simple, but sometimes is a difficult and critical decision (*Sections 7.3.1, 7.3.2 and 7.5*).

People

Who is in the team working on the brand, and in particular who is the brand owner? Who has the final say in its financial health?

It is important to identify early the main decision-makers, because they must be involved in the financial planning of accountability from the start (*Section 2.1*). Their identification of objectives and benefits is essential – and cannot be assumed by others.

Budget

Are you familiar with the details of the brand's budget? For example, how are gross margin per unit and total contribution defined?

Since accountability involves both finance and strategy, you must understand this and the next heading. Accountability is impossible if you dash straight into analysing results in the marketplace without measuring tools and a list of goals (*see Chapter 4*).

Business Objectives

What are the purposes of the brand, from the point of view of the firm?

Note the priority given to business results – marketing and communication tasks depend on the ultimate purposes. Note also that there is very likely to be more than one objective. The objectives are likely to be a mix of strategic outcomes, often long term, and of financial criteria (*see Sections 2.1, 2.5 and 2.7*).

You may be analysing a competitor's performance, in fact it is recommended that you spend as much time understanding the competition as your own results. You will then have to guess the answers for the two sections above, based on what you know of the competitor's history and current situation, and on what their advertisements say.

Budget Benefits of Achieving Objectives

If the chosen objectives are achieved, in what ways will the brand's budget look different?

Here the financial targets are spelled out (*see Section 2.8*). Note that the firm does not inevitably look for short-term profit improvement. It may be worth paying out, in order to establish some other goal. So the criteria may not include a simple 'pay back the advertising investment this year'.

10.2 Searching for Materials

Data

What relevant data do you have?

Obviously, all data about the objectives and about communications are relevant. Information about the competitors and the category are nearly always needed. Hence, you will review marketplace data – about retail sales

Ideally, if you had alternative explanations before, all but one can be rejected. At this stage, the results may show that more is going on than you have data available to explain. This is acceptable, provided you have believable estimates for the sizes of the effects of those variables you want to evaluate.

10.6 Build the House

Marketplace Data + Budget

Add the budget data to your marketplace model.

There are revenues and costs associated with the variables in your model. From these you will be able to estimate the profitability of the relevant activities, which is often a key part of the original objectives.

Benefits Revisited

Did we get the benefits?

We all hope to find the easy cases (described in *Section 9.2*), but spend much more time on the difficult ones. When the direct effects of advertising are clearly uneconomic, and other benefits are being judged, it is often the character of the firm and of its key executives – thrusting and optimistic, or cautious and disbelieving – which determines the evaluation.

More generally, you will be able to say whether the original objectives were or were not met, and at what cost. In many cases, advertising is part of the entry fee for doing business, and it was agreed at the beginning that managers did not expect a simple payback.

Hence, looking backwards, the activities have been made accountable (*Chapter 9* is relevant – *Section 9.1* for examples, *9.2 to 9.7* for the simpler cases, *9.9 and 9.10* for the more complex).

10.7 Live in the House!

Benchmark

Could you have done it differently? Better?

This is the point of benchmarking – how did we do, compared with how competitors did? We compare the effects of our own activities with previous years or other countries. We compare each of our activities with the others (*see Section 9.8*).

Forward planning

What have you learned for next year?

Looking forwards, and with some forecasting, you will be able to help plans for the future (*see especially Chapter 6, and Sections 7.8.4, 7.8.5*).

The difficult part of evaluating marketplace and budget scenarios is representing the effects on the marketplace. Adding the budget dimension is comparatively straightforward, and normal work for accountants. Nevertheless, the addition is made even more rarely than modelling itself.

Many firms have by experience, often unquantified, learned to operate with sensible brand budgets, and major improvements in the business plans are not expected. These are the hardest cases of all, where changes will not have major effects. What sort of guidance can analysis offer?

The choice of direction (higher price or lower, more adspend or less), is the first decision to make. If this is really hard, you are probably near optimum. How far to go is a more difficult decision and again the character of the firm plays a part. Also, you are edging into strategy and war games, where the prediction of competitors' moves may be critical.

Provided you have arrived at a sensible model for your own brand, the output of marketplace plus financial models can give the team great assistance. If all those concerned have had a say in building the model, and especially after it has passed its first forecasting tests and has earned trust, the work will be repaid a hundredfold.

As postscript to this book, I echo what Goethe said about his play *Iphigenie*,

> Though you will not, of course, find in its pages what I should have written, you will at least be able to guess what I would have liked to have written.
>
> *– Italian Journey*

Appendix

Glossary

Accountable: An activity is accountable if there is convincing evidence that it has or has not met management objectives. Often, an objective is to influence consumer behaviour, so that overall profit is increased, or at an acceptable cost. More in Section 1.2.

Activity: What is paid for by the marketing budget and is intended to affect our target, such as advertising, other communications and temporary price changes.

Adstock: Cumulated, decayed TV ratings, representing the current pressure from advertising. Adstock is calculated from the schedule of ratings. More in Section 8.2.

Advertising: Paid-for communications with a group of people, usually in the mass media – TV, newspapers, and so on. There are other ways of communicating; some are listed in Section 1.3.

Analysis: In this book, using numerical data about the brand and the category, in order to help evaluation of activities and managers' decision-making. The numbers not only have to be manipulated in order to yield up their meaning, they have to be understood in a business context.

Brand: A brand is a product or service seen through the eyes of the consumer, and the reason why your product is chosen, not a competitor's. Other definitions are given in Section 2.2.

Branding: Some theorists have doubted whether the 'brand' includes product properties, and hold that a product is 'branded' by processes other than manufacture. It is preferable to see the 'brand' as starting with design, while raw material and manufacture itself are part of creating the brand.

Brand audit: A review of your brand, and a comparison with competitors. This is expanded in Sections 3.2 and 7.3.

Brand equity: This phrase is avoided in this book as it can have many different meanings, as described in Section 3.2. See Consumer Brand Equity.

Brand essence: In this book, the output from a process, carried out by management, of reviewing the brand. See Section 2.3. The phrase is used loosely elsewhere, often as a synonym for the brand proposition or for the major item in brand image.

Brand image: How consumers describe the brand. Often as quantified in a survey.

Brand valuation: The sum which would be paid for the brand if it were up for sale. See Section 3.2(d).

Breakeven elasticity: The elasticity at which a small change in the activity results in no change in profit.

Category: A group of brands which compete directly with each other. Sometimes this is hard to define. See Sections 3.4.2 and 7.5.

Communications: Any paid-for way of passing a message to the trade, purchasers or consumers. Advertising (in mass media) is one such way. See Section 1.3.

Consumer Brand Equity: The result of a calculation on the volume share of the brand, removing the effects of price and of distribution. One brand has higher Consumer Brand Equity than another with the same distribution if it sells more at the same price, or sells the same volume at a higher price. More in Section 8.7.

Consumer: Strictly, the person who 'consumes', eats, drinks, wears or views the brand. More loosely, the buyer too (a mother 'consumes' baby foods).

Cost, fixed: In the brand's budget, the total of those costs which do not change if the amount sold varies (within limits).

Cost, variable, per unit: In the brand's budget, the average paid to make and deliver an extra unit, including for example the cost of raw materials. *Variable cost* is the product of units sold and variable cost per unit. More in Section 4.1.

Distribution: For groceries, this usually means 'listings' which is the percentage of outlets or shops (weighted by the total turnover through each outlet), which have agreed to stock the brand. It may mean this figure modified in various ways to make it closer to availability: by subtracting 'out-of-stocks' which is the percentage of outlets which temporarily did not carry the brand, or measuring 'front of shop' which means actually on the shelf, excluding times when the brand was officially in stock but only in the storeroom. Also the quality of distribution may be measured, by position in store, or the number of facings, or feet of shelf occupied, or percentage of the chiller cabinet occupied.

Econometrics: In this book, a synonym for modelling. More generally, the application of statistics to economic data.

Elasticity (of an activity like advertising): The percentage by which sales volume changes, when the activity increases by one per cent.

Equity: When used loosely, this means the 'value' or 'worth' of the brand. In this book, it is used as an abbreviation for 'Consumer Brand Equity'.

Framing: The process by which advertising directs the consumer to an aspect of the product which is confirmed or perceived when the consumer uses or consumes the product.

Gross margin, per unit: In the brand's budget, revenue per unit, or the money received when a unit is sold, less variable cost per unit. *Gross margin* is the product of units sold and gross margin per unit.

Half life: The time by which half the total effect of an opportunity-to-see has been felt.

Manufacturer: Strictly, a firm making a physical product. The term is often stretched to include those who buy products and re-sell them in bulk. Or those who do very little actual manufacture, more assembly and packaging. It extends even to those whose products are services, or physical in only a token sense, such as a credit card, an insurance policy, a building society account or a TV programme.

Marketing: Designing, making (in the widest sense – see Manufacturer) and selling brands, while taking the consumer's views explicitly into account.

Marketplace: The real world, where buyers make their brand decisions, opposed to the *office* (where we deal in summaries and ideas), the *laboratory* (where real buyers are not present and emotions ideally play no part), and the *interview* (or focus group, where people say what they feel and do, rather than do it).

Model: A representation of the marketplace behaviour of the brand by an equation.

Modelling: Representing the marketplace behaviour of the brand by equations. The work to do this. In this book, these equations are usually fitted by regression. This is the subject of Chapter 8.

OTS or Opportunity-to-see: Loosely, a person is said to have an opportunity-to-see who is in the room when a TV commercial is on. For a more precise definition, see the details of how ratings are measured in the system you are using. Other media have equivalent definitions.

Parameter: A term in an equation which determines the size of the effects of the relevant activity – see Regression.

Plots: Presenting data as lines, symbols or bars against two axes – the X or horizontal axis, and Y or vertical axis.

Plots, scatter: Plots where symbols are used and the X-axis is not time (it is price, distribution, etc).

Plots, time series: Plots when the X-axis is for weeks, months, etc. Usually a line plot.

Rating or TVR or TV rating; outside the UK, GRP (Gross Rating Point) or TARP (Television Audience Rating Point): The percentage of the defined universe (eg female housewives), who had an opportunity-to-see when the commercial was transmitted. One hundred ratings means that, on average, everyone in the universe had a single opportunity-to-see.

Regression: The calculation needed to 'fit' a 'dependent' variable (eg sales share) by one or more 'explanatory' variables (eg price). The fit is by an equation (eg sales share = A + B x price). The method in this book is OLS or 'ordinary least squares'. The result is that the 'parameters' (eg A and B) are chosen so that the 'residuals' (differences between the original values of the dependent variable and the fitted values), are as small as possible. Strictly, it is the sum of squares of the residuals which is minimised. More in Chapter 8.

Residual: The difference between the value of a dependent variable and the corresponding fitted value – see Regression.

Response function: In this book, how brand volume share responds to more or less pressure from advertising (eg from adstock). More in Section 8.8.

R-squared: This number is part of the output when a regression is carried out. The higher the number, the better the fit. The maximum is one. It is the proportion of the variability in the dependent variable which is accounted for by the explainers. 'Variability' is the sum of squares of differences from the mean.

Target: The group of buyers or consumers whose behaviour we have decided to influence.

Trade: The channels through which the product moves from the manufacturer to the final sale.

TVR: see Rating

T-value: Part of the output when a regression is carried out. It indicates how well the coefficient of an explanatory variable is determined – the larger the t-value, the better determined. More in Section 8.3.

Value: The value or worth of a brand means in this book its Consumer Brand Equity. The phrases have a more general meaning: worth paying more for (than competitors).

Volume: A measure of how much of a product is sold. The units depend on the nature of the product and are not restricted to the literal sense, for example litres or gallons. Weight (kilograms and tonnes) and numbers (of standard cases) are included. The number of packs is rarely used, because packs vary in size.

References and Notes

In this section, references are given for further reading, and some notes are added. The author of the papers and books is Simon Broadbent unless otherwise stated.

This book is not a *review* of its subject: it does not describe the many alternatives which have been put forward to meet the firm's needs. For a review, see Paul Feldwick, *Evaluating Advertising*, to be published by John Wiley. Here I concentrate on the way I recommend analysing data and making decisions. Do not expect to find here every way the job might be done.

How to Use This Book

The Advertising Budget was published by NTC for the Institute of Practitioners in Advertising in 1989, following an American version I worked on in 1986–87. Those books also mentioned accountability and evaluation; they described modelling as understood at the time. This was about short-term effects, and so the books said little about strategic issues and indirect results. We have all now learned more, through the IPA Awards papers and in other ways. The process described there still seems sound to me and I do not repeat it here; we can now do parts of it more thoroughly, in particular through the Continuous Budgeting process described in Section 9.10.

Questions from the finance department have become more probing and inescapable. The marketing director has to sell his plan harder internally, as well as manage his own affairs more prudently. Determining the budget sensibly has become second fiddle to justification, though they play the same tune. The earlier book described the process inside the marketing department and understated the current need for marketing to reach decisions alongside the rest of the brand team – a phrase not often heard then.

The 'woolly answers' quotation is from a letter to the *Times* by William Gaskill, on 29 June 1996.

Chapter 1

The 1995 survey quoted was carried out by the Marketing Forum, The Leo Burnett Brand Consultancy and Arthur Andersen. The 1996 survey was commissioned by the IPA and KPMG, and the results are quoted from the *Economist*, 8 June 1996.

Chapter 2

A personal view of the situation facing the marketing department is in 'Changes in the way marketing is managed', *Journal of Marketing Management*, 1995, Vol 11, pp 285–293. This is summarised by 'Marketing has tried to be accountable in the same way as other departments but has usually failed.' This book is an attempt to correct the failure.

The importance of the personal view is emphasised in 'Through the factory gate – what you see depends on who you are', *Admap*, September 1994, pp 16–18.

Patrick Barwise's definition of a brand was given in a Centre for Marketing Workshop, London Business School, October 1995. Tim Ambler's is from *Marketing from Advertising to Zen, a Financial Times Guide*, Pitman, 1995. Stephen King's comment is from *Developing New Brands*, Pitman, 1973.

David Aaker's headings for brand equity are from *Managing Brand Equity*, The Free Press, 1991.

A review of the subject is Paul Feldwick's 'What is Brand Equity anyway, and how do you measure it?', *Journal of the Market Research Society (JMRS)*, **38**, No 2, pp 85–104.

Chapter 3

Brand essence workshops are described in Helena Rubinstein's 'Brand chartering – getting to a common understanding of the brand', *Journal of Brand Management*, **3**, No 3, 1996, pp 145–153.

Chapter 4

More about the brand's budget, with reference to communications in general and advertising in particular, in *The Advertising Budget*, NTC Publications for The Institute of Practitioners in Advertising, 1989.

More about advertising and price elasticities in 'Price and advertising: volume and profit', *Admap*, November 1980, pp 532–540. Breakeven elasticities are derived there, and further, the condition is given that we can increase both price and adspend, yet leave volume unchanged – if these increases are in the proportion of (actual advertising elasticity) : (minus actual price elasticity). The condition that profit is unchanged is also given. Such guidelines are best treated as no more than suggestions: the real effects of changes in our marketing plan are not completely summarised in one or two numbers like these.

The averages of measured elasticities obviously depend on the cases used (countries, years, brands and market situations, budget sizes), and on the techniques (which are also varied). An average relevant to your situation is hard to find. An old collection from four different sources is in the 1980 *Admap* paper quoted just above; another, later but still not up to date, is in the Marketing Sciences Institute (MSI) 1988 reference under Chapter 8.

Chapter 5

The quotation from Paul Feldwick is from an overview of advertisement and campaign evaluation, 'The four ages of ad evaluation', *Admap*, April 1996, pp 25–27.

Chapter 7

I have been using a spreadsheet system similar to the one described here since the late 1980s. It is called SMT (sales, media, tracking) and is more fully described in 'Using data better', *Admap*, January 1992, pp 48–54.

The review of categories from which the summary was drawn is 'Diversity in categories, brands and strategies', *Journal of Brand Management*, 1994, Vol 2, No 1, pp 9–17.

A general account of *Best practice in Campaign Evaluation* is in a booklet with that title published by the Institute of Practitioners in Advertising, 1995. Much of this is descriptive.

Chapter 8

Adstock modelling has been the subject of a series of papers in the Journal of the Market Research Society in 1979, 1984, 1990, 1993 and 1995. The most recent was with Tim Fry and is called 'Adstock modelling for the long term', *JMRS*, **37**, No 4, pp 385–403. Applications described include fitting tracking study data (also in 'The shifting base – an approximation for the awareness index', *Admap*, March 1991, pp 27–29), short-term blips in sales data and long-term effects.

Two comments on the system are now given, the first by C. F. Jex, University of Lancaster, and the second by Tom Corlett, J. Walter

Thomson. 'The Box-Jenkins transfer modelling confirms the Broadbent type model as being the most appropriate,' *JMRS*, 1985, **27**, pp 293–297. "Now a very common principle in market modelling – the use in the model not of the 'raw' advertising input in each period but what might be called a 'pre-modelled' ... version of it ... known to most UK readers from Simon Broadbent's elegant developments and lucid expositions of it under the name 'adstock'. Recent experience has increased my confidence that this general picture of how advertising effects decay over time is sound." 'Modelling the sales effects of advertising – today's questions', *Admap*, October 1985, pp 486–494.

It is a fallacy that, because advertising elasticities are numerically smaller than price elasticities, advertising has little influence and advertisers shift correctly towards price and promotional discounts. This is exposed in 'What is a small advertising elasticity?', *Admap*, December 1988, pp 34–36. Incidentally, the American collection of elasticities which gave rise to the gaffe averaged 0.22 for advertising and –1.76 for price: *The price elasticity of selective demand: a meta-analysis of sales response models*, G. T. Tellis, MSI, Report 88–105, 1988.

The analysis of both sales and media exposure information from the same informant, Single-Source data, discussed in Section 8.13, came back into debate in 1995 through the work of John Philip Jones in *When Ads Work*, Lexington Books, 1994. His findings and conclusions are controversial: see 'Single-source – the breakthrough?', *Admap*, June 1995, pp 29–33, and later papers there on this subject. My own conclusions from a first look at the BehaviorScan data were in 'Two OTS in a purchase interval – some questions', *Admap*, November 1986, pp 12–16. As I write, the best description of work with this type of data, though from the marriage of separate sources, is by Andrew Roberts, 'What do we know about advertising's short-term effects?', *Admap*, February 1996, pp 42–45.

In the UK the largest source so far is called AdLab, which was funded by Meridian TV and is now owned by Carlton UK Sales. This panel ran for four and a half years up to March 1990. Currently, a different technique is operated by Taylor Nelson-AGB, called TVspan; this can be used for experiments. Another was run recently by Nielsen in the US, but is now discontinued; some of the findings were the subject of *When Ads Work*. The method lives on successfully in Germany, also run by Nielsen. IRI have collected such data in the US for many years.

As can be seen, the method has had a patchy history and the data are not routinely available to most European advertisers. Methods of analysis have not, as I write, been generally agreed. Therefore I do not give the subject much space, even though the opportunities offered by single-source data are important, and are currently one of my major preoccupations.

An easy analysis was suggested by John Philip Jones – divide all purchase occasions into two groups: 'ad-exposed' (defined for this purpose as those where the housewife has 'seen' at least one commercial for the brand during the seven days before the occasion), and 'non-exposed' (the rest). The brand share of occasions is defined by the number of times the brand is chosen. The shares in these two groups usually differ. Dividing the share for the ad-exposed by the share for the non-exposed gives an index which he calls STAS (short-term advertising strength). He claims it measures the short-term sales effect of the commercials seen. An earlier definition of 'exposed' by Colin McDonald counts the opportunities to see in the interval between successive purchases; in this case purchases are divided into two groups by whether they were for the same brand, or were switches between brands.

Here we have an example of an apparently simple measure of advertising effectiveness, so attractive to many managers. There are two difficulties. The first is that possible confounding is ignored: the measure is affected by any relationship which may exist between weight of viewing and brand share (called the purchase/viewing bias). Second, the underlying mental model is that advertising is there to make consumers rush out and buy. This can be one effect, but it is rarely large or economic.

A further analysis attempts to measure the response function by calculating the brand share for occasions with one, two, three ... OTS in the previous week. Results are not published by brand in *When Ads Work*, but an overall average is given: receiving only one exposure gives 111 for STAS, which is little below the average, 114, for any number of exposures. This implies sharply diminishing returns. Unfortunately, this does not compare like with like. Those shoppers who receive two or more exposures are not the same as those who receive none or one only, as can be seen when their viewing weights are compared.

The argument is put forward in *When Ads Work* that there can be no long-term effect unless the instant reaction, measured by STAS, is obvious. I know, from using both short and long-term adstocks in modelling, that one can take place without the other. The definition of long-term effect given in the book is dubious (the measure gives unadvertised brands almost the same 'long-term advertising effect' as the advertised brands), so the argument need not be taken seriously.

Chapter 9

The summary of the IRI BehaviorScan experiments is from L. Lodish & B. Lubetkin, 'General truths? Nine key findings from IRI test data', *Admap*, February 1992, pp 9–15.

Tables

Table 1: Data Collected to Describe a Category (sales & media)

	Volume share %	Value share %	Relative price	Distribution	Share of voice	Share of voice – share of market
1994						
A	16.7	20.0	119	95	33.4	3.5
B	13.7	14.8	108	93	19.4	4.6
C	8.8	9.4	106	92	6.2	–3.1
OL	28.3	24.2	85	80	–	–24.2
Other	32.4	31.7	98	–	41.0	9.3
1995						
A	17.3	21.1	122	96	35.8	14.7
B	14.7	15.7	107	93	23.8	8.0
C	6.7	7.4	110	91	2.9	–4.5
OL	31.2	26.9	86	82	–	–26.9
Other	30.2	28.9	96	–	37.6	8.7

Table 2: Rearranging a Tracking Scores Table

A. Scores from the tracking study, 1995

Attribute	Our Brand B	Brand A	Brand C
A	30.7	47.8	20.9
F	58.9	61.3	54.6
G	49.3	47.1	41.7
H	44.9	44.1	40.1
J	16.1	15.9	16.9
K	7.4	9.2	8.3
W	21.1	15.1	19.8

B. The same data, rearranged and formatted

Attribute	Brand A	Brand B	Brand C	Average
F	61	59	55	58
G	47	49	42	46
H	44	45	40	43
A	48	31	21	33
I	24	26	20	23
W	15	21	20	19
J	16	16	17	16
K	9	7	8	8
Average	33	32	28	31

C. Differences from expected

Attribute	Brand A	Brand B	Brand C	Index
F	−1	−1	2	7
G	−2	2	0	9
H	−2	1	1	6
A	12	−3	−9	244
I	−1	2	−1	5
W	−5	2	3	36
J	−2	−1	2	8
K	0	−1	1	2

Attribute	D. Reduced table Brand A	Brand B	Brand C
Brand Awareness	48	31	21
Worth it	15	21	20
General	34	34	30

Table 3: Summary of Tracking Scores to Add to a Category Table

In Table 1, the main sales and media characteristics of the selected brands or groups were summarised. In Table 2, a number of tracking scores were reduced to three for each brand. When this work is done for both years and all the brands or groups to be studied, we get a summary of tracking scores which can be added to Table 1. In this case, it is reasonable to summarise the own label brands, but the group of others is so diverse we do not try to do so.

	Brand awareness	Worth it	General
1994			
Brand A	46.0	15.6	33.1
Brand B	28.2	20.2	31.6
Brand C	22.3	20.1	31.2
Own Label	41.9	31.9	28.3
1995			
Brand A	47.8	15.1	33.6
Brand B	30.7	21.1	33.7
Brand C	20.9	19.8	30.3
Own Label	42.3	29.5	27.4

Table 4: Annual Differences, from Tables 3 and 4

The category table has entries for two years. It is easier to use this data if we concentrate on the latest year and on the differences from the previous year. A table of these differences shows who is winning and who is losing. It is usually clearest to show percentage changes for figures like volume share, but actual changes for share of voice, the aggressiveness of the media activity (share of voice less the brand's share of value in sterling) and so on. The numbers are formatted to make the important differences stand out.

	Volume share %	Value share %	Relative price	Distribution
		Percent changes, 1995 on 1994		
Brand A	3	6	2	1
Brand B	7	6	−1	0
Brand C	−24	−21	4	−1
Own Label	10	11	1	2
Others	−7	9	−3	

	SoV	SoV – SoM£	Ad aware	Worth it	General
		Actual changes, 1995 on 1994			
Brand A	2	1	2	−1	1
Brand B	4	3	3	1	2
Brand C	−3	−1	−1	0	−1
Own Label	0	−3	0	−2	−1
Others	−3	−1			

Table 5: From Half Life to the Fade Parameter

Normally, half life is stated in weeks and the data period is either weeks, four weeks or months.

Half life is the time by which half the total effect has been felt. The fade parameter f tells us the ratio of the effect in each period on the period before (except for the period in which the advertising was seen, since the 'first period counts half' convention is used when the periods are weeks or longer – *see Section 8.2.2*).

The equation which gives us half life when f is known is:

$$h = \log\{(1 + f) / 4\} / \log(f)$$

which is calculated for a given f easily enough. In this expression and the next, logarithms may be to the base 10 or e – either will do.

To solve it for f, given h, which is what we usually need to do, is not trivial.

Three ways are recommended. The first is to use Table 5.1. This gives the values most often used, for weeks, four weeks and months. It also gives in the last column the solution of:

$$h = \log(0.5) / \log(f)$$

which is appropriate when 'first period counts full' – *see Section 8.2.1*. This is appropriate when single-source data is available, and we know the actual *day* of exposure to the advertising and the actual *day* of purchase.

The second way, and the one used to create the table, is a recursive calculation, called Newton's method of successive approximation. Given h, and any suitably close approximate f, a closer approximation is given by subtracting from the first approximation the correction:

$$[h.\ln\{f\} - \ln\{(1 + f) / 4 \}].f.(1 + f) / [h.(1 + f) - f]$$

In this expression, logarithms must be to the base e. We then repeat the process until the correction is very small (such as 10^{-15}). This can be built into the program we are using, or into a spreadsheet as a macro. Or, it can be written as a couple of short columns (ten rows is enough), as follows:

Divide the half life (example, six weeks) by the number of weeks in the period in the data (for months, this is 4.3333). Here, we have 1.3846.

Choose a starting value for f; suppose this is 0.1.

Then the two columns give, first, the successive approximations, and second, the correction for which the formula is above – see Table 5.2.

Table 5.1

Half life Weeks	Weeks f	Data period Four-weeks f	Months f	Half life Days	Data period Days f
0.5	0.0718			0.5	0.2500
1	0.3333	0.0040	0.0025	1	0.5000
2	0.6404	0.0718	0.0558	2	0.7071
3	0.7607	0.2011	0.1692	3	0.7937
4	0.8215	0.3333	0.2946	4	0.8409
5	0.8578	0.4421	0.4043	5	0.8706
6	0.8819	0.5260	0.4901	6	0.8909
7	0.8990	0.5903	0.5578	7	0.9057
8	0.9119	0.6404	0.6110	8	0.9170
9	0.9218	0.6801	0.6536	9	0.9259
10	0.9297	0.7122	0.6881	10	0.9330
15	0.9533	0.8093	0.7931	15	0.9548
20	0.9651	0.8578	0.8457	20	0.9659
26	0.9732	0.8911	0.8819	26	0.9737
39	0.9822	0.9297	0.9218	39	0.9824
52	0.9866	0.9461	0.9415	52	0.9868

Table 5.2

Approximation	Correction
0.10000	−0.14665
0.24665	−0.16052
0.40717	−0.07413
0.48130	−0.00870
0.49000	−0.00001
0.49009	$-1.1E-08$
0.49009	$-2.1E-16$

where for example 0.24665 is 0.10000 + 0.14665.

In the third way, we interpolate from a plot as overleaf. Here, weeks and four-weeks values are given. This helps to choose starting values for the second method.

It is also possible to use a goal-seeking tool in a spreadsheet, but this is less precise than the successive calculation above.

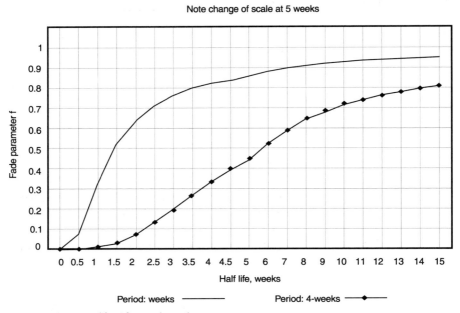

Note change of scale at 5 weeks

Period: weeks ——————   Period: 4-weeks ——◆——

Figure 31 Half Life and Fade Parameter

Table 6: Calculation of Adstock

The period here is weeks and the half life chosen is four weeks, so the fade parameter f is 0.821468 (this is by the method explained in Table 5).

The method used here is explained in Section 8.2.4. We repeatedly need the quantity $(1 - f) / (1 + f)$, so it is handy to calculate this next; it is 0.098015.

The previous rate of advertising in this case was 26 TVRs per week.

Column 1 holds the TVRs. Adstock is the sum of the entries in columns 2 and 3.

Notes 1. 2.55 is given by 0.098015 x 26
2. 23.45 is given by 2 x 0.821468 / (1 + 0.821468) x 26
3. This and the entries below are 2 x 0.821468 times the entry in column 2 in the row above, plus 0.821468 times the entry immediately above.
4. Entries in this column are 0.098015 times the TVRs in the same row.

Year & week	TVRs Column 1	Column 2	Column 3	Adstock
	2.55^1		23.45^2	26.00
9401	0	0.00	23.45^3	23.45
9402	0	0.00	19.26	19.26
9403	0	0.00	15.83	15.83
9404	0	0.00	13.00	13.00
9405	0	0.00	10.68	10.68
9406	0	0.00	8.77	8.77
9407	0	0.00	7.21	7.21
9408	0	0.00	5.92	5.92
9409	0	0.00	4.86	4.86
9410	0	0.00	3.99	3.99
9411	0	0.00	3.28	3.28
9412	0	0.00	2.70	2.70
9413	0	0.00	2.21	2.21
9414	0	0.00	1.82	1.82
9415	0	0.00	1.49	1.49
9416	0	0.00	1.23	1.23
9417	0	0.00	1.01	1.01
9418	0	0.00	0.83	0.83
9419	0	0.00	0.68	0.68
9420	17	1.67^4	0.56	2.23

continued→

Year & week	TVRs Column 1	Column 2	Column 3	Adstock
9421	20	1.93	3.20	5.13
9422	27	2.62	5.80	8.42
9423	34	3.31	9.07	12.38
9424	41	4.00	12.89	16.89
9425	44	4.31	17.15	21.46
9426	42	4.12	21.17	25.29
9427	40	3.92	24.15	28.08
9428	38	3.73	26.29	30.01
9429	21	2.05	27.72	29.76
9430	21	2.09	26.13	28.22
9431	22	2.13	24.90	27.02
9432	22	2.17	23.95	26.11
9433	62	6.03	23.23	29.26
9434	52	5.06	28.99	34.06
9435	42	4.10	32.14	36.24
9436	32	3.13	33.13	36.27
9437	4	0.39	32.37	32.76
9438	4	0.34	27.23	27.58
9439	3	0.29	22.94	23.23
9440	2	0.24	19.32	19.57
9441	9	0.92	16.28	17.19
9442	12	1.22	14.88	16.10
9443	16	1.52	14.22	15.75
9444	19	1.83	14.19	16.02
9445	37	3.61	14.66	18.27
9446	29	2.88	17.97	20.85
9447	22	2.16	19.50	21.66
9448	15	1.44	19.57	21.01
9449	0	0.00	18.45	18.45
9450	0	0.00	15.15	15.15
9451	0	0.00	12.45	12.45
9452	0	0.00	10.23	10.23
9501	0	0.00	8.40	8.40
9502	0	0.00	6.90	6.90
9503	0	0.00	5.67	5.67
9504	0	0.00	4.66	4.66
9505	0	0.00	3.83	3.83
9506	0	0.00	3.14	3.14
9507	0	0.00	2.58	2.58
9508	0	0.00	2.12	2.12

continued→

Year & Week	TVRs Column 1	Column 2	Column 3	Adstock
9509	0	0.00	1.74	1.74
9510	0	0.00	1.43	1.43
9511	0	0.00	1.18	1.18
9512	0	0.00	0.97	0.97
9513	12	1.16	0.79	1.95
9514	18	1.74	2.56	4.30
9515	24	2.32	4.96	7.28
9516	30	2.90	7.89	10.79
9517	73	7.11	11.25	18.36
9518	85	8.37	20.93	29.29
9519	98	9.62	30.93	40.55
9520	111	10.87	41.22	52.09
9521	81	7.96	51.72	59.69
9522	67	6.59	55.57	62.16
9523	53	5.22	56.48	61.70
9524	39	3.85	54.97	58.82
9525	9	0.92	51.48	52.40
9526	9	0.93	43.80	44.73
9527	10	0.93	37.51	38.44
9528	10	0.94	32.35	33.29
9529	43	4.23	28.12	32.35
9530	57	5.54	30.05	35.59
9531	70	6.86	33.79	40.64
9532	83	8.17	39.02	47.19
9533	80	7.88	45.48	53.09
9538	18	1.79	45.45	47.24
9539	14	1.34	40.28	41.62
9540	9	0.90	35.30	36.19
9541	0	0.00	30.47	30.47
9542	0	0.00	20.56	20.56
9544	0	0.00	16.89	16.89
9545	12	1.18	13.87	15.05
9546	18	1.76	13.33	15.09
9547	24	2.35	13.85	16.20
9548	30	2.94	15.24	18.18
9549	67	6.58	17.35	23.93
9550	54	5.26	25.07	30.33
9551	40	3.95	29.24	33.19
9552	27	2.63	30.51	33.14

Table 7: Data for Regression of Brand Awareness on Trend and Adstocks

Year & week	Awareness	Trend	Ads4	Ads5	Ads6	Ads7	Ads8
9401	7.70	1	71.54	77.43	81.53	84.54	86.84
9402	7.86	2	32.58	41.92	49.32	55.23	60.04
9403	5.49	3	14.83	22.70	29.83	36.08	41.51
9404	6.53	4	6.76	12.29	18.05	23.57	28.70
9405	6.53	5	4.74	7.96	11.98	16.31	20.62
9406	6.57	6	42.82	37.74	35.60	35.26	35.99
9407	9.10	7	104.84	92.01	83.05	76.91	72.78
9408	9.64	8	111.12	103.74	97.01	91.48	87.15
9409	10.86	9	135.82	127.23	119.51	112.90	107.40
9410	10.52	10	103.13	104.88	103.99	102.00	99.67
9411	8.23	11	65.05	71.69	75.57	77.64	78.63
9412	10.07	12	81.79	82.44	83.12	83.44	83.42
9413	8.86	13	56.27	61.38	65.11	67.77	69.64
9501	6.95	14	25.62	33.23	39.39	44.28	48.15
9502	6.27	15	11.67	17.99	23.82	28.93	33.29
9503	6.40	16	5.31	9.74	14.41	18.90	23.01
9504	8.20	17	24.33	23.10	23.73	25.31	27.31
9505	11.16	18	140.30	119.21	105.13	95.48	88.70
9506	13.36	19	242.36	215.83	194.50	177.57	164.10
9507	13.27	20	168.86	167.54	162.11	155.52	148.95
9508	13.29	21	155.77	155.51	153.00	149.26	145.05
9509	14.45	22	225.92	214.76	205.07	196.26	188.20
9510	13.23	23	178.14	181.03	180.60	178.31	175.02
9511	12.01	24	92.94	108.42	118.46	124.74	128.44
9512	9.56	25	64.53	76.76	86.87	94.63	100.35
9513	10.92	26	120.59	117.67	117.74	118.78	119.93

Table 8: Category Volume and Value at Consumer Purchase Level

Four weeks	Tonnes	£000	£ per kilo
9201	9,157	45,720	4.99
9202	10,064	50,312	5.00
9203	10,250	51,698	5.04
9204	12,655	63,614	5.03
9205	11,467	57,534	5.02
9206	9,096	45,700	5.02
9207	10,340	51,771	5.01
9208	9,895	49,492	5.00
9209	10,263	51,321	5.00
9210	10,395	51,666	4.97
9211	10,634	52,755	4.96
9212	13,468	66,634	4.95
9213	9,255	46,489	5.02
9301	9,157	45,909	5.01
9302	10,064	50,470	5.01
9303	10,250	51,569	5.03
9304	12,655	63,586	5.02
9305	11,467	57,625	5.03
9306	9,096	45,567	5.01
9307	10,340	51,804	5.01
9308	9,895	49,668	5.02
9309	10,263	51,475	5.02
9310	10,395	52,181	5.02
9311	10,634	53,838	5.06
9312	13,468	67,378	5.00
9313	9,255	46,341	5.01
9401	9,332	47509	5.09
9402	10,231	52087	5.09
9403	10,300	52571	5.10
9404	12,837	64954	5.06
9405	11,557	58612	5.07
9406	9,218	46317	5.02
9407	10,457	53589	5.12
9408	9,992	50593	5.06
9409	10,363	52723	5.09
9410	10,653	54163	5.08
9411	10,896	55196	5.07
9412	13,506	68332	5.06
9413	9,470	47852	5.05

continued→

Accountable Advertising

Four weeks	Tonnes	£000	£ per kilo
9501	9,415	47362	5.03
9502	12,033	60749	5.05
9503	8,776	44149	5.03
9504	9,440	47693	5.05
9505	10,475	52412	5.00
9506	9,927	49909	5.03
9507	11,253	56428	5.01
9508	8,813	44379	5.04
9509	9,735	48697	5.00
9510	10,967	54952	5.01
9511	13,136	65951	5.02
9512	11,911	59539	5.00
9513	8,009	40211	5.02

Table 9: Sales Share Modelling with Price, Adstock and Other Explainers

The data here is for our brand, for two years and for weeks. The ratings were given in Table 6, so other adstocks could be worked out, but they have already been calculated here for two half lives. At the end of the table the modelling is explained.

	Vol%	RelPr	Dis	Promo	Ads2	Ads39
9401	13.81	110.00	95.40	0.0	14.30	28.37
9402	13.69	109.00	95.20	0.0	9.16	27.86
9403	13.57	109.00	95.00	0.0	5.87	27.37
9404	13.45	108.00	94.80	0.0	3.76	26.88
9405	13.23	106.94	92.94	0.0	2.41	26.40
9406	13.18	106.62	92.49	0.0	1.54	25.93
9407	13.13	106.30	92.03	0.0	0.99	25.46
9408	13.08	105.98	91.58	0.0	0.63	25.01
9409	13.78	105.04	91.45	0.0	0.40	24.56
9410	13.43	105.93	91.51	0.0	0.26	24.13
9411	13.09	106.82	91.57	0.0	0.17	23.70
9412	12.75	107.71	91.63	0.0	0.11	23.27
9413	11.43	112.49	92.39	0.0	0.07	22.86
9414	10.59	112.76	92.59	0.0	0.04	22.45
9415	10.55	113.02	92.79	0.0	0.03	22.05
9416	11.32	113.29	92.98	0.0	0.02	21.66
9417	11.71	109.92	92.34	0.0	0.01	21.27
9418	12.53	108.73	92.73	0.0	0.01	20.89
9419	13.34	107.54	93.12	0.0	0.00	20.52
9420	14.16	106.34	93.51	0.0	3.73	20.30
9421	16.48	104.70	94.89	0.6	9.10	20.27
9422	16.95	104.56	95.26	0.9	14.46	20.32
9423	17.42	104.43	95.63	1.1	20.41	20.50
9424	17.89	104.29	96.01	1.4	26.75	20.80
9425	15.87	106.67	95.68	0.5	32.50	21.19
9426	15.74	107.00	95.57	0.5	36.19	21.57
9427	15.61	107.32	95.46	0.5	37.84	21.92
9428	15.48	107.65	95.35	0.5	38.19	22.23
9429	15.98	106.90	95.27	1.0	34.37	22.35
9430	16.54	106.79	94.87	1.0	29.62	22.33
9431	16.51	106.68	94.48	1.0	26.71	22.32
9432	15.87	106.56	94.09	1.0	25.00	22.31
9433	15.86	106.53	92.90	0.7	32.60	22.66

continued→

	Vol%	RelPr	Dis	Promo	Ads2	Ads39
9434	15.58	106.43	92.81	0.6	40.84	23.26
9435	15.29	106.33	92.73	0.4	42.58	23.68
9436	15.00	106.22	92.64	0.3	40.15	23.92
9437	14.86	105.63	94.35	0.0	31.08	23.81
9438	14.45	105.88	94.16	0.0	21.23	23.45
9439	14.03	106.13	93.96	0.0	14.74	23.09
9440	13.62	106.39	93.76	0.0	10.41	22.73
9441	13.35	106.43	91.83	0.0	9.07	22.43
9442	12.85	107.59	91.56	0.0	9.85	22.22
9443	12.35	108.74	91.29	0.0	11.46	22.08
9444	11.85	109.90	91.02	0.0	13.61	21.99
9445	10.94	113.37	92.22	0.0	19.40	22.09
9446	10.82	113.96	92.16	0.0	24.04	22.29
9447	10.71	114.56	92.11	0.0	24.36	22.35
9448	10.59	115.16	92.05	0.0	21.93	22.28
9449	11.02	114.50	90.90	0.0	16.11	22.01
9450	11.47	112.96	91.00	0.0	10.32	21.62
9451	11.92	111.42	91.10	0.0	6.61	21.23
9452	12.36	109.88	91.19	0.0	4.23	20.85
9501	13.56	104.27	92.52	0.0	2.71	20.48
9502	14.72	103.95	92.73	0.0	1.73	20.12
9503	14.68	103.64	92.93	0.0	1.11	19.76
9504	13.44	103.32	93.13	0.0	0.71	19.40
9505	11.11	109.50	91.38	0.0	0.46	19.06
9506	11.35	109.71	92.09	0.0	0.29	18.72
9507	11.60	109.91	92.80	0.0	0.19	18.38
9508	11.84	110.12	93.51	0.0	0.12	18.06
9509	15.31	106.08	96.96	0.6	0.08	17.73
9510	16.00	105.47	97.63	0.9	0.05	17.42
9511	16.70	104.87	98.29	1.1	0.03	17.11
9512	17.39	104.26	98.96	1.4	0.02	16.80
9513	15.78	104.62	97.90	0.7	2.61	16.61
9514	15.56	105.19	97.27	0.6	7.23	16.58
9515	15.35	105.76	96.64	0.4	12.32	16.65
9516	15.14	106.33	96.01	0.3	17.70	16.83
9517	14.66	109.25	94.56	0.0	31.40	17.45
9518	14.79	109.23	93.92	0.0	49.01	18.54
9519	14.91	109.22	93.27	0.0	64.88	19.85
9520	15.03	109.20	92.63	0.0	79.65	21.36
9521	16.05	105.96	92.43	0.0	84.39	22.69
9522	16.67	105.57	92.40	0.0	80.19	23.61

continued→

	Vol%	RelPr	Dis	Promo	Ads2	Ads39
9523	16.68	105.17	92.37	0.0	72.47	24.26
9524	16.10	104.77	92.34	0.0	62.49	24.66
9525	14.50	106.92	93.03	0.0	47.59	24.65
9526	14.79	106.56	93.27	0.0	33.87	24.38
9527	15.09	106.20	93.51	0.0	25.11	24.11
9528	15.38	105.85	93.75	0.0	19.52	23.85
9529	18.30	103.01	94.09	0.6	23.31	23.90
9530	18.63	102.94	94.06	0.9	33.38	24.36
9531	18.96	102.88	94.04	1.1	44.65	25.06
9532	19.28	102.81	94.01	1.4	56.69	25.98
9533	17.83	104.86	93.71	0.7	65.62	26.98
9534	17.19	105.55	93.36	0.6	68.53	27.83
9535	16.56	106.25	93.01	0.4	66.47	28.47
9536	15.92	106.94	92.66	0.3	61.23	28.91
9537	15.76	106.20	91.65	0.0	50.91	29.02
9538	14.87	107.24	91.63	0.0	39.82	28.87
9539	13.98	108.27	91.60	0.0	31.07	28.64
9540	13.09	109.30	91.58	0.0	23.83	28.34
9541	11.18	112.69	92.92	0.0	16.54	27.91
9542	10.98	113.07	92.97	0.0	10.59	27.41
9543	10.78	113.45	93.03	0.0	6.78	26.92
9544	10.57	113.83	93.09	0.0	4.34	26.44
9545	12.09	111.02	92.19	0.0	5.41	26.08
9546	12.47	110.55	92.08	0.0	9.10	25.88
9547	12.84	110.09	91.96	0.0	13.61	25.80
9548	13.21	109.62	91.84	0.0	18.66	25.82
9549	13.08	110.00	92.19	0.0	30.88	26.23
9550	13.27	110.00	92.08	0.0	40.98	26.84
9551	13.47	110.00	91.96	0.0	42.61	27.19
9552	13.66	110.00	91.84	0.0	38.83	27.31

When we regress the volume share on the explanatory variables, we find that the preferred fit uses all these explainers. The output looks like this:

	Regression coefficient	SE of coefficient	t-value
Relative price	−0.393	0.017	−23.6
Promotions	−0.605	−0.156	10.3
Distribution	0.213	0.036	5.9
Ads2	0.036	0.002	16.7
Ads39	0.040	0.015	2.6
Intercept	34.510		

R-squared = 0.963, Durbin-Watson = 0.91, standard error of estimate = 0.43.

This means that the fit is 34.51 – (0.393 x relative price) + (–0.605 x promotions) and so on.

96.3% of the variation is explained by this fit, and the estimates given by it are in error by only 0.43 on average.

The low Durbin-Watson number shows that the data is serially-correlated, as is normal, so the statistical tests are not very reliable.

The coefficient for price, –0.393, divided by the standard error for this estimate, is –23.6, and this large number shows that the coefficient is well-determined, despite serial correlation.

The mean volume share is 14.61, while average price is 106.7, so price elasticity is –0.393 x 106.7 / 14.61 = –2.9.

Table 10: How to calculate Consumer Brand Equities

Table 1 presented the key numbers about the main brands in our category. From these we now make Consumer Brand Equities, following Section 8.7. The formula is explained in Section 8.7.2. We already know V (the volume share for each brand), P (its relative price), D (its distribution) and D_A (the average distribution over the brands in 1995, which is 90.679). We cannot get a number for 'others' since distribution is not a meaningful concept for a group of brands.

In Table 1 the numbers were given to one decimal only; for the calculations we are going to do, we need them more precisely:

	V	P	D
1994			
A	16.720	119.436	95.100
B	13.674	108.327	93.199
C	8.840	105.770	92.480
Own Label	28.340	85.439	80.420
1995			
A	17.260	122.140	95.930
B	14.657	107.336	93.497
C	6.740	109.884	91.320
Own Label	31.180	86.204	81.970

We have not decided yet which elasticities to use. We make plots of the changes in the variables (price and distribution), against changes in shares. The plots include any changes in equity which may be happening – and below we see evidence that equities *are* changing. We get one estimate from that source, and another from the regressions we do for individual brands, as in Section 8.6.1 and, for example Table 9. We decide to use a price elasticity of –2.8, and a distribution elasticity of +1.

For Brand A, in 1994, Consumer Brand Equity is given by:

$$16.720 / [\exp\{-2.8 \times \ln\{1.19436\}\} \times \exp\{+1 \times \ln\{95.100 / 90.679\}\}]$$
$$= 16.720 / [\ 0.6082 \times 1.0488\ ] = 26.21$$

Being 19% above average price in the category would make equity considerably above the volume share: 1 / 0.6082 is 1.64, so the rise is 64%. Distribution is only a little above average: 1 / 1.0488 means a drop of 5% from volume share to equity. Together, price and distribution make equity 57% above volume share.

In this way we make the following table:

Accountable Advertising

	1994	1995	% change
Brand A	26.2	28.6	9.0
Brand B	16.6	17.3	4.1
Brand C	10.1	8.7	−14.1
Own Label	20.6	22.8	10.7

Table 11: Changes in Share, Equity, etc

The percentage changes in equity in Table 10 can be linked to other numbers we have now produced. This was discussed in Section 8.7.2.

As an example, take the increase of 4.13% in our brand's equity, compared with our volume increase of 7.1% between 1994 and 1995.

There are two other reasons why our share might have increased: we dropped relative price and we improved distribution slightly.

Our price drop was from 108.3 to 107.9 or 0.9%. With price elasticity of −2.8, we expect a share increase of 2.6% from this factor. Our distribution rise from 93.2 to 93.5 implies a share increase of 0.3%.

So +7.2% in volume share comes from:

```
relative price:  +2.6%
distribution:    +0.3%
equity:          +4.1%
```

These produce the overall gain: 1.026 x 1.003 x 1.041 = 1.071.
We can do these sums for all the brands to make this table:

	% change in volume share	Due to rel price	Due to distribution	Due to equity
Brand A	3.2	−6.1	0.9	9.0
Brand B	7.1	2.6	0.3	4.1
Brand C	−23.8	−10.9	−1.3	−14.1
Own Label	10.0	−2.5	1.9	10.7

Thus Brand A grew despite its price rise because the equity gain was larger than the fall expected from price. Brand B had both a price cut and an equity improvement. Brand C fell most because of the equity drop but also because it put up price. Own Label grew mainly because of its equity rise.

In general, volume share changes were due more to price and equity changes, than to distribution changes.

Table 12: Data for Budget Allocation over Time

Week	Seasonality index	£ cost of 100 TVRS	Value/Cost index	1995 actual TVRs	Recommended* TVRs
9501	84	17,000	113	0	85
9502	88	17,100	119	0	85
9503	91	17,100	123	0	85
9504	94	17,100	127	0	85
9505	93	17,100	125	0	85
9506	89	20,100	102	0	65
9507	94	20,100	108	0	65
9508	96	20,100	110	0	65
9509	95	20,100	109	0	65
9510	94	21,300	102	0	45
9511	100	21,300	108	0	45
9512	97	21,300	105	0	45
9513	97	21,300	105	12	45
9514	96	22,900	97	18	45
9515	101	22,900	102	24	45
9516	99	22,900	100	30	45
9517	104	22,900	105	73	45
9518	105	22,900	106	85	45
9519	103	25,700	92	98	25
9520	107	25,700	96	111	25
9521	108	25,700	97	81	25
9522	114	25,700	102	67	25
9523	108	24,800	100	53	25
9524	108	24,800	100	39	25
9525	107	24,800	99	9	25
9526	115	24,800	107	9	25
9527	117	23,400	115	10	35
9528	114	23,400	112	10	35
9529	112	23,400	110	43	35
9530	115	23,400	113	57	35
9531	110	23,400	108	70	45
9532	109	20,300	124	83	45
9533	112	20,300	127	80	45
9534	111	20,300	126	69	45
9535	110	20,300	125	59	45
9536	109	25,400	99	48	25
9537	111	25,400	101	23	25
9538	107	25,400	97	18	25

continued→

Week	Seasonality index	£ cost of 100 TVRS	Value/Cost index	1995 actual TVRs	Recommended* TVRs
9539	105	25,400	95	14	25
9540	102	27,700	85	9	0
9541	101	27,700	84	0	0
9542	95	27,700	79	0	0
9543	94	27,700	78	0	0
9544	95	27,700	79	0	0
9545	97	26,800	83	12	0
9546	99	26,800	85	18	0
9547	105	26,800	90	24	0
9548	105	26,800	90	30	0
9549	102	21,700	108	67	0
9550	88	21,700	93	54	0
9551	48	21,700	51	40	0
9552	49	21,700	52	27	0

*The recommendation is for a long half life of 39 weeks

Table 13: Continuous Budgeting

In Section 9 Continuous Budgeting is described. Here the actual application is given in detail. Only a single year is set out, 1996, though the full model runs from 1992 to 1997. It is built on the marketplace experience of 1992 to 1995, described in Chapters 7 and 8. Only the original scenario is described, but it is made clear how what-if questions are put and answered.

A complication in this case is that accounts are kept by months, and TV plans are also written for months, but marketplace data, and so the model, uses four weeks as the unit. The decisions and output are therefore set out in months in the first table below. Later, the four-week detail is explained. Movement between the two sorts of table is by converting to weeks and back again.

Months: Decisions and Results

	Adspend £000	Cost £000 per 100 TVRs	TVRs	Ex-factory price £000 per tonne	Volume tonnes	Profit £000
Jan 96	693	188	369	3.93	1,982	773
Feb 96	309	221	140	3.93	1,847	778
Mar 96	423	234	181	3.99	1,978	477
Apr 96	506	252	201	3.99	2,697	2,003
May 96	0	282	0	3.99	1,957	1,420
Jun 96	0	272	0	3.99	1,624	674
Jul 96	126	257	49	3.99	2,177	1,701
Aug 96	582	224	260	3.99	2,081	508
Sep 96	67	279	24	3.99	1,875	922
Oct 96	120	305	39	3.99	2,303	1,940
Nov 96	229	295	78	3.99	2,038	1,341
Dec 96	0	239	0	3.99	2,098	1,681

In this table, three decisions are made: how much to spend on TV – here £3,315k in total, the allocation across months, and the ex-factory price to retailers. So in using the model, the what-if questions are asked by changing the entries in these columns.

Using the forecast of TV costs, the numbers of TVRs which will be bought are worked out. These TVRs are moved into the next table, after transformation to four weeks.

In the last two columns are the results, moved back from the third table. The volume of sales ex-factory has been predicted. From this, profit is calculated as follows.

Income each month starts with the gross margin forecasts, which this year are £1,850k per tonne. This multiplies the tonnes sold, suitably lagged to allow for when payment is received. From this, three items are deducted. First, fixed costs, which are £2.2 million per month. Second, spend on promotions and print advertising. Third, spend on TV media costs, shown on the table but again lagged.

The system also calculates annual and quarterly profit forecasts, compares key figures with previous years and provides useful plots. The current net worth of the decisions is shown by cumulating future profits with a discounting factor. It was these estimates which provided the raw material for the recommendations in Chapter 6.

Four weeks: Preparation for Modelling

Yr, 4-wk	TVRs transformed	CAds39	Ads2	Category tonnes	£/Kg
9601	217	3,013	212	9,265	5.01
9602	160	3,127	168	10,598	5.01
9603	171	3,246	170	9,894	5.01
9604	120	3,366	127	11,897	5.00
9605	0	3,482	17	11,242	5.00
9606	10	3,589	10	9,334	5.00
9607	39	3,691	35	10,598	4.99
9608	260	3,797	230	9,649	4.99
9609	24	3,905	53	10,156	4.98
9610	31	4,007	33	10,603	4.98
9611	66	4,105	62	11,325	4.98
9612	19	4,199	25	13,088	4.97
9613	213	4,295	187	8,997	4.97

In order to run the model, the TVRs we expect to buy are moved into the four-week table above, and adstocks are calculated. The model requires cumulated adstocks with a 39-week half life, to create a floating base as described in Section 8.10. There is also a short-term, two-week half life, effect.

Since the model relies on price relative to the category, and produces a forecast for volume share, the category forecasts are shown.

Four weeks: Application of the Model

Yr, 4-wk	RelPr	Dis	Promo	Fit Vol %	Vol tonnes
9601	107	93.5	0	15.4	1,761
9602	108	93.5	0	14.8	1,933
9603	109	93.5	1	16.5	2,023
9604	109	93.5	0.5	15.3	2,247
9605	109	93.5	0	13.4	1,860
9606	109	93.5	0	13.4	1,545
9607	109	93.5	0	13.7	1,790
9608	110	93.5	1	17.4	2,081
9609	110	93.5	0.5	14.9	1,875
9610	110	93.5	0	13.8	1,809
9611	110	93.5	0	14.1	1,974
9612	110	93.5	0	13.8	2,231
9613	110	93.5	0	15.3	1,698

When we come to run the model, we now have all the terms needed. From our decision about the price to retailers, with a suitable factor to translate this to the price to consumers, and the category average, we have our relative price. The estimate for distribution and decisions about the timing of promotions are shown. We already have the adstocks which, with a trend term, give the floating base and short-term effect. Hence our forecast share, and from the category forecast our retail tonnage. It is from the last column, using both a factor and suitable lagging, we got the ex-factory volume we saw in the first table.

Index